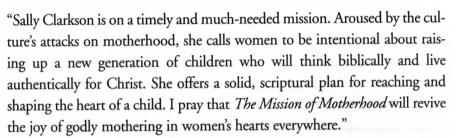

"Sally Clarkson is on a timely and much-needed mission. Aroused by the culture's attacks on motherhood, she calls women to be intentional about raising up a new generation of children who will think biblically and live authentically for Christ. She offers a solid, scriptural plan for reaching and shaping the heart of a child. I pray that *The Mission of Motherhood* will revive the joy of godly mothering in women's hearts everywhere."

—NANCY LEIGH DEMOSS, author and host of *Revive Our Hearts Radio*

"In true Sally Clarkson form, *The Mission of Motherhood* touches the heart. Sally faces some hard questions and thought-provoking ideas about what the Bible has to say on motherhood. With tenderness and compassion, combined with a wonderful knowledge of the Scriptures, she unfolds to us God's plan for the family. A true work of art."

—LYNN VANWINGERDEN, wife, mother of 23 children,
and grandmother of 7

"Contained in these pages are help and hope for *every* mom. Sally's book is thought-provoking yet practical. I highly recommend *The Mission of Motherhood.*"

—LINDA DILLOW, author of *Calm My Anxious Heart, Intimate Issues,*
and *Gift-Wrapped by God*

"Sally Clarkson has achieved a beautiful balance of biblical teaching and the heart of a mother in *The Mission of Motherhood.* She gently takes the reader by the hand and stands with her before the truth of her calling. Readers will be entertained by her personal stories, empowered by God's call to mothers, and encouraged by Sally's teaching."

—VICKI CARUANA, author of the best-selling *Apples & Chalkdust*
and founder of EncourageTeachers.com

"In *The Mission of Motherhood*, Sally Clarkson invites the reader into her family and into her heart to see 'mother' in action: teaching, comforting, training, enriching, and blessing. This book elevates the mission of motherhood and sends the reader back to her children 'pumped.' "

—JEAN FLEMING, author of *A Mother's Heart*

"Sally hasn't one impolite bone in her body. She so politely passes on what is actually a powerful message. Those who seek affirmation of the value of traditional motherhood will find it here, wrapped in biblical principles and a certain sympathetic sweetness."

—KAREN ANDREOLA, author of *A Charlotte Mason Companion*

THE

MISSION *of*
MOTHERHOOD

THE

MISSION *of*

MOTHERHOOD

Touching Your Child's Heart

for Eternity

SALLY CLARKSON

WATERBROOK
PRESS

THE MISSION OF MOTHERHOOD
PUBLISHED BY WATERBROOK PRESS
2375 Telstar Drive, Suite 160
Colorado Springs, Colorado 80920
A division of Random House, Inc.

ISBN 1-57856-581-2

Library of Congress Cataloging-in-Publication Data
Clarkson, Sally.
   The mission of motherhood : touching your child's heart for eternity / by Sally Clarkson.
   — 1st ed.
      p. cm.
   Includes bibliographical references.
   ISBN 1-57856-581-2
   1. Motherhood—Religious aspects—Christianity. 2. Mothers—Religious life. I. Title.
BV4529.18C53 2003
248.8'431—dc21

2002011002

Printed in the United States of America
2003

10 9 8 7 6 5 4 3

To the Lord Jesus,
who had such a great idea when he invented mothers

CONTENTS

ACKNOWLEDGMENTS

As I look back over the years in which God prepared this message in my heart, it was as though the message found me. I didn't pursue it—but here it is. I want to thank the Lord for years of his faithfulness to me and for showing me that he does care about the desires of my heart and my dreams.

When my husband, Clay, and I first decided to host conferences for mothers, the Lord raised up several friends and their families who supported us through all of the years of building our ministry, followed us all over the United States, and worked tirelessly at our conferences. They have also faithfully supported me throughout the writing of this book and prayed for me each step of the way. Thank you, Dana Clay, Lynn Custer, and Kathy Jackson, for working so hard and reaching out to so many women. Thanks to your committed husbands and wonderful children for working too—at registration, setup, and cash registers—and for serving the moms at our conferences so enthusiastically. Haven't we got some great memories?

Linda Dillow, you are the catalyst in my life who opened doors for this book and for our family to have three great years in the mountains. I'll always be grateful for your friendship, help, enthusiasm, prayers, and passion for our Lord.

Phyllis Stanley, your life embodies what I hope to become. Your care, time, and friendship help to sustain me and give me energy and hope for my many tasks.

Lynn van Wingerden is my friend who called and encouraged me throughout the whole process of this book and checked on me when I returned from each speaking trip. Keep checking on me, Lynn—I need it. Shelley Rose is the best neighbor in the world and was available for our children to invade her home any time of day. Lynn Bradshaw prayed and wrote me sweet notes and sent chocolate.

Thanks also to Mom and Nana for praying for us every day.

A special thanks to sweet Sarah for all that you do to help me and for being my kindred spirit. There will be jewels in your crown for your faithfulness in the hundreds of small ways you serve the Lord and me each day. Thanks to Joel for willingly helping me with my tasks and loads and encouraging me and bringing out my tender side because of your gentle spirit. Nathan, thanks for being so fun and loving, for being proud of me and affirming me as a creative person, and for being my friend. And thanks to Joy for your beautiful, responsive heart, your loving pats and hugs, your enjoyment in our relationship, and your patience when I sit in front of my computer. I appreciate all you kids for having such great hearts for your mom and dad and for believing in our projects.

To Clay, my comrade in arms, who has led our ministry and worked so faithfully through all the years to reach out to parents—how privileged I am to have you as a lifelong partner. May God give wind to your wings as you continue to pursue so many great ideas and projects and books and still work to leave a legacy of righteousness to our children. I'll always have a cup of tea waiting for you.

Thank you, God, for Anne Christian Buchanan, who has partnered with me as my editor and helped to bring my thoughts out in the clearest possible way. Thanks so much for your patience and a generous spirit throughout the ending process of this book, as I was packing to move, preparing for trips, living life, and making it through the stomach viruses that attacked the kids, Clay, and me all on the same crucial weekend!

Hearts and Hands

As I look back to the memories of my childhood, a strong image that comes to my mind is that of my mother's loving hands. I thought they were the most beautiful in the world. In many ways, I still feel that way.

Because I had been a premature baby, I was often sick with a variety of respiratory illnesses, including chronic asthma and occasional bouts with pneumonia. My memories of these illnesses, however, are mostly pleasant, because my mother would gently stroke my brow as she talked softly or told me stories and gave me her full attention. I remember feeling very loved from such focused attention.

At other times, when I fidgeted in church services, I remember my mother's hands massaging my own, pulling and squeezing each of my fingers as she quietly played finger games with me. As a young child, sitting next to her in a big overstuffed chair, I would watch her hands as she read to me from an oversized children's book. Her fingers would point to the enticing, heart-delighting pictures and turn the pages of the large volumes as we leisurely sat together and talked and read.

And during the period when I was having a recurring nightmare—one I still remember!—I especially remember the comfort of my mother's hands when she came to my bedside. She would take my hand in hers as she knelt to pray with me, soothing away my fears and comforting me as she entreated God to take all of my bad thoughts away.

Now, many, many years removed from my mother and a thousand miles away, these memories of my mother's hands are still strong in my heart. Those hands are now old and wrinkled and aching with arthritis, yet still, as an adult, I often wish she were with me to stroke my brow in the midst of illness and exhaustion, to massage away the frustration and boredom of tedious days, to open windows to the world while reading to me in a big old chair, and to take my hand in prayer and cast away all the fears of my life. The touch of a mother's hand and the power of a mother's love indeed has carried me through many moments of my life.

As I look to the needs of children of today, I am convinced they need the same things from their mothers that I needed—and received—from mine. They need not only the gentle touch of a mother's hands, but her focus and her attention on a daily basis. They need a champion and a cheerleader, someone who has the time and energy to give encouragement along life's way and comfort in dark times. They need a directive voice to show them how to live.

These needs are not frivolous demands. They're part of the way God designed children. And meeting those needs is not an option or a sideline for mothers, but part of his design as well. Perhaps because I was fortunate enough to have a mother who met my own needs so beautifully, God has put on my heart a desire to encourage other mothers by showing them the significant role they play in the life of their precious children—and by assuring them that their deep desire to devote time and energy to their families is a vital part of God's call on their life.

For quite a few years now, my husband and I have been privileged to travel all over the United States and to other parts of the world, conducting seminars on the biblical vision of the family. Wherever we travel (usually with our children in tow), I meet mothers from so many stations of life—from stay-at-home moms and homeschoolers to professional career women, from sweet young moms pregnant with their first babies to older mothers trying to reach the hearts of their teenagers. Though the choices and circumstances of these women may be very different, their hearts and desires are basically the same—to do the best job they can at loving and nurturing their children and to bring meaning and continuity to the life and relationships in their families. They all want to be the very best parents they can. They want to do motherhood right.

And yet, increasingly, I find that these women are unsure of what it means to be a good mother. They are confused by a culture that sends them drastically mixed messages about the importance of a mother's influence and what her priorities should be. As a result, so many mothers I meet are baffled and frustrated. They don't know how to reconcile these conflicting messages with the calling of God on their hearts and lives.

What's the cure for this confusion? I believe it lies with a rediscovery of the traditional mission of motherhood, a rediscovery of what God had in mind when he first designed families. That fundamental design is still valid, although its specific shape in a given home may vary widely. And the fundamental mission of motherhood now is the same as it always was: to nurture, protect, and instruct children, to create a home environment that enables them to learn and grow, to help them develop a heart for God and his purposes, and to send them out into the world prepared to live both fully and meaningfully. It's up to us to embrace that mission as our own, trusting God to walk us through the details and to use our willing mothers' hands as instruments of his blessings.

It is my heart's desire to encourage each precious mom who reads this book by affirming the significant role a mother plays in the lives of her children. I hope to remind moms of the value God places upon their lives and to help them respond wholeheartedly to his call on their lives. As we explore together what it means to cultivate a heart for God, a heart for our children, and a heart for our home, I will attempt to create a complete picture of how we are called to live as mothers, so that the integrity of our own lives will reflect the beauty of God's original design.

I do not, however, consider myself to be a perfect mother. My aspirations and what I can idealize oftentimes far exceed my ability to live up to them in reality. Yet it is in being able to visualize the dreams of my heart and beauty of God's design that I have found a standard of maturity to move toward.

As I reflect on my own life, I feel that I have learned so much—the hard way, by making many mistakes. Many moments of stress and struggle could have been handled so much more easily if I had had a wiser, older woman to shed light on my stages of life. It was through writers like Edith Schaeffer that I was encouraged and helped along my way. My hope is that in some way, I might be able to provide that same encouragement and inspiration.

But I'm still learning, and the lessons God has taught me as I sought to embrace his mission for motherhood have been truly life changing—and a source of unbelievable blessing. No matter what our culture tells us, I've discovered, and no matter what directions our own desire may push us, the only way to true joy and peace is God's way.

May your heart be warmed, encouraged, and lifted as you read this book, and may God hold you in his own capable hands as you strive to fulfill the mission of motherhood in your own life.

PART ONE

A MOTHER'S CALLING

CHAPTER 1

A Journey Like No Other

Discovering the Mission of Motherhood

But a woman who fears the LORD, she shall be praised.
Give her the product of her hands,
And let her works praise her in the gates.

PROVERBS 31:30-31

Nocturnal asthma was the mysterious name the doctors gave to define the severe condition my three-year-old had developed. Each morning within five minutes of 1:30, little Joy would wake up with spasms of coughing and wheezing, gasping for breath.

We had tried nebulizers that administered strong asthma medicines, natural and homeopathic medicines, and nutritional routes of healing. The one thing that seemed to work best, however, was a home remedy. After giving Joy her normal dose of medicine, I used the old "croup" method to calm her until the asthma medicine began working—I sat on a small stool in the middle of a hot steaming shower and cradled Joy in my arms. For distraction during these times, I often made up heroic "Joy" stories in which she rescued a small dog or bird, or helped a hurting child, or did some creative or thoughtful deed to encourage her friends or family. We usually did this for forty-five minutes or until the hot-water heater was empty.

One such evening, at the end of our little ritual, Joy stood shivering outside of the shower with sopping wet hair and glassy brown eyes that looked like saucers in her sallow little face. She smiled at me with a thoughtful expression as I wrapped her in a large towel.

"Mommy! You know what? When I was growing inside your tummy, I always hoped and hoped that when I came out, I would have a mommy just like you who would take care of me when I was sick and tell me Joy stories!"

In her own childish way, Joy articulated what I believe is a profound need of every child: to be loved, cherished, cared for, and protected by her very own mother, whose womb was her first home. And it's not just a need but an important part of God's design for shaping human beings according to his will.

The beautiful design of nature itself shows us that a child grows inside its mother's body hearing the specific sound of her voice, comforted by the beat of her heart, intimately connected to her very being. Upon arrival into the world, the mother's arms are her first cradle, and the mother supplies the first food and comfort and security. Because of the intimacy of that first relationship, the child's heart is naturally open to the mother. Children automatically turn toward their mothers as their first source of protection, love, and spiritual, emotional, and mental support. This is all a part of the design of mother, child, and family as unfolded for us in the Bible—a design that, from the beginning, God pronounced as very good.

After a journey of eighteen years into motherhood, I can heartily affirm Joy's profound thoughts and her deep desire to be cared for and loved by a mother who is committed to her care. I can confirm wholeheartedly that God's design for the family is indeed very good. I have also come to believe that motherhood, while demanding, is one of the most fulfilling and meaningful roles a woman can fill.

But I didn't reach these conclusions without a struggle. For me, it took years of personal search and study—as well as a lot of trial and error as a mother—to understand the importance of my role as a mother. In a sense, I think my journey parallels that of many other moms who are trying to understand their mission in the context of a culture that is deeply ambiguous about both mothers and motherhood.

Recently I took a trip to the East Coast. On the way I sat next to a woman who was a professor of physics at a prestigious California university. Obviously proud of being the only woman on the faculty in this department, she talked of her pleasure in her career—pleasure that was marred only by her desire to spend more time with her new baby. Just as she had started building her lab, she had given birth to a little girl. Even though her childcare arrangements were satisfactory, she still felt a need to be with her baby and to share the precious moments of her first year. "She's just so captivating. I can't resist being with her! But we've got a good nanny. So now I'm just trying to figure it all out."

Coming back from Boston, I found myself next to another articulate young woman, this one a professor at Harvard University. After talking about some of the issues concerning families, she shared with me a little about her own broken family background. She also told me that she and her "partner," the man with whom she had been living, had been involved in personal counseling for a year. "You see, I can't explain it, but I have a deep longing to get married and to have a child. But I don't think you can really have an intense career and still give a child all that he needs in life. My partner thinks that he and my career should be enough. But I feel a deep longing to have a child and be a family— to bring a sense of completeness to our lives. I even think I would like to get married."

As I travel throughout the United States, Canada, and Europe, I continue to meet woman after woman who expresses the same needs and desires. Though many with whom I speak are not Christians, still they feel there is a design in their hearts for motherhood and family. They long to have a center for life—a home where love, marriage, and children are a part of the complete picture.

I am also amazed at the maternal instincts that women express over and over, in spite of their educational background, social status, or religious preferences. As I have been writing this book in early 2002, the United States is fighting a war against terrorism in Afghanistan, and the news often features scenes of Afghan refugees fleeing to Pakistan for protection and shelter. Even amid the poverty and danger, however, there are images of Afghan mothers holding their children close, gently and lovingly, and feeding them meager offerings of food—a poignant picture of mother love and sacrifice that transcends boundaries of culture.

Clearly, God has written *motherhood* in the hearts of women wherever they live. And he has written it in my heart as well. What a worthwhile journey it has been to rediscover the wonderful significance God prepared for me in motherhood when he gave me the gift of my children.

A MOTHER'S JOURNEY

For thousands of years the view of motherhood described in the Bible was generally respected in Western culture. Motherhood was seen as a noble and important calling. Women considered themselves blessed to bear many children, and it was considered normal and good for home and family to be the central focus of a woman's life. This is not to say that mothers were always well treated—after all, sin has been with us since the very beginning. But the office of "mother" was usually respected and revered, and it was generally assumed that entire generations were shaped during the time they spent at the mother's knee.

By the time I became a mother, however, the American culture had dramatically redefined the role of motherhood, and the biblical model of motherhood no longer drove the imagination of culture. Somehow, over the course of the last century, traditional motherhood had become a lifestyle option—and to many, a lesser option—rather than a divine calling.

When I had my first child at almost thirty-one years old, I had not seriously considered the importance of motherhood in light of my whole life. I was thrust into the role and then realized that I needed to discover God's perspective in my life. I had been raised in a traditional American home, where my father went to work and my mother stayed home to care for her children. My mother had left her job as a systems engineer with IBM to stay home with my brothers and me. As a child, however, I never considered the significance of her decision.

At school I had been taught to embrace a very different model of womanhood. Friends and teachers encouraged me to do something "important" with my life, which meant choosing a career and a type of work that would make the best use of my talents and personality. I could marry and have children if I wanted, but not at the expense of "fulfilling my potential." Even many of my Christian friends and mentors managed to convey that being "just a wife and mother" would somehow be less than God's best for me.

Because I had an enthusiastic, passionate personality, I looked forward to doing something meaningful with my life. By the time I graduated from college, I was ready to take on the world. I just knew God was calling me to serve him in dramatic, exciting ways. While I hoped that I would someday be married and I looked forward to having a life partner, I didn't often think about having children. I had grown up as the only girl with two older brothers and had never even been around younger children very much.

The next few years were indeed exciting. I worked with women across the United States in the areas of leadership development and spiritual training. I moved to Europe and worked for three years behind the Iron Curtain, teaching and training young Christian leaders in four communist countries where Christianity was forbidden. I traveled alone or with another single woman into highly stressful and challenging situations. Eventually I moved to Poland to learn the language and train the first Eastern European staff women for the ministry of Campus Crusade for Christ. We lived with these precious women, even though our presence was illegal and offensive to the secret police.

By the time I returned to the United States, I had been on my own for quite a while, and I was emotionally vested in my independent lifestyle. I liked keeping my own schedule, eating my own meals, buying lovely clothes that suited my speaking profession, and traveling whenever I wanted. I moved back to Denver, Colorado, where I spent two more years traveling and speaking. Finally, in my late twenties, I married Clay. We had been friends for almost eight years and had finally decided to spend our lives together. At this point, he was in seminary preparing for full-time Christian ministry.

I welcomed marriage and rejoiced in finally having a life companion and partner for ministry. I really looked forward to starting a family as well. But I was also fully entrenched in my own identity and independence and my work as a Christian speaker and leader. So two years later, when I became pregnant, I was filled with confusing, diametrically opposed feelings about my role as a mother.

One part of me was absolutely dreamy eyed about the prospect of having my own precious baby to love and care for. But I was also excited and scared and concerned about how this new development might change my life.

Conflicting advice from well-meaning friends further blurred my understanding.

One confidante told me, "The most important thing you can do with your life is invest it in your children. Their lives are more important than building a career!" And what she said certainly seemed to ring true in my spirit.

But other advisors assured me that I could handle the challenge of balancing children with career—after all, most of the mothers I knew were doing just that. One woman, an older missionary, even advised, "Don't let your children control your life! You've got lots of gifts and messages and a ministry to share with the women of the world! It would be a waste of your time and experience to focus too much on your children and lose your ministry! Don't have more children. It will take up too much time."

Confusion and questions began to flood my soul. *What is right? I love teaching women's groups! I don't want to lose what I've spent so many years developing! And hasn't God called me to this work? Don't I have a stewardship—an obligation to continue in my ministry in order to help others? But I have waited so long to have a child. Shouldn't this child have first priority in my life?*

I simply couldn't decide what I would do when my baby came. But I soon discovered that life has its own ways of helping us choose. What happened was that my tiny baby girl arrived and took my life completely by storm.

I had read every childbirth book I could find. After preparing perfectly through nutrition and exercise to have a natural birth, when I finally came to the hospital to deliver this baby, I was in for a shock. After twenty hours, two and a half of which she was stuck in the birth canal, Sarah Elizabeth Clarkson made her way into the world—tiny, beautiful, and with meconium-filled lungs.

She was immediately placed into intensive care. One of the neonatal nurses told me that babies with problems like hers often died of sudden infant death syndrome—not the words I needed to hear as a brand-new mother less than twenty-four hours after giving birth. I looked at this beautiful, bright-eyed baby girl, and suddenly nothing else in the world seemed important but caring for her and helping her to thrive.

Sarah was finally released from the hospital, and I delighted in her every moment. Her smiles that were reserved just for me; the way her tiny fingers patted my chest as she nursed filled my emotional cup. Watching when she seemed to dance on her back each time the musical toy played "You Are My Sunshine" convinced me that she was indeed the most intelligent, charming, and beautiful baby that had ever been born. I didn't actually sit down at that time and think, *This is it; I'm choosing traditional motherhood over my career.* I simply wanted to be with my daughter as much as possible. I wanted to woo her, love her, care for her, and serve her and find joy in each moment that she required. So when opportunities arose to speak or to teach a women's group, I was very selective and allowed my career to be a secondary choice.

Not long after Sarah was born, Clay finished seminary, and we moved to Austria to work in the international community of Vienna. By the time Sarah was two and a half, our second child, Joel, was born. Clay's job allowed us to work with a wide variety of people—from diplomats to refugees, from opera singers to music students. I was also involved in the ministry, reaching out to the numerous people who visited our home frequently. But I was not actually employed, so I devoted most of my time to my children at home. Yet, in the process of taking care of my little ones, I often felt overwhelmed by the routine nature of my tasks.

Before Sarah was five, I had three babies, had moved to Colorado and then to California, had lurched through hundreds of sleepless hours, and had coped with myriad asthma attacks and ear infections and respiratory problems. Chronic exhaustion, a house that seemed perpetually messy, the inevitable stresses of moving so often, and days of "quality time" with little ones who were often fussy and demanding caused me to doubt my sanity! I began to realize that my mothering honeymoon was over and my confusion was back.

What had I gotten myself into? A challenging career suddenly seemed more productive to me because I could measure the results of my work. These precious little ones had endless needs. They were busy little sinful creatures who demanded all of my body, time, life, emotions, and attention! As much as I loved my children, I often felt like a failure. Surely someone else could do a better job with these precious ones than I. And what exactly was I supposed to be accomplishing anyway? Was I wasting my time? What had this husband, who professed to love me, done to me?

With overwhelming feelings of discouragement, multitudes of questions, and a deep-felt need to make sense of my life, I began to search for the answers to my questions. I read every book I could get my hands on about family, motherhood, and children. And although I found much that was helpful, my reading also seemed to heighten my confusion. I was amazed at how many conflicting and antithetical views of motherhood and womanhood itself I found even among my fellow evangelical Christians.

I finally decided that I needed to search the Scriptures to find out for myself just what God, the Designer himself, had in mind when he created the role of mother thousands of years ago. This search has been well rewarded. In fact, it changed my life. My personal study of biblical motherhood—which I'll outline more fully in the next chapter—has helped me not only to realize that God has an important mission for mothers, but to embrace that mission as a source of deep joy and fulfillment in my own life.

CALLED TO MOTHERHOOD?

God designed motherhood to be a deeply meaningful role. We mothers have the opportunity to influence eternity by building a spiritual legacy in the lives of our children. Through our teaching and influence, morality can be learned and modeled, love and kindness are taught and received, purpose and vision are ignited and passed on.

The real ability of a mother to secure such a spiritual legacy is based on the strength of her relationship with her child. As we tenderly care for our children, meeting their needs, teaching them and guiding them, praying for them and modeling our faith, we are also anchoring their hearts to our home, our values, and our beliefs. These ties are built over a period of many years, through the small ways we spend the minutes of our days and the large ways in which we celebrate the momentous events of our lives.

The mother who reaches the heartfelt needs of her children by helping them feel loved and secure, by believing in their dreams, by noticing when they stray and gently steering them back in the right direction, and by teaching them what they need to know to live full and meaningful lives accomplishes a great work for the Lord.

As I have thought about these issues for many years, I have come to picture the heart of each child as a treasure chest. Each chest is empty and needs to be filled with the riches of unconditional love, spiritual nurture, and the emotional heritage of family and traditions; with mental stimulation that comes from excellent sources of truth, morality, and inspiration; with a sense of physical and emotional security; and with guidelines for all of life, including purpose, relationships, and proper behavior.

Each child whose treasure chest is full will have abundant resources on which to draw in the midst of life's demands. As a woman now pushing fifty, I realize that those foundational years in the life of a child—those same years when I sometimes thought I was accomplishing nothing—have a lasting effect on almost every aspect of the rest of that child's life.

I can still hear my mother's voice in my heart as I face different situations. I still have a need for a cheerleader who believes in me when I have failed, who will pray for me in the stressful moments of life, lend me money when I need it, and help me through times of difficulty with wisdom and perspective. A mother's relationship with her child is one that will encompass a lifetime. How blessed is a child who has that anchor of strength and support.

And yet over the years I have come to realize something else about my role as a mother. As important as my role is, and as important as my children are, they are not to be the center of my life, and my central calling is not to motherhood.

That would not only make for very selfish children, but it could even become a form of idolatry.

My calling as a mother is the same as any other Christian's: to fulfill God's will for our lives and to glorify him. This means I am to follow the Lord's design for my marriage—cleaving to my husband, supporting him, honoring him, loving him as my own flesh. I am to be a careful steward of the world in which I live. I am to seek opportunities to bring God's message of redemption to others, to make full use of the gifts and talents he has placed in my life to bring him glory and further his kingdom. And I am to delight in him and worship him and praise him in whatever circumstance I find myself.

But that's just the point. Because God has blessed me with a husband and children, a part of his call to me is to follow his plan for families. And that means I am to shepherd the hearts of the children whom he has providentially placed in my care. I am to care for them tenderly and to partner with God and my husband in leading my children to know and love his Word and to follow his will.

This design doesn't mean I have to lose myself in my children's lives. On the contrary, following God's design for living is the true key to finding myself—to becoming the person he had in mind for me all along. And saying yes to the mission of motherhood has certainly not meant giving up my ministry. To a great extent, it *is* my ministry.

I will grow into the kind of person God wants me to be as I live out my life in faith and seek to be faithful in my walk with God; as I nurture and honor my commitment to my husband and children and family and home; as I exercise my skills, training, and gifts toward those whom God has placed on my path; as I seek to give to the poor and minister to the needy and those in my neighborhood and church while living a life of bold faith in a great and wonderful God. At the same time, my children, in the context of walking with me through my life, will gain a clear model of how they can live as well.

This journey of discovering God's design for motherhood has filled me with purpose, peace, fulfillment, and excitement. In fact, I have come to believe that being a mother encompasses all that is best within me. To embrace the mission of motherhood requires that I understand God and his design for life and can relate deep theological issues to the everyday minutes of my life. It requires that I become a mature counselor, ready at any moment to make decisions judiciously. It also requires that I develop skills in hospitality, nursing, intellectual prowess, diplomacy, leadership training, and more, and that I stretch my creativity to the max.

God's design provides a completeness to the circle of life. Our family is a vital piece of the puzzle of his design that was intended to give all children the opportunity to be lovingly nurtured so they could live their own lives well. The mission of motherhood is strategic in providing the next generation with whole-hearted, emotionally healthy, and spiritually alive adults. It is not simply a lifestyle choice. It is a divine calling that will indeed affect eternity.

I have heard others speak about the challenges and rewards of traditional motherhood. And I'll have to admit there was a time when I would listen to such talk and feel it was just mothering rhetoric with little relevance to my life. Yet, as I have focused my vision and expanded in my own experience and confidence, I have come to see how true it is in my own life. I've learned that my influence on my children is limited only by the smallness of my dreams and my lack of commitment to the Lord and his purposes.

The scope of my mothering and my life lived for God's purposes has expanded over the years as I have matured. As I have learned to go to God and listen to his voice, my goals for my family and for myself have grown bigger and grander.

This is especially true now that my children are entering young adulthood. They are my best friends and closest companions. Expanding interests and broadening spheres of influence, coupled with increasing spiritual maturity and ongoing training, have developed my children into loving, vital people. Together we have learned to look at the world and say, "Lord, in the power of your Holy Spirit, what work do you have for our family this year? How can we expand your kingdom? How can we glorify you together?"

Life as a mother, in other words, is more exciting to me now than ever before—especially as I begin to see the fruits of my earlier labors. The foundations that were laid in my children's lives, little by little, have given them the ability now to reach for the sky.

Each of my children, like Joy, has a built-in desire to have me fulfill God's great call on my life for their sakes. How thankful I am that God showed me his path so that I can relax in each stage of childhood and find joy in my moments with my sweet ones, knowing that in my acceptance of his call, my children can rest in the peace and security of my commitment to them.

For Thought and Reflection

Something to Think About...

When Clay and I were a young married couple in Vienna, we went to a department store to purchase a simple computer desk. We found a "put it together yourself" model and enthusiastically attempted to jump into the project as soon as we got home. We dumped the pieces of wood and nails and screws on the floor and began to assemble it by intuition.

Pretty soon we realized that we were making a mess of things, but the directions for the project were in German, and we couldn't read them. So we offered our trusty friend Klaus a home-cooked dinner in exchange for a translation. Once we understood the instructions, we knew exactly how the pieces were designed to fit together to match the picture on the box. Our furniture soon stood complete.

God had a design in mind when he created the family. When we follow his instructions and design, we emerge as a productive, flourishing family. God's Word gives us the instruction manual to his design. Consider these verses as you review your own philosophy of motherhood.

1. *Psalm 127:1.* In the Old Testament, the word *house* is often used to express the same concept as the English words *family* or *home*. What, according to this verse, is the secret to the success of a godly family? What will happen to the work of the house building if parents are not following God's path?

2. *Psalm 127:3.* What does this verse indicate about God's view of children? When God blesses us with children, why does he consider it a reward? How does this verse contrast with the prevailing view of children in contemporary culture? How does this compare to your own feelings about your children?

3. *1 Thessalonians 2:7.* When Paul wanted to communicate how dearly he loved the people in Thessalonica, he used a picture of motherhood. What is the attitude or the heart of the mother reflected in his example? How does this picture compare to the way that you care for your children?

4. *Titus 2:4-5*. What are the elements of responsibility that the older
    women are required to teach to the younger women? Why would this
    need to be taught? What does it mean to be a worker at home? In what
    ways do women who obey these standards keep from dishonoring the
    Word of God?

Something to Try...

When the busyness of life and its demands cloud my vision for the priorities of
my life, I often try to get away for a few hours so I can rethink what I am called
to do with the moments and months and years of my life. A local five-star hotel
offers an inexpensive refuge where I can go for a cup of coffee, a roll, and as
much time as I want to sit and think and pray. Taking advantage of one of the
beautiful lobbies around the hotel, I usually park myself in a quiet corner and
spend several hours with my Bible, a prayer journal, a date book, and a pen. This
time with the Lord helps me determine what to cut out from my life and what
to add. It gives me a clear perspective on how to proceed with life.

- Schedule a personal planning time to evaluate your own goals. Write
  down your goals for your family. Write down your goals for each child.
  Consider how you are falling short of your goals. Plan specifically how
  you can do better and what you need to do in the next six months to
  move toward your goals. Then spend time in prayer, committing this
  plan to the Lord.
- Put pictures of your family or favorite snapshots of the kids in a prominent place where you can see them during your prayer times. Use these
  pictures as a joyful reminder as you pray for your family or as you plan
  the priorities of your life.
- Buy a blank book for each child. In each, write the story of the child's
  birth and his or her first few months of life. Add to this journal each
  year on their birthday to document all of the ways they have grown
  and to highlight the special events that took place in their lives. You
  can either share these journals with your children as they grow or save
  them as a gift for their twenty-first birthdays.

CHAPTER 2

Beautiful by Design

Exploring the Meaning of Biblical Motherhood

See to it that no one takes you captive
through philosophy and empty deception,
according to the tradition of men,
according to the elementary principles of the world,
rather than according to Christ.

COLOSSIANS 2:8

The hotel ballroom was packed full of women from all over California. The hum of excited conversation, laughter, and discussion filled the room. We had just finished the first evening of a conference on becoming a wholehearted mother and were moving toward the exit doors to get some needed sleep. A few women lingered to ask me questions about their children and home or to encourage me about the messages being shared.

One woman, however, stood behind me, conspicuously alone, pulling away from the crowd. With downcast eyes and slumped posture, she waited quietly until all the other women had gone. Then she timidly approached me and said, with tears streaming down her face, "I don't know if I should talk to you or not. You see, I would love to be a great mother to my children, but I don't know if I can. What you spoke about tonight is meaningless to me. My mother was an alcoholic, married three times. My stepfather abused me. I have never experienced a loving relationship in my life. So how can I do something that I have never even seen in real life? I've always longed to feel and give real love, but I don't know if I am capable."

She was describing the fruit of brokenness in a family that had turned away from God's design for the family. She had experienced anger, rejection, and isolation from her own mother. She sincerely wanted to be healed, but she didn't know where to start. She wanted to be a good mother, but she found that hard to do when she herself felt like an orphan.

As I travel throughout the United States, Canada, and Europe, I continue to meet women who express these same needs and desires and frustrations. Some have suffered the brokenness that results when God's design is ignored. Others, like the women I described in chapter 1, feel confused and adrift in a culture full of conflicting messages about what it means to be a mother.

Many with whom I speak are not Christians; yet they identify a design in their hearts, a deep longing to have a center for life—a home where love, marriage, and children are part of a complete picture. At the same time, they feel uncomfortable with these desires. Either they have little confidence in their mothering abilities, or they simply can't reconcile their heart longings with their mental image of a successful woman. They long for purpose and meaning and a sense of peace in their homes, but they have no understanding or clear idea of how to grasp what is already written in their hearts.

I think that these women express these desires because they were designed by God to enjoy and affirm in their hearts what we were made to live out in our lives. Yet many have become confused by voices that try to define femininity apart from marriage, physical design, motherhood, or family—and many have been directly damaged by their own families or by a culture that has drifted far from God's design. The yearnings of their hearts are often belittled or subdued by the stronger cultural voices that picture feminine success in terms of emotional independence, career accomplishment, and a kind of personal fulfillment that may have little to do with God's design on their lives and therefore cannot bring real happiness or satisfaction.

I don't think we need to delve into the extremes of feminist issues here with a debate about women's roles and society. But it is important to acknowledge that this sense of brokenness is real and deeply felt in the hearts of women in our culture. Actually, it has been felt long before now, because the problem is not just a cultural one, but a matter of the heart—a direct result of the fallenness of the human race.

The heart of motherhood has been broken by sin's perversion of God's design throughout all of history. Families have been broken apart. Parents have failed in their calling, and children have rebelled. Men and women have demeaned and mistreated each other and their offspring, and those offspring have passed along the painful results to their own children.

Yet the longing for a stable and secure home and a desire for a defined and meaningful family heritage have remained a foundational part of the human psyche, built into the yearnings of each person. To understand where this came from and why it has persisted, we must go back to the Word of God to examine his original design for mothers and families—and to some of the ways that our culture makes it difficult for women to live as God intended.

God's Word, you see, gives us the map or plan for the family so that we might better understand what he had in mind for us. Few things will last after we die, but our children and their children will live throughout eternity. What we do as mothers, therefore, has eternal significance, so it's especially important to understand God's original intentions in this regard. Exploring his design for families and for motherhood cannot only help us understand what has gone wrong, but also how, with God's help, we can move closer to the joyful, fulfilling, and vitally important role he intended for us from the very beginning.

Even as I write this, I am aware that there are countless interpretations and philosophies concerning motherhood, a woman's role, and what the Bible has to say about all of this. These issues have been addressed at length by scholars more educated and intelligent than I. And it is certainly not my desire to write a theological treatise or a sociological exposé. Instead, I would like to simply share with you the beauty of God's design as I have come to understand it from my study of God's Word. The story begins in the book of Genesis, with the creation of the first man, the first woman, and the first family.

IN THE BEGINNING—CREATED FOR A PURPOSE

It is important to note at the beginning that God started families when the world was perfect and no sin had taken place—that the role of "mother" was a part of God's core design of a perfect life. The family was to be the unit of life through which all of life was organized. Each person would come into this world through a mother and father who would work together to give the family stability and purpose.

The first chapter of Genesis gives us a clear picture of God's intentions when he created the first man and the first woman:

Then God said, "Let Us make man in Our image, according to Our likeness; and let them rule over the fish of the sea and over the birds of the
sky and over the cattle and over all the earth, and over every creeping
thing that creeps on the earth." And God created man in His own image,
in the image of God He created him; male and female He created them.
(1:26-27)

Though whole books have been written about these verses, I'd like to focus on
a few points that are especially pertinent to our focus on motherhood.

First, both men and women were made in the image or likeness of God.
God is, among many other attributes, intelligent, wise, creative, righteous, powerful, loving, and moral. And we were made to be like him, to display these
attributes as well. We were designed, unlike the other animals, to be replicas of
God in his created world. Both men and women were created to reflect his likeness in and through their work, their leisure, and the purpose of their lives.

Second, we notice that men and women were given a joint purpose from the
first of creation. They were made to rule over all of God's creation. Even as a king
or queen has a dominion, a country or area over which he or she exercises
authority, so we humans were given authority over the world that God made.

Genesis 1:28 gives us a further idea of what God had in mind in giving us
this authority. This verse is essentially a pronouncement of blessing on Adam
and Eve:

And God blessed them; and God said to them, "Be fruitful and multiply, and fill the earth, and subdue it; and rule over the fish of the sea and
over the birds of the sky, and over every living thing that moves on the
earth."

This one little verse speaks volumes about what God intended for families
from the beginning. It indicates that men and women are to "fill the earth" with
children and that being fruitful is part of his blessing. It also states that men and
women have the privilege and responsibility to "rule over" and to "subdue" the
rest of God's creation. The Lord blesses them, out of the goodness and love of
his heart, that they might flourish in his design for them. "Subdue" carries with
it not just the idea of ruling over, but also bringing something to productivity.

A few years ago, when we moved to Colorado, Clay and I found a piece of land on which a builder was about to construct a home. It was a beautiful lot with stunning mountain views. After we put a contract on the home, we witnessed the process of construction as the plot of land gave way to what would become our home. To me, this building process gives a picture of the real meaning behind the word *subdue*. First we selected a suitable building site—away from the road, with the best possible views, and with optimal drainage on the side of our mountain, so that the melting snows would not damage our home. A crew cleared away the brush where the house would be built. Then we began planning a home that would suit the site as well as our particular needs and tastes.

We wanted the outdoors to seem an intrinsic part of our rooms, so we planned for picture windows in the living room, dining room, master bedroom, and kitchen. A deck running the length of the house would let us enjoy meals outdoors while looking down over sparkling city lights and peaceful mountain views—not other houses. The interior of the home—architecture, paint, and fixtures—would not only suit our tastes but also fit the needs of our large family, with a spacious kitchen, wide-open and well-lit rooms, and low-maintenance wall and floor surfaces that could stand up to the tromping of four children, their friends, and their pets. Two fireplaces would give the living spaces a sense of warmth, and every room would be filled with favorite and familiar antique furniture, knickknacks, pictures, and candles.

The outdoor spaces, too, were planned to suit our family's particular needs. An expansive lawn in front of the house—along with a playground and playhouse on top of a spread-out sand pile under the shade of our old pine trees— would give our children room to run. And we would plant hundreds of flower bulbs, wildflower seeds, bushes, and aspens to make our already-beautiful land even more wonderful.

All these plans took awhile to come to fruition. Turning that raw land into a home required years of saving our money and investing our hard labor. But gradually, under our watchful eyes, it became something useful, beautiful, and suited to our specific needs. It is also, we hope, through the raising of our children and an ongoing ministry of hospitality, instrumental in bringing about God's kingdom on earth.

This is just a small picture of the word *subdue* as used in this passage. The Hebrew word for *subdue* implies making something subject to your authority. It means being responsible for making it useful and beautiful, caring for it rather than exploiting it. As Clay and I worked to subdue the land and make it our home, so are we humans to subdue the whole world for God's glory.

This, in a nutshell, was what God intended for the first man and woman when he made them in his image and gave them his blessing. God's blessing on Adam and Eve was a way of saying, "As you live out your life, may you be successful in bringing the earth under your authority, caring for it, and making it even better than it is now."

So originally, each of us, man and woman, was given the purpose of partnering with God to rule over the world and to make it productive—in an infinite number of areas—government, the arts, architecture, food production, worship, and so forth. Each of us is created with a capacity and purpose to be productive and creative in life—according to our drives, gifts, and strengths—and to glorify God as we rule over the specific dominion he has entrusted to us. And each of us will be required to give an accounting of how we handled this responsibility—how we invested our lives in God's purposes to subdue our own little corner of the earth—the circumstances of our particular life—for his glory.

THE BLESSING OF CHILDREN

God's blessing on Adam and Eve contained another important element as well. Not only were the man and the woman to rule over and subdue the earth; they were also to "be fruitful and multiply, and fill the earth." They were to have many children!

Before the Fall, in other words, one of man and woman's greatest privileges and most important responsibilities was to bring other human beings into this world from the purposeful partnership of their marriage. These offspring were also to know the design of God. In the context of family, they would learn what it meant to be made in the righteous image of their Creator, to subdue the earth for God's glory, and to populate the earth with their own children, thus producing a godly heritage.

This idea that children are a blessing and that bearing children is a vital part of God's design for mothers continues to be assumed and supported by the rest of Scripture. In Psalm 127:3-5, for example, we read:

Behold, children are a gift of the LORD,
The fruit of the womb is a reward.
Like arrows in the hand of a warrior,
So are the children of one's youth.
How blessed is the man whose quiver is full of them.

Psalm 128:1-4, another psalm about Gods blessing in a person's life, paints a beautiful picture of the blessing that comes from fruitfulness.

How blessed is everyone who fears the LORD,
Who walks in His ways.
When you shall eat of the fruit of your hands,
You will be happy and it will be well with you.
Your wife shall be like a fruitful vine,
Within your house,
Your children like olive plants
Around your table.
Behold, for thus shall the man be blessed
Who fears the LORD.

The fruitful family was even the foundational place in which the Son of God was placed in which to represent his Father in this world. When God chose to bring Jesus into the world, as a full reflection of his glory and being, he chose to bring him into a simple family with a mother and father and, eventually, siblings. It was within the context of this home that Jesus was trained and instructed and loved and nurtured, both protected and prepared for his ministry ahead.

Throughout his life, Jesus upheld and affirmed the original design of marriage and family and stressed the needs and concerns of children. In Luke 2:51-52, for instance, we read that Jesus willingly submitted himself to the authority of his parents and that he prospered in this role of a son to parents. Even from the cross, Jesus expressed his respect for family, requesting specifically that his disciple John take care of his mother, Mary.

Jesus also demonstrated a consistent concern and affection for children and considered them important to the work of God's kingdom. Again and again the Gospels show him spending time with children, talking to them or blessing them or drawing them onto his lap. He even told people directly that they needed to become like little children in order to enter into his kingdom.

Clearly, nothing in God's mind had changed between the time of the Old Testament and the New in regard to the design of the family and the centrality of children in his plan to bless and redeem the earth. I think we can assume as well that the Lord's view of children and what they mean in a family and a society is the same today.

WOMEN AND MEN: DESIGNED TO BE DIFFERENT

What else about God's design do we learn from Genesis 1? One important thing to note is that gender differences were a part of God's good creation from the very beginning, when God created us "male and female."

Later passages in Genesis give a little more detail and perspective about these differences and hint at differing roles for men and women—roles that later scriptures explain in more detail. In Genesis 2, for instance, we are told that God created Adam first and assigned him a number of specific tasks, such as cultivating the garden for God (Genesis 2:15) and naming the animals (Genesis 2:19-20). As Adam was involved in these tasks, God allowed him to notice his own loneliness and need for a companion who could help him to fulfill his purpose on the earth.

Adam had longings in his heart that were not met. He wanted to talk to someone—to share his ideas, to have someone to sympathize with his minor pains and irritations, to share a moment of his enjoyment in the earth around him and his satisfaction in the productivity of his work. Longings for a partner to share in his work and burdens and vision deepened his sense of loneliness. He was beginning to realize he longed for a peer, for someone with whom he could share his whole life. Adam also longed for physical fulfillment. He needed the warmth of another with whom to be close, and he felt passions in his body that longed to be fulfilled. The physical drive of manhood flowed through his body without a way to fulfill his needs.

But God was already planning the remedy for Adam's loneliness: "Then the LORD God said, 'It is not good for the man to be alone; I will make him a helper suitable for him'" (2:18). And so Eve was created as a partner for Adam, to help him in accomplishing his calling of subduing the earth and glorifying God. But she was to be so much more than just a helper. She was also to share Adam's thoughts and dreams. She was to be a comfort and joy to him within the intimacy of a committed relationship—to share in the joy of his passions, to comfort him in the intimacy that God designed for marriage, and to receive his comfort and love in return. Genesis 2:24-25 confirms: "For this cause a man shall leave his father and his mother, and shall cleave to his wife; and they shall become one flesh. And the man and his wife were both naked and were not ashamed."

The differing design of the two sexes was originally fraught with purpose and meaning. Man and woman were called together not only to subdue and rule over the dominion of the earth, to provide companionship for one another, and to produce children. God intended this relationship to be mutually a blessing to both the man and the woman. And to help ensure this blessing, he created the man and the woman with different physical and emotional attributes and with correspondingly different roles.

The man, for instance, was bigger, stronger, and more muscular than the woman—more suited to hard physical labor. He was blessed with strong protective instincts, a focused intellect, and a drive to make his mark on the earth.

And what about woman? She had many of the same basic traits as her husband, but she was smaller and softer. Though physically weaker, she had a powerful stamina. And she was blessed with a particular ability that made her vital to the survival of all God had made. She was able to bear children.

Genesis 3:20, for instance, points out that the first woman was named Eve, meaning "life" or "living," because she was "the mother of all the living." She was the first woman, as God's creature, made in his image, to be able to bring the life of another human being into the world—which was a part of God's blessing.

This is a beautiful picture—that God equipped a woman from the very beginning to bring life into the world from her own body and to nurture growing families. How wonderful that he gave her a womb to bear a child, breasts to feed it, a more padded physique suited for cradling babies, and the emotional makeup, with all of the right hormones, to be able to nurture and care for her children and to maintain relational connections in her family. According to recent research, he even structured our brains to make it easier for us to handle several tasks at once—as the tasks of caring for a household and small children demand.

From the very beginning, then, God equipped women for a specific role in the family—that of bringing life into the world and nurturing it. He created us

with a helping nature and a predisposition for relationships. And though Genesis doesn't spell this out specifically, the whole of biblical tradition supports
another element of God's design for women—that a woman's primary responsibility in a family, especially if she is blessed with children, is that of establishing
and maintaining a home.

Proverbs 31:10-31, for example, gives us a fuller picture of both a woman's
specific gifts and the wide variety of ways she can use them in fulfilling her
God-ordained role. The activities listed in these verses all revolve around her
home—the preparation of food (verse 14), clothing (verses 13,21), ministering
to others (verses 17-20), teaching her children and others (verse 26), spiritual
life (verse 30), business (verse 16), future and well-being (verse 25), and productivity (verse 27), as well as meeting her husband's needs (verse 11). The
chapter is summed up by saying, "She looks well to the ways of her household"
(verse 27).

The word *household* itself is used four times in the passage. The woman
described in this passage was clearly living up to her mandate from Genesis by
fulfilling her God-ordained role in the family. She was partnering with her husband, helping him to fulfill their mutual destiny by nurturing the life God had
commanded them to have.

The New Testament, too, supports the idea that women have been given
charge of the domain of the home. Titus 2:4-5, for example, specifically says that
older women are to "encourage the young women to love their husbands, to love
their children, to be sensible, pure, workers at home." In other words, women
were to be productive in providing emotional stability and encouragement,
physical sustenance, and spiritual encouragement for their families, as well as
managing and directing the necessary work of running the household.

Both of these passages underline the importance of being able to establish
and maintain a household and to hold it together. Every home needs not only
an emotional center, but an overseer who can plan, organize, and manage the
productive and creative life of the home. Without such management, no foundation will be laid upon which to build the rest of life.

Man, meanwhile, was called to fulfill a different but complementary role—
one implied in Genesis and supported through the rest of Scripture. Physically
equipped with stronger muscles, enhanced mental focus, and "adventurous"
hormones, they were beautifully suited for the roles of provider and protector.

In addition, they were to instruct their children in righteousness (Proverbs 1:8; Ephesians 6:4; Deuteronomy 6:6-9), meet their wife's needs (1 Corinthians 7:3), and even to lay down their lives for their families (Ephesians 5:25-29).

A "VERY GOOD" DESIGN

Many in our culture today look at the biblical view of family, children, and gender roles with much disdain and difficulty. But we must nonetheless consider that God himself directed through his Word that it was a "very good" design, the best plan for bringing about his purposes on earth and for blessing all people. We cannot arbitrarily throw out the verses that don't seem to fit with today's cultural norm of a woman's role. When God's commands are obeyed, people flourish because they are living in harmony with the way they were designed—and the One who designed them.

As a younger woman, I struggled with many of the scriptures referring to a woman's role in life. But the more I have lived, the more I have come to appreciate the beauty and wisdom of my God-given assignment. As a free-spirited person who generally thinks outside the box, I have found deep fulfillment and satisfaction in exercising my gifts, strengths, and personality to bless my family, neighbors, and friends from the strength of my home. Establishing my household as a place in which the greatness of God and a devotion to him is lived out each day has given me focus. Loving my children and nurturing their hearts and minds while training their characters and leading them to know the Lord and his purposes has satisfied my soul's need for purpose.

At the same time, I have come to believe that, within the basic outlines of God's design, there is a lot of room for diversity, creativity, freedom, and redemption. Not every woman, for instance, will marry. Not every woman will be able to have children. And yet all women have the God-given capacity to live in ways that beautifully and purposefully express their life-giving feminine design—their helper or cooperative approach to tasks, their ability to multitask, their nesting instincts and creative spirit. A woman's body was made, in part, to bring life into the world, and that's a good thing from God's point of view. However, the common purpose for all women is to glorify God in whatever circumstances and boundaries of life we find ourselves, trusting him to show us how we can best use our gifts for him.

Similarly, although I think the Bible clearly indicates that a mother's first responsibility is to her home and her children, it never spells out that a woman absolutely cannot work or earn money—or that a man cannot take an interest in the organization of his home. In our own family, though I have chosen from the beginning to be at home with our kids, I have also found various ways to supplement our income from this home base. Because my husband happens to be a supremely organized and practical human being, I have benefited greatly from his input on running our home more smoothly. We have both used our talents to design our home and build our ministry, and we have done it all, we believe, in accordance with our understanding of God's design for our family.

In fact, as Clay and I have partnered in building on the foundations of God's Word in our unique way, we have been amazed at what God has built from our partnership. Our mutual commitment has provided us with a strong emotional glue that has given our marriage meaning in the midst of life's inevitable ups and downs. Our vision of serving the Lord together through our family keeps us ever moving forward.

WHAT HAPPENED TO GOD'S DESIGN?

Though there are so many other scriptural issues that could be discussed, I want to do a quick summary of what all of this says about my role as a mother. First, from Genesis through the New Testament, family is at the center of God's design for all people and, moreover, is a center of life from which God's work and redemption will begin. Men and women were created in God's image and were called together to a lifetime commitment. They were meant to live as partners and to rule over God's earth together.

Second, children were an integral part of God's plan from the beginning. A woman was to receive her ability to bear and nurture children as a gift, and biologically she would be the one through whom her children were made to receive nourishment and nurture from the beginning.

Third, men and women were created with biological differences and corresponding roles within their overall calling. Central to a woman's design—though not the whole of it—is the privilege of bearing children, caring for them, and overseeing her home and household.

The family, incorporating the man and woman and children, was designed from the beginning to be a secure and stable foundation from which all of life could flow. Mutual partnership, with man and woman working together, was a picture of unity and stability. The love and commitment of parents and children would provide for a clear vision of life to be handed down to each succeeding generation. The family as a whole was called to a bigger purpose than any one of them could accomplish alone.

And God, when his design was complete, pronounced it very good. Throughout the rest of his Word, he reaffirmed and elaborated on the goodness of his family plan.

Which leaves us, of course, with the question of what happened. We can easily observe that normal life for a twenty-first-century family often looks quite different from God's original design as set forth in Genesis. And though there are many historical and sociological reasons we could explore for why our current family culture is what it is, we don't have to look that far for the fundamental answer as to *why* it happened. It's right there in Genesis 3. What happened to God's design for men, women, children, and families was human sin!

Genesis 3:1-6 tells us the story of the temptation of Eve. She chose to give her allegiance to Satan and ate from the tree that God had forbidden. She shared the forbidden fruit with Adam, and thus both men and women were separated from God. This meant that humans no longer reasoned as God reasoned, and they began to make up their own theories about their purpose in life.

Romans 1:18-21 describes this process in depth. It tells us that people suppressed truth in unrighteousness, that they became "futile in their speculations, and their foolish heart was darkened."

Since the beginning of time (Genesis 3:1; Job 1:1-7), Satan has sought to destroy God and all of the goodness of God's design (1 Peter 5:8-9). Destroying the foundation of the family, which was designed by God to be the stable foundation of life, is a natural place for Satan to attack.

So what does this have to do with motherhood? As we look at history and our current American culture, it's easy to see the implications. As sinful human beings persisted in living according to their own philosophies, God's original design for families has been constantly in danger of being lost. Over the centuries it has teetered between various distortions.

Jesus' discussion with the Pharisees about divorce in Matthew 19:3-12 was really about such a distortion—the "hardness of heart" that led men to easily divorce wives who no longer pleased them. Other, later distortions included laws and customs that treated wives and children as property or political pawns and practices like slavery or child labor that tore families apart for financial gain.

Until the twentieth century, however, the concept of traditional motherhood somehow held its own in Western culture. Though life was often difficult for mothers and for families, the basic institution of motherhood was still respected and valued, and the idea that a mother would focus her efforts on running her home and raising her children was understood as valid.

Today, however, for a variety of reasons, that concept is rapidly being lost. Practically speaking, the ideas that marriage is a partnership with a purpose, that children are a blessing to be cherished, and that home and children should be a woman's primary responsibility have come to be scorned or simply dismissed as irrelevant. This attitude, I believe, has developed to the great detriment of women, children, families, and society in general.

WHEN GOD'S DESIGN IS FORGOTTEN OR IGNORED

What happens when the God-ordained purpose for the marriage relationship—that of working together to build a family and a heritage and to glorify God as the center of the relationship—is lost? We see it every day in the marriage announcements, the divorce decrees, and the *Dear Abby* column. Marriage outside of God's design becomes primarily an institution where men and women try to meet their personal needs for companionship, sex, and housekeeping.

That's not to say it's always a cold, calculated transaction. Men and women still hunger for real love and want to find a soul mate. But beneath that romantic ideal is still a basically selfish purpose: *I want you because you're good looking and make me proud to be seen with you* or *because you turn me on* or *because I have a lot in common and feel comfortable with you* or *because I'd like you to complete me and give me purpose* or *because other people my age are getting married and I don't want to be different.*

The problem is that the self-centeredness implied in such a relationship is a formula for relational failure. No sinful, imperfect human being can ever fully satisfy the longings in another person's soul for love, security, and purpose, especially over the long course of a human lifetime, because neither partner was *intended* to have these needs met apart from God. The glue that was intended to hold a marriage together is just not there.

What happens then is that some people divorce and start searching for the perfect mate all over again. Some spend their whole lives jumping from relationship to relationship, looking for the elusive love that is found only in the movies. Others stay married and look for fulfillment outside the family—in work, in affairs, in sports or charities and hobbies, or in outside friendships. Some, especially women, even turn to their children as sources of meaning.

This brings us to the next consequence of leaving behind God's plan for families—which is a change in the way children are viewed by parents and society. When passing on God's ways to the next generation and building a godly heritage is no longer an integral reason for getting married, children tend to lose their proper place and value in the scheme of life. Instead of being welcomed as blessings from God and part of God's divine calling for parents, they come to be valued by how well they fill the parents' own needs.

This development can express itself in different ways. Some parents, as indicated above, may turn to children as primary sources of emotional fulfillment. They have children for essentially the same reasons they marry—to make themselves feel good. So the children are considered as blessings—as long as they fulfill this function. Parents who depend on their children to fulfill their own needs may shower the children with affection and material goods. But they also put an unhealthy pressure on the children to perform in such a way as to meet the parents' expectations and emotional demands. At the same time, they teach the children to be self-centered and self-absorbed, passing on a legacy of emotional neediness rather than godliness.

Another, opposite consequence of straying from God's plan for children is that they come to be regarded as a burden, the often-inconvenient by-products of sex. When the mission and reason for having children is lost, they easily come to be seen as a time drain, a monetary expense, a career impediment, and a curtailer of personal freedom.

Such devaluing of children can have devastating effects on both personal and societal levels. It leads naturally to a preoccupation with birth control, a high abortion rate, and to child abuse and neglect, all of which are evident in our culture. More commonly, it results in a tendency to pass the buck when it comes to the actual work of raising children. Because children are not considered important enough to occupy the lion's share of a mother's time, childcare quickly becomes a growth industry (although the actual childcare providers, too, tend to be undervalued and underpaid). The responsibility of instilling morality, conscience, intellect, emotional stability, and spiritual understanding is relegated to day care, teachers and schools, the media (especially television), and peers. Emotionally, spiritually, and often physically as well, children tend to be left to their own devices—left to flounder for love, purpose, and meaning in a culture that values time, efficiency, and measured productivity above the real needs of a human being. Consequently, children feel exploited and demoralized and act out their frustration in numerous negative ways.

And once children lose their value in a culture, so does the work of bringing them into this world and tending them once they are here—a third consequence of moving away from God's design. Instead of being revered, respected, and supported by society, mothering is devalued. Even when lip service is paid to the value of family, there is still the underlying assumption that only "real" work—financial performance, career achievement, or some other contribution outside the home—counts in terms of value and success. Often, as a result, women feel confused and torn between the cultural messages they hear about what is important for them to do and the eternal message God has written on their hearts.

If they absorb the cultural message, they may avoid having children at all or radically limit the number of children in order to leave enough time and energy for their "real" work. They may come to consciously or unconsciously resent the children who keep them from being "productive." Or, more commonly, they will exhaust themselves trying to have it all—a successful career and a vibrant home life. They try to fit too many activities into their days and end up feeling that they are not successful at anything they do.

A whole generation of children, as a result, ends up feeling rushed and pushed, with little or no sense of the comfort and stability of a satisfying home life. Without a strong, supportive structure for passing down righteousness, the morals of the culture become relative to the personal fulfillment of those within the culture. When the biblical mission of motherhood is devalued and disappears from culture, the whole next generation suffers morally, emotionally, and spiritually.

Meanwhile, the minority of mothers who choose to devote their lives to the nurturing of a godly heritage by focusing on their home as the center of life find themselves unsupported and unaffirmed by a culture that does not value their contribution. The hard, daily, repetitive work of making a home a haven, providing healthy meals, correcting and training little ones, and constantly cleaning up messes is perceived as menial labor instead of the stuff from which godliness is built. The result is that the mothers who do attempt to follow God's design for families may suffer from feelings of isolation, loneliness, and discouragement.

GOD ISN'T FINISHED WITH US YET

So where does all this leave us as mothers? It is certainly easy, at this point, to look at the state of our culture and perhaps the state of our families and feel like giving up.

Some women have said to me, "If all you are saying about God's design is true, then my whole life is a mess. But what can I do about it now?"

Others tell me, "I love my job, and I think the work I do is important. Surely you can't mean that I'm supposed to give up my career and way of life to come home and be a traditional mom!" (I'll have more to say about that in the next chapter.)

Often I hear, "I'm a single mom, and I know the design of family for my children is already destroyed. I feel condemned and hopeless! But I certainly can't afford to quit my job and stay home with my kids!"

And I also hear, "What's the big deal? Our family isn't perfect, but we love each other, and we're doing all right. The kids like their day care (and their school, and their baby-sitter, and their after-school care), and I make a special effort to spend time with them when I'm home. Besides, I'm working to pay for their college education. So who are you to say I'm violating God's design?"

To which I respond: I'm *not* here to say that at all! How well you are following God's design is truly a matter for you and your family and the Holy Spirit to decide.

And yet I am convinced that many women have become casualties of a culture separated from God's design for families. Like the woman who came to me at the end of the conference, they are tempted to despair because they don't know how to repair the damage done in their lives and their children's lives or how to make their lives whole.

The purpose of this book is not to tell you how to live your life. And it's certainly not to make you feel guilty. The purpose of this book is simply to hold up God's ideal for the role of motherhood, to remind us of God's design and how we can use our role to stitch together the pieces that will help make our families whole. We need to know where God wants us to go in order to create a plan to get there. Each person must find where she is on this path of motherhood so that she may know how to travel forward from this point. No matter where you are on this road of discovering and living out the mission of motherhood, you can take steps forward.

Even more important, you can trust God to bring you forward. After all, the message of redemption in the Bible is just as strong as the message of family. We serve a redeeming God, a God of second chances, a God whose whole history has been that of seeking out his wayward people and bringing them back into his fold.

He didn't have to put Adam and Eve out of the garden and onto the farm after they sinned. He could have killed them on the spot! He didn't have to bring the Hebrews out of Egypt, put them in the Promised Land, and send them prophets and kings to warn them of the consequences of forgetting their covenant with him. He didn't have to discipline his people when they disobeyed or forgive them when they repented. And he certainly didn't have to send his Son to redeem us, to model wholesome living for us, or to die for our sins.

Jesus came to forgive, redeem, and give us a renewed life. In 2 Corinthians 5:17, God says, "If any man is in Christ, he is a new creature; the old things passed away; behold, new things have come."

Romans 3:23 tells us that all have sinned and fallen short of the glory of God. None of us is any worse or more sinful than anyone else—we are all in the same boat! Although Romans 6:23 warns us that though the wages of sin is death, it also assures us that the free gift of God is eternal life.

So I repeat: We serve a God of redemption and second chances. When we acknowledge our shortcomings and failures to him, he is faithful and just to cleanse us from all unrighteousness. We can always start off with a fresh slate with the Lord and trust him to show us how to return to his original design. He has promised to support those whose hearts are completely his (2 Chronicles 16:9).

The most important factor in being successful as a mother is to turn our hearts to God, to seek his will, and to allow him to begin making sense out of the messes we've made of our lives. He who created motherhood is the gentle teacher whose ways and input we must seek.

As we move ahead in the next chapters, our understanding of motherhood and God's design will become more evident. We will begin to put our plan together so that we will know the steps we must take to find fulfillment in the mission of motherhood.

However, if we reject God's design from the outset, our children and their children and their children will reap the consequences of our unfaithfulness. When we face the Lord at the end of our lives, he will ask us, "What did you do with those precious eternal human beings that I entrusted into your hands? Did you sacrifice your own life to give them my life? Did you pass on my purposes? Did you do the work in your children that will result in praise to my name throughout all of eternity?"

Let us hope that we may all answer yes and that we may hear, "Well done, my good and faithful servant!" For it is in finding God and submitting to him that we will find the purpose and meaning that he designed us to experience. As we learn to fulfill the design for which we were created, we will find the love, peace, and freedom that we long for.

FOR THOUGHT AND REFLECTION

Something to Think About...

When I was a small child, the living room was almost a sacred place to me. We were restricted from playing in this room when our parents were gone because of the many breakable objects my mother had placed around the room.

One evening when our parents were out to dinner, my brothers and I began to throw a ball around in the living room! We were sure that nothing would happen. Sure enough, one of us missed our catch, and the ball came down on a hand-painted gold-leaf plate propped up on a side table. The plate broke into three pieces. I can still see them lying there on that table.

With fear and trembling, my brothers and I confessed our mistake to our parents when they returned home. After being disciplined, I went to my mom and told her how truly sorry I was to have broken something so dear to her. She reassured me by saying, "You leave it in my hands, and we'll see if it can be fixed."

The next week the valuable plate was back on its stand looking as good as new. In my mother's masterful hands, what had been broken was skillfully repaired.

Often we have broken pieces of our lives that cause us great sadness and despair. Yet God, the masterful artist of life, can take our lives into his hands and repair our hearts, souls, and minds. If your family has experienced brokenness, God can begin to redeem it, to bring it back to himself and rebuild and repair the damage that has been done. All we need to do is willingly place our children in his hands and obey his instructions.

1. *Genesis 3:20.* What is the significance of the name that Adam called Eve? What meaning does it have in relationship to our identity as women? How would you describe woman's original purpose as indicated in Genesis. How has this sense of purpose changed in our culture today?

2. *Genesis 1:26-28.* What does it mean to be made in God's image? In verse 28, when God blessed Adam and Eve, what was the first part of his blessing? How does having children and filling the earth with them correspond to our responsibility of subduing the earth and ruling over it? In what way has God prepared you to subdue the world? In what ways have you neglected your stewardship in this matter? What impact would you like to make in the world for the purposes of God? How are you sharing this mandate from God with your children?

3. *Colossians 2:8.* What are some of the philosophies of man concerning family that have taken people captive today? What are the results of these deceptions? In what ways have you been influenced by cultural expectations that conflict with God's design? What impact has this had on your family?

4. *Romans 8:1.* What does this passage say about the guilt of people who have fallen below God's standards? What is the condition for escaping the condemnation we deserve from God? Who are those "who are in Christ Jesus"? Do you feel condemned for the mistakes you have made? Why or why not? How can you be freed from the feeling of guilt? (See 1 John 1:9.)

Something to Try...

When I was a sophomore in college, I was confused about life. I lacked a sense of love, for which I longed desperately. I also had a vague sense of guilt for the ways I had strayed, but I didn't know how to get rid of those feelings. I decided to go on a college trip for young adults. We traveled to Mexico for the two-week retreat, which was in a beautiful resort area. A gifted teacher taught us from the Bible each morning, and we were free to spend the afternoons as we wanted.

One evening the crisis in my life came to a head. I was on a hotel balcony in the dark crying about the pain and sorrow I felt. At just that time the teacher happened by. He took my hands gently into his own and said, "Sally, God loves you through and through. He loves you even though he sees every part of you. He knows all the things you have done wrong, and he still loves you. You are precious to him."

The teacher suggested I take out a sheet of paper and write down all the ways I had sinned and fallen short of God. When I had written a list of what was in my heart, he took the paper and, without looking at it, wrote the words of 1 John 1:9 across it. Then he tore it into tiny pieces and threw them in the garbage can.

"Sally," he said, "according to this verse, all of your sins are forgiven and forgotten. You will never have to worry about them again."

That moment changed my whole life. For the first time I felt a sense of freedom and peace. For the first time I was certain I was loved.

- Take a piece of paper, and write across the top "Ways I Have Fallen Short of God's Standards." Now make a list of all the sins and rebellious acts against God for which you feel guilty.
- Next, look up 1 John 1:9, and write the verse at the top of the page. Then consciously give this list into God's hands. Ask him to wash your heart with his love and grace. When you are finished, tear the paper into pieces and burn it or throw it away. Thank God that you are forgiven and will never have to be responsible for these sins again. Enjoy your peace with God.

CHAPTER 3

The Undivided Heart

Committing Our Lives to God's Design

The wise woman builds her house,
But the foolish tears it down with her own hands.

PROVERBS 14:1

A few years ago I was having some medical problems, and I sought the help of a new young doctor. Her office was light and modern and filled with patients. Her staff was friendly and efficient. The doctor herself seemed knowledgeable and professional, but she also seemed distracted and a bit absent minded. She even misdiagnosed a simple problem regarding my health. As we talked, I learned that she was the mother of a baby, and before long she was sharing some of her frustrations.

"I spent all this time and money to become a doctor. I have my practice, a nice office, and employees. I've supposedly made it in the world, and all of my friends and family are impressed by what I have accomplished. But I feel so torn because I'm not doing a very good job of taking care of my baby, and I love her more than anything! I'm exhausted when I go home at night. I don't have time to relax and enjoy the moments of discovering life with my little one. She gets my leftovers, not my best. But I'm not concentrating at work as well as I should either. What am I supposed to do?"

I felt deeply for this frustrated mom, because I understood her dilemma. It's the same one confronting so many loving, well-intentioned mothers. When they were preparing for life, they focused on career preparation and assumed that motherhood and a home life could be tucked in around the edges. The importance of motherhood, marriage, and the legacy they would leave in the lives of their children didn't enter into their training or planning. So they were not prepared for the reality that motherhood, especially when it is carried out according to God's design, is more than a full-time job. It's an absorbing task that demands all the resources God has given us—our physical energy, our intellectual abilities, our creative gifts—and involves powerful emotional attachments as well.

No wonder this young doctor felt torn. It's not easy to live with a divided heart. And that's exactly what happens when today's mothers attempt to juggle jobs, families, needs, and expectations. More specifically, it's what too often happens when moms attempt to achieve the ideal of this culture—a successful career, a perfect family (but not at the expense of the job!), a dynamite love life, and a beautiful "self-actualized" spirit. They smash into the reality that it's simply impossible for one person to do it all well. No wonder so many mothers feel like failures!

A MATTER OF THE HEART

As I approached the writing of this chapter, I knew that many readers would misunderstand what I am trying to say. Even in the process of getting this book published, I kept running into women, many of them publishing professionals, who looked at my proposal, then stared at me with disbelief. "But surely you're not saying I should quit my job and just stay home with my children."

Well, in a way I *am* saying that—or at least I am saying that women should consider the possibility more seriously than many do. But my real concerns are more with matters of the heart than with the nuts and bolts of whether women should have careers.

I am not opposed to women working or even to mothers having careers. I love my work as a writer and a speaker, and my husband has always encouraged my abilities, skills, and strengths in this area. Women have been gifted by God to be insightful and skilled in most areas of work, and many families would find it hard to manage without a mother's income. I have a variety of friends with many different lifestyles who are working out God's will for their lives within the limitations of their finances, circumstances, and family needs.

I support a woman's freedom to walk by faith and work out her own solutions to life's problems and challenges within the framework of biblical priorities. So I am not writing to propose a single solution for every reader. At the same time, I think it's a mistake to assume—as the dominant culture today does—that a mother can maintain a full-tilt career and a full dedication to her home without shortchanging one or both. There is a strong case to be made for full-time, wholehearted motherhood—and this is something women rarely hear anymore.

So many mothers today, like my doctor, have never considered full-time motherhood as an option; they have never even stopped to consider a choice their hearts are really longing to make. They are unprepared for the deep love and connection they feel to the babies whose lives began in the womb.

Others, influenced by the language of feminism, remain confused because they think of the issue in terms of a choice between equal alternatives. "Well, some mothers choose to stay home with their children," they say, "and that's fine, but it's not for me. My choice is to work and use my skills."

The implication is that one choice is as good as another—like choosing between fish and chicken in a cafeteria line. But life really isn't a cafeteria, and the choices we make about how to care for our children are not neutral. Choices have consequences. How we choose to focus our priorities and time in light of our children's lives will have great consequences not only for their individual futures but for the future of our society as well.

Most of the moms I know, whether they go to work or stay at home, have a great concern and love for their children. Yet in this generation the issues at stake in our children's lives have not often been discussed or evaluated so that we can really think through the ramifications of our decisions. Traditional, home-based, full-time motherhood at least deserves to be a part of the discussion.

Children do not accidentally become righteous leaders or emotionally healthy and productive adults—any more than seeds thrown randomly to the wind grow to be part of a thriving garden. Simply throwing children into a cultural tornado and hoping for the best gives them little chance of living up to their potential or coming out unharmed. Someone needs to take responsibility for their nurture, protection, nourishment, intellectual development, manners, recreation, personal needs, and spiritual development. Someone needs to commit time and energy into staying close to them as they grow, encouraging and correcting and teaching.

Doesn't it make sense that a wise God, who ordered the rest of creation in an intricate and systematic way, would also have provided such a person to care for children—to commit wholeheartedly to creating the right environment for them to grow and to prepare them to live throughout eternity bearing his image?

I am convinced that God designed us as mothers to be that person in the lives of our children. He intended it to be a fully committed job, not something we do on the side. For me that has meant choosing full-time, at-home mothering as my top priority. Yes, I have continued to speak and to write and to tackle a variety of projects to earn extra money during lean years. But instead of pursuing a career with mothering tucked in around the edges, I have chosen to focus first on the mission of motherhood. My reward for this decision has been both simple and profound. I have been able to know the joys of mothering without a divided heart.

But it took some time and a great deal of study for me to come to this point. Like the young doctor at the beginning of this chapter, I had thought a lot about my life and work when I was growing up, but I had never really thought about what priority motherhood would take. More to the point, I had not yet given myself wholeheartedly to the mission of motherhood.

Yes, I loved my family and wanted to do a good job as a mother. But when up to my elbows in the tedious responsibilities of life, I spent much of my mental energy thinking about when I would have more time for myself and my own interests. *When my children are six,* I would think, *there will be no more children in diapers, no more naps, and my life will be freer. Then I will have more time to write and speak and spend time on me—to do the important stuff!*

As I began to seek God in this area, however, he gently began to put his finger on the real source of my dissatisfaction, which lay not on my specific choices or my skills as a mother, but in my divided heart. How could I put all of me into my time at home if I was always thinking about a future time when I could escape the routine tasks of motherhood?

Though I slowly made progress, it took me years to embrace totally and joyfully my calling and commitment to motherhood and to accept the sacrifices that I needed to make. Failure was a familiar part of my early life as a mother, and many of my lessons were hard learned.

I remember one particular moment when I was bathing my four-year-old and two-year-old in the double kitchen sink. It had been a rough day, and I was desperate to get everything tucked away for the evening. Suddenly little Joel, my toddling boy, exuberantly stood up in the sink and began splashing water and bubbles all over the floor.

That did it! I screamed at Joel and threw out some words about making messes and making more work for Mommy. His sweet face fell, and I immediately felt remorseful. I knew he didn't deserve the anger I had unleashed on him.

I gently picked him up, wrapped him in a towel, cuddled him, and asked for forgiveness. And he gave it to me—sweetly and beautifully. He smiled and said, "Don't worry! Joelly loves Mommy!"

In that moment the two conflicted drives of my heart stood out in stark contrast—my commitment to motherhood versus my lurking desire to have life my own way. And from that moment on, I became a little clearer about which path I needed to follow if I really wanted to reflect God's design. I began to see my children's care and nurture as God's best will for my life during my season as a mother.

I needed to accept days like this—my children's neediness, the myriad mindless tasks, and even my own occasional discomfort—as part of my partnering with my husband toward our mutual goal of building a godly heritage for Christ. I needed to nurture my children with my songs, my words, and my physical labor, treating each day as sacred in their development toward becoming healthy, mature adults. I needed to face the reality that all of the "important stuff" I was longing to do had far less eternal significance than what I was involved in doing. If I didn't commit myself wholeheartedly to the demands of motherhood, I would never be able to do my best, because my heart would always be somewhere else.

WHOLEHEARTED MOTHERING
IN A HALFHEARTED SOCIETY

As soon as I made the commitment to wholehearted motherhood, however, I began to realize that this kind of mothering can be a challenge in today's culture. We often hear of the gains women have made over the past 150 years. We can vote. We are more educated than our great-grandmothers were 100 years ago. We have access to the same professions as men and, in many cases, the same or more pay.

But I wonder if anyone realizes some of the losses these developments have caused in the lives of many mothers. As more women work outside the home and the two-income family is considered the norm, I believe it's become harder, not easier, to be a family.

For one thing, as a culture we have lost the vision of the crucial role mothers play in the life of the next generation. When women are not encouraged to embrace motherhood with a whole heart, as an occupation worthy of a full life's devotion, a part of the basic design of our femininity is devalued. Women were designed to nurture, to provide a life-giving environment in the home—to provide a center of life for all who live there. But as the women's movement has gained ground over the course of the century, women have felt less and less free to follow this design. No longer do we have the moral support of a culture that applauds what we are doing—or even the practical support of other women in our neighborhood. (They're mostly at work during the day.) In a cultural sense, we have all but lost the right to focus wholeheartedly on creating a home.

At the same time, as women have moved out into the world, our lives—and especially our children's lives—have lost much of the richness and simplicity we once enjoyed. What we have gained in lifestyle options and material goods we have lost in terms of time, flexibility, peace, and personal attention.

How difficult it is to fit in doctor's appointments, birthday parties and celebrations, shopping for food and clothes, keeping house and washing clothes, and cooking in the time that is left after a mom gives her most energetic and creative eight hours (or more!) to her job or career. When is there time or energy to do more than the basics for her children, much less have time for creative or inspiring activities? Such satisfying homely pursuits as gardening, canning, baking, or sewing have been relegated to hobbies instead of meaningful home life, and for many women these pursuits fall into the category of "things I'll do someday if I have the time" or "things I like to watch on Home and Garden TV when I collapse at the end of the day."

It's so easy, in this era of divided hearts, for women's souls to become withered and dried up because we have so little time to read, to think, to enjoy the beauty of nature or the joy of relaxing with a friend or loved one. We buy fast food or prepared food instead of cooking nutritious homemade meals. Instead of creative, homemade gifts, we buy ready-made synthetic flower arrangements and cellophane-wrapped gift packs made in China. Instead of playing pretend with our children or taking the time to blow bubbles, we park them in front of an impersonal box that baby-sits them for hours with no real love, touch, morality, or truth to give.

Our children, meanwhile, miss out on the time and devoted attention from an adult who has made a commitment to be there for them. Discovering inter-esting books, beautiful music, captivating art, and fun, playful moments within an intimate loving relationship nurtures the souls of children. What happens too often instead in this era of divided hearts is that little ones must seek to find their own footing and search for love and inspiration from impersonal institutions where children are overstimulated, under-rested, and have little opportunity for individual attention.

I don't mean to say that all day-care situations fit this nightmarish scenario —although some do. And I certainly don't mean to imply that women who work do not love or nurture their children! Most of the women I have met truly want to do what is best for their little ones.

My point is that a divided mind that comes from a lack of wholehearted commitment to the home, as well as the simple time pressure that comes from supporting a dual career of home and family, tends to rob mother and children alike of the freedom they need to grow and thrive.

Instead of being rocked and nursed and sung to by a mother who has time to stay until all childish fears are at rest, they tend to be rocked and nursed and put to bed by a loving mother who is desperate for them to go to sleep so she can sleep too. Instead of being allowed to play imaginatively for hours in their own yard with their own swing set or homemade tent, they may have an hour or so of play between the end of after-school care and the onset of darkness. Reading from Mom's favorite books or being served Mom's best chocolate-chip cookies are rare treats instead of daily staples. Time to explore and discover in the rich environment of a well-planned and artfully designed home is no longer a possibility for children who are awakened early to be rushed off to day care or school before Mom's workday begins.

The loss isn't just imagined; it's real, and children feel it acutely. *Time* mag-azine ran an article on April 30, 2001, based on the largest study ever done on this subject by the National Institutes of Health. One of the conclusions of the study was that "the more hours children spend away from their mothers, the more likely they are to be defiant, aggressive and disobedient by the time they get to kindergarten."

In the face of evidence like this, child psychologist Dr. James Dobson stated in an interview in the August 2001 issue of the *Focus on the Family* magazine how important it is to have a mother at home: "I have never said publicly what

I will share now—and I will be criticized for saying so in this context—but I believe the two-career family during the child-rearing years creates a level of stress that is tearing people apart. And it often deprives children of something that they will search for the rest of their lives."

As I began to read books and articles on these subjects, I was overwhelmed by the statistics of increased problems in children's lives during the past fifty years as more women entered the workplace and traditional motherhood ceased to be the society-approved norm. The problems ranged from peer and drug dependence and lower school test scores to teen pregnancy, violent crimes, runaways, and suicide. I could spend the rest of this book quoting from these articles. Instead, I'd rather focus on the ways that following God's design for wholehearted, traditional motherhood can help prevent or solve such problems, at least with our own children.

If a woman chooses to stay at home with her children, she has the opportunity of nursing her baby in the peacefulness of her own home, caressing her precious little one, singing sweet lullabies to comfort and please the child's deepest emotional desires. She can offer them the restfulness of long, quiet naps in their own bedrooms. She has time to enrich the home environment with beautiful sights and smells—from the aromas of homemade soup bubbling on the stove to the beautiful pictures in books—and arrange outings that foster budding intellects and awaken curiosity. And she has the flexibility to change her schedule to respond to teachable moments—those times when children's natural curiosity leads them to question and learn.

Best of all, when a mother chooses to stay home, she has the time and opportunity to craft the kind of relationship with her young children that only extended time together can foster. And from such a relationship she has a much better chance of building a strong moral and spiritual foundation in the heart of her young child, teaching a system of truth and values without the constant challenge of authorities and peers whose lives are totally different. When these advantages are taken away from a child, how can we not count them as a loss to a whole generation of children who are hungry for direction, love, stability, and individual attention?

This is not to say that the life of a woman who makes the choice for wholehearted, full-time motherhood will always be peaceful and relaxing. Anyone who has ever lived with a toddler—or a teenager—knows better than that. Even under the best of circumstances—and even with the extra time and flexibility that traditional motherhood does provide—parenting can be a challenge as well as a blessing. But this is precisely my point, which is that being a mother is a full-time job—demanding as well as deeply fulfilling. It is a responsibility that rightly commands our primary attention and calls for an intentional commitment. We owe our children—and ourselves—our full hearts, not whatever is left over after a busy day at the office.

MY PRIMARY RESPONSIBILITY

As I prayed about my own life, I realized that because I was a mother, I was automatically under a different set of responsibilities than my unmarried friends or my married friends who had no children. With the privilege of bearing children comes the responsibility to commit wholeheartedly to the care of those children.

God holds us accountable for our stewardship of his blessings. And that means I am responsible for the ways in which I choose to care for the children he has given me. At the Judgment, I know I will give an account to him for these precious lives he entrusted into my hands.

As a woman who has enjoyed a career of teaching, speaking, counseling, and writing, I have had to make many difficult decisions to cut my career opportunities in order to focus on my family priorities. However, I have come to realize that embracing God's call to the duties of motherhood doesn't diminish my abilities to use my gifts, strength, and training, but fulfills a part of God's design.

Loving my children, protecting them, and building them into a godly heritage is a life's work worth far more than any money or status I might find in a career. If the mother who gave her children life is not willing to do what it takes to provide security, love, protection, instruction, and stability for her own children, then who will be willing to do so? Many will be orphans in a crowded world, longing for the security they were supposed to find in their own family.

If we want to experience the blessing of God and have a sense of wholeness to our lives, we must seek to understand his original design as clearly as possible. We will then have a map by which to travel toward God's destination. But we need to do more than understand. We also need to commit to living as mothers with undivided hearts—dedicating ourselves fully to the task of building a home and nurturing our children.

CHOICE AND SACRIFICE

Once we have made the choice for wholehearted motherhood, other decisions will fall into place. The practical questions—such as how it can be done and where the money will come from—will find answers, although this will sometimes involve a lot of creative problem solving.

Clay and I experienced many times of financial difficulty during our parenting years. When we were starting our ministry, we went almost five years without a regular salary. Those times were quite challenging. There were even times when I felt guilty going to the grocery store because we didn't seem to have enough money to go around.

And yet even in those years, we found ways to make ends meet while enabling me to honor my commitment to be at home full time with the children. I sold homemade cinnamon rolls to a coffee house, sold books through a party plan, wrote articles, and gave stamp parties in desperate times when our ministry did not provide enough money for us to live. Our entire family even worked in a professional musical production during the summers just to put food on the table. The memory of our time working together is cherished by all of our children.

Even though those times were hard, the Lord provided and sustained us. Those lean years turned out to be precious ones, years in which much of my foundation of faith was laid.

So many moms I know who have made the choice for wholehearted motherhood have discovered the same thing. Through a combination of creative problem solving and active trust, they have learned that whatever the Lord requires, he also enables. I know moms who have chosen to remain in smaller homes and to drive older cars in order to live on one income and spend more time with their young children. Others have started home-based businesses or juggled interesting work hours. A nurse friend works evenings, when her husband can be home with the children. I have written books from half past four until eight in the morning so I could be free and undistracted in my time with my children. Each of these moms I know have sought creative ways to provide financially while staying committed to having time to nurture their children.

Recently I was speaking to a large conference of women. A young single mom who had four children sat down with me to tell me her story. Her Christian husband had run away with another woman and had left her to fend for herself and her children. She told me, "I panicked and despaired about what I would do with our lives. Everyone at church told me that it was my responsibility to immediately go to work to pay all of our bills. But I knew my little ones were already struggling with the emotional upheaval of the divorce, and I didn't feel right about leaving them. Oh, you can't imagine the criticism I received from 'well-meaning Christians.'

"I decided to move into a trailer in the backyard of my mom and dad's home, which in itself was humbling. I spent time with my children and prayed that God would show me a way to stay home with them. I can't tell you how many times, when we were down to our last penny, that God helped to provide for our needs. It has been a hard road, but now, three years later, my children are flourishing, and we are finally getting on our feet financially. And I can look back and see what strength we all gained from each other by working through these life problems together and building a strong, peaceful, and spiritual home."

This young woman's story had a powerful impact on me, because it testified so beautifully to the ways that God provides for those who commit to doing things his way. Her particular solution might not work for everyone. Each of us is different, each of us finds herself at a different point on this path of motherhood, and our individual decisions will reflect the difference in our circumstances. But once we commit to embrace the vision of motherhood, God always provides the creative guidance we need to keep moving toward our goal.

WISE BUILDERS

One of the most important ways God guides us, of course, is through the words of Scripture. My husband and I have often said that, in the absence of biblical convictions, people will go the way of their culture. Without biblical conviction, the tendency is to blindly accept the norms or standards of the people with whom we spend time. That means we can allow the media and our peers to shape our ideas about motherhood and family instead of basing our decisions on the eternal truth of Scripture.

We have already spent some time in this book examining God's basic design for motherhood as set forth in his Word. But the Bible also has some specific guidance for making choices and commitments that can help us as we journey toward mothering with an undivided heart.

The first thing the Bible tells us about committing to motherhood is that we need to be aware of what we are doing when we make our choices. Proverbs 14:1 tells us that the wise woman builds her house and the foolish tears it down with her own hands. The Hebrew word that is translated here as *house* really has three different meanings in the Old Testament—an actual, physical dwelling; a home or household; and a heritage. I think the context in Proverbs 14 refers more to a heritage of godly children. And the clear implication is that the process of building our heritage requires wise attention.

If we are to build such a heritage, we must know what we're doing. All houses have a design and a cost and a systematic way in which they must be built. If we want to build strong homes, we must think ahead and do what is necessary to lay a strong, stable foundation. And then, as we build, we need to check our progress along the way, keeping our overall purpose in mind and making choices that keep our building on the right track. We must assess our choices honestly to determine whether they are helping or hindering what we are trying to do.

I have never met a mother who has told me she willingly set out to tear down her house or heritage with her own hands. Yet many a mother has shared with me her regrets that she unwittingly did just that—either because she didn't know what to do or because her misplaced priorities or divided heart kept her from doing what she needed to do for the sake of her children. If we want to be wise mothers, we must recognize our need to commit to what we're doing. We need to plan for building our house, and we need to keep monitoring our progress to ensure we're not tearing down what we mean to build.

The doctor I described at the beginning of this chapter had never done this, and I believe this failure was at the heart of her frustration. She longed in her heart for something she didn't quite understand. She had a God-given desire to build her home and not destroy it—to be with her baby, to love her and answer her cries, to protect and provide for her, and to know her deeply. But because she had never understood that her desires were part of a divine calling that required her full attention, she was living in confusion and pain.

Scripture tells us plainly that we are to count the cost of the choices we make and the tasks we undertake (Luke 14:28). When we can do this as mothers— understanding what we are called to do and committing ourselves wholeheart- edly to the work of nurturing children—we will indeed be wise mothers who build our houses and don't tear them down.

ETERNAL TREASURES—AND LIVING SACRIFICES

A second important thing Scripture tells us about our commitment as mothers has to do with the eternal significance of our choices. Matthew 6:20-21 encourages us: "Lay up for yourselves treasures in heaven, where neither moth nor rust destroys, and where thieves do not break in or steal; for where your treasure is, there will your heart be also." We are instructed to set our hearts on choices with eternal results, not choices with only temporal significance.

As I pondered these verses, the realization that my children are eternal human beings whose lives and souls will last throughout all of eternity struck me powerfully. God has given them into my husband's and my hands to protect and lead and shepherd them through this life on earth; in his sight, they are my first priority. Committing myself to fulfilling God's design falls under the admonition to seek first his kingdom—the kingdom of heaven where we will live for all eternity. The kingdom of this world and all of its pleasures last only for a time.

My children will become treasures in heaven if they indeed learn to love God and serve him with their whole hearts. This is eternal work—to train the hearts, minds, and consciences in righteousness. This is the vital work of building a morally, emotionally, mentally, and spiritually strong generation of children who will be prepared to function responsibly for the rest of their lives. But before I can do this work effectively, I have to come to a point of yielding my heart to God's will. I have to surrender my old expectations of who I thought I was to the calling of the Lord on my life. And if I have been blessed with children, I have to surrender myself wholeheartedly to my role of being a mother after God's design.

This brings us to a third thing that Scripture tells us about our commitments as mothers. Romans 12:1 provides a vivid picture of what it means to give our whole selves to the Lord's way of doing things: "I urge you therefore, brethren, by the mercies of God, to present your bodies a living and holy sacrifice, acceptable to God, which is your spiritual service of worship."

To fully experience our fulfillment in Christ and fulfill his will for our lives, we must come to the point where we give our whole selves to him—our freedom, our time, our bodies, all of our possessions and gifts—trusting him to show us how to use all that we are for his glory. To sacrifice means to give up or surrender something of value. We are living sacrifices, which means that moment by moment, out of our worship of him, we are to surrender our own needs and expectations for the greater value of pleasing our Lord.

What a contrast this image of sacrifice makes to the philosophy of our world today. Everywhere we turn—whether on television, magazines, newspapers, or radio—we are encouraged to make time for ourselves, to take care of our own needs first, to look out for numero uno!

But Jesus says just the opposite. He clearly states, again and again, that if we lose our lives for him, we will find our lives—the joy and fulfillment we long for.

I knew this scripture quite well when I first became a mother so many years ago, but I didn't really understand how it applied to my calling as a mother. I had no idea what it would mean to sacrifice myself for my family, how much it would cost to follow God's design for the journey of motherhood. If I had understood more of what to expect, what I was called to do, and the intrinsic significance of my role, I think I might have had an easier time of yielding myself to God's purposes. Perhaps I wouldn't have had to struggle through so many self-ish attitudes, to fail so often in meeting my children's needs, and to fight so many unnecessary battles.

As it is, after eighteen years of learning the truth of living sacrificially, I have found that embracing God's call to motherhood once and for all has brought me great peace. Instead of seeing fusses and messes as irritations in my day, for instance, I am more likely to see them as opportunities to train my children to be peacemakers and to learn to be responsible for their own messes. Instead of resenting the interruptions in my schedule, I am more likely to accept them as divine appointments. More and more, I have learned to see my children through the eyes of God and to accept the stages of growth through which he has designed them to grow.

How do we make the commitment to give the area of motherhood over to God as a sacrifice of worship to him? We yield our personal rights into his hands. We give up our time and expectations to him—and also our fears and worries about how we will manage. We trust him to take care of us and our family. We let him redirect our thinking and expectations and adjust our dreams. And we wait in faith to see the fruit of our hard labor in the lives of our children, knowing that he will be faithful to honor our commitment to him.

A friend of mine told me that when she first came to one of our mothers' conferences, she had never heard of God's design for motherhood. She had two different nannies for her children—a daytime nanny and a nighttime nanny. Her professional life was fulfilling and lucrative. And yet she still felt that something was off kilter in her life.

"When I heard these messages," she told me, "I suddenly realized how empty I felt. My children were more attached to their nannies than me. I didn't like who they were becoming. I gave it all up and stayed at home with my children. My friends thought I was crazy, but I feel like I'm sensing the intimacy of close relationships, the joy of my children growing and developing more toward my goals and values in life, and the unity in my marriage that I always longed for. Before we were all going in different directions, but now our home is the center of life. You can't imagine how my life has changed, but it's going in the right direction."

As I see my own children now in their teens, I am so glad that the Lord gave me the opportunity to understand this commitment in an early part of their lives. The cost has been great, but the sacrifice was well worth it. I can honestly say that my children are my best friends. No, they're not perfect—and neither am I—but we're all growing and blossoming in all areas of life. I see now that the fruit of God's design tastes sweet to my soul. And with that fruit, there are no regrets.

FOR THOUGHT AND REFLECTION

Something to Think About...

About ten years ago, during a particularly stressful time in my life, I was pregnant with what I thought would be my fourth child. As I approached the thirteen-week mark, I sighed in relief, knowing that I had passed the "miscarriage window." Suddenly one evening when I went to bed, I felt something almost snap in my womb. I feared that the stress was taking its toll on my body.

The next morning I began to spot, and within a short period of time I was bleeding heavily. Because I was new in town and didn't have a maternity doctor yet, a friend called a midwife she knew to come to my aid. By the time she arrived, I was resting in the bathtub, because my miscarriage was in process, and I was quite messy with the evidence.

A slight young woman came into the room, laid her coat on the cabinet, and stooped down to my eye level. She said, "Hello, precious one. I am so sorry for your pain, and I am here to take care of you." She took my hand and stroked it gently as she asked me to tell her what had taken place. During the next hour, Heather very gently and humbly cleaned me up, treated me medically, and helped me determine what steps I needed to take to get further medical attention. Her voice was a constant flow of soft encouragement. In all of my life, it is one of the times I felt most loved.

After I returned home from the hospital, I called Heather and told her how very special she had made me feel and how meaningful her generous care had been to me, even though I was a total stranger. "When I gave my life to Jesus," she gently replied, "I realized that he wanted me to give my life wholeheartedly to comforting and serving those moms he blessed with pregnancy. I consider that each time I help someone, it is as though I am serving the Lord Jesus himself, and I give him the best love that I can give."

I learned through this precious woman something of the beauty of wholehearted commitment. What a picture for me as I pour myself out to meet the needs of my children. For me, it has become a constant reminder that when I serve my family, I am serving the Lord Jesus himself. So I am learning to give the best love I can give!

1. *Proverbs 14:1.* What does it mean to build our house or family? In what ways do we tear it down? To build a physical home, a plan must be made. What does the plan for building your family look like? What changes need to be made?

2. *Matthew 6:20,33.* What are the treasures Jesus is talking about in verse 20? In what way does it apply to the eternal work of building a heritage through our children for eternity? What does it mean to teach our children to seek his kingdom first? How do we model this in our own home?

3. *Galatians 6:7.* What does this verse mean? How do we sow in a meaningful way in our children's lives so that the seed we plant will bear spiritual

fruit? What are some of the negative things that are sown in our children's lives through the media? What materialistic values do they encounter in the general culture? What can we do about these "weeds" that spring up as a result?

4. *Romans 12:1-2.* According to these verses, what does God consider to be the most effective kind of worship? In what ways can we do this, and how does it apply to the way we live as parents? According to verse 2, how do we keep from being conformed to this world? In what way can we transform our minds? (See 2 Timothy 3:16.)

Something to Try...

A few years ago I did a study on the word *cup* as used in the Bible. It usually represents our lot in life or the portion that God has given. When Jesus was about to be crucified, he prayed to the Father, "If it is possible, let this cup pass from Me; yet not as I will, but as Thou wilt" (Matthew 26:39). I am so glad that he was willing to drink his cup so that I might be forgiven. He lived his life and obeyed God with grace.

To help me remember this, I bought a miniature teacup and placed it on the top of my desk. Whenever I see it, I pray that I will drink my own cup with as much graciousness as did my Lord. I have also made a collection of pictures and figurines of mothers and children. These pictures are full of love and life and point me back to the commitment I have made to God to embrace my calling as a mother. As one more reminder, I have framed many of the snapshots taken of my children over the years and placed them throughout the house. I have made a commitment to pray for them whenever I see their pictures.

- Spend personal time with the Lord, and make a commitment to present your whole self to him as your spiritual service of worship. Write in a diary the time and scope of your commitment to him so that you can always review it and have it as a spiritual marker in your journey of motherhood.

- Collect books, pictures, quotations, verses, or mementos to remind you of your commitment to the Lord. Let these symbols encourage you in your commitment to be the mother God designed you to be.

❧ Start a Mom's Night Out or support group with other moms you know. Meet once a month in one another's homes or in a favorite restaurant to share your stresses, questions, needs, and frustrations—or just to have fun. Be sure to keep this time as an adult time, without the kids, so that you can enjoy the fellowship and prayer without any distractions. Studying and discussing a book together, like this one, can add substance to your group and give it direction and purpose.

PART TWO

A MOTHER'S HEART *for* HER GOD

CHAPTER 4

The Servant Mother

Mothering with the Heart of Jesus

Greater love has no one than this,
that one lay down his life for his friends.

JOHN 15:13

It was 4:30 in the afternoon, and I was pooped! We had been out on a hotter-than-normal afternoon in a car without air conditioning. It was Joy's sixth birthday, so we had enjoyed lunch at her favorite restaurant and played at a playground with friends. Grocery shopping and errands had followed. Now I was longing to sit down with a cup of tea for just fifteen minutes to relax and regroup. But dinner still needed to be made. Groceries sat on the kitchen cabinet, waiting to be put away. Joy's birthday cake needed to be frosted.

If I can have just a few minutes alone, I thought, *I'll be okay.* But as I was sneaking into my room for a short reprieve, the phone rang. Sarah, who had borrowed the car as soon as I got home, was calling to tell me she couldn't get the gas tank open. Did I know what was wrong?

I gave her a couple of suggestions, then hung up and reheated my tea water. Ringgggggg!

"By the way, Mom. I found a movie I would like to get for my birthday." Sarah was so excited she couldn't wait until she got home to tell me. I did my best to share her enthusiasm, but all I could think about was that chair and my cup of tea.

As I hung up the phone, Joel called from the den.

"Mom, can you please take a picture of me for my Web site? It will just take a minute!"

We set up the camera, and he posed with his guitar. But the camera wouldn't work. The battery pack was dead. We tried to plug it in, but the cord wouldn't reach the outlet. Finally, after moving a wooden hutch, we were able to plug in the camera and take the picture Joel wanted.

By now I had given up on my tea! I went to the kitchen to unpack the groceries and noticed that no children seemed to be around to help. Just as I was stashing an armload of vegetables in the crisper, Joy urgently called from her downstairs bedroom, "Mommy, come quickly!" I raced to see what was up. "Look, Mommy! I made a pen to put my Beanie Babies in! Isn't it neat?!" After affirming her genius, I trudged back up the stairs. Again the phone rang. This time it was Clay.

"Hi, honey! Did you know John [my nephew at the Air Force Academy] is coming over for the birthday dinner and needs someone to pick him up?" I quickly phoned Sarah to ask if she could do it. As I hung up the phone, Nathan called out from downstairs in a panic.

"Mom, can you help me find my T-shirt for our meeting tonight? I have to wear it, or I don't get points for my badge."

After searching the house, we found the shirt in a laundry basket. At least it was clean!

The phone rang again. It was the next-door neighbors, ready to take Nathan to his meeting.

I glanced up at the fridge as I hung up the phone. Tacked up with a magnet was a card with a phrase from an old chorus: "If you want to be great in God's kingdom, learn to be the servant of all!" For a second I was tempted to take the verse off of the door and stick it in the recycling bin. Then I just had to laugh at the Lord's sense of humor.

The truth is, serving others in the ordinary moments of life is not something that comes easily to me. I'm the kind of person who tends to be attracted to the grand sweeping accomplishments in life. I am challenged by stories that offer great vision and depth of commitment. When it comes to motherhood, I like the idea of being a mom who inspires my children to great accomplishments in medicine (developing the cure for cancer) or statesmanship (a future president of the United States) or the arts (a Christian movie producer). The everyday realities of running a household just don't have the same appeal.

But such humdrum activities, of course, comprise the majority of a mother's experience. Before I had children, I never realized this. I really had no clue that admiring a Beanie Baby's pen, taking a picture, finding a T-shirt, and helping to unlock a gas cap would be the kinds of sacrificial acts required of me most often while I attempted to fulfill the mission of motherhood.

As I have grown through the past eighteen years of motherhood, however, I've come to appreciate the importance of the many thousands of routine moments in a mother's life, for it is in these moments that real greatness tends to be taught and caught. It is certainly important to grasp the great calling of motherhood and respond to a vision for what a family can be. But it's the way I respond to my children in everyday moments that gives me the best chance of winning their hearts. If I have integrity and patience in the small moments of life that are so important to my children, and if I approach them with a servant's heart, then I have a far better chance of influencing them in the larger and more critical issues of life.

THE MODEL OF A SERVANT LEADER

I have often looked to Jesus' relationship with his disciples as a model for how I am to lead my own "disciples." And one of the stories from the Lord's life that has powerfully affected my thinking in terms of how to relate to my children is found in John 13. This passage of Scripture contains the familiar but still amazing account of the last supper Jesus shared with his friends the night before he was crucified. To me it also contains a beautiful picture of what Jesus thought about leadership and what he expects from me as a mother:

> Now before the Feast of the Passover, Jesus knowing that His hour had come that He should depart out of this world to the Father, having loved His own who were in the world, He loved them to the end. And during supper,…Jesus, knowing that the Father had given all things into His hands, and that He had come forth from God, and was going back to God… (John 13:1-3)

Let's stop here and consider what these verses are saying. First of all, before the night even began, Jesus had in mind his position in the universe. He knew "that the Father had given all things into His hands"—in other words, that he owned the stars, that he had created the heavens and the earth, that he had command over legions of angels. He even governed history and had the freedom from God to say yes or no to sacrificing his life. He knew "that He had come forth from God, and was going back to God"—in other words, that his home was in heaven, where thousands of angelic beings sang songs of his greatness and worthiness day after day, and that someday every person who ever lived would bow before him.

Now, if I were Jesus and I knew how really important I was—how powerful and authoritative and worthy—I would want someone to throw a banquet in my honor. I would at least want my closest friends to sympathize with me about the difficulty ahead or somehow acknowledge my greatness.

Yet, as we read on, we see the most amazing thing. Instead of demanding deference and respect from his disciples on his last night, Jesus chose to serve them:

> [He] rose from supper, and laid aside His garments; and taking a towel, He girded Himself about. Then He poured water into the basin, and began to wash the disciples' feet, and to wipe them with the towel with which He was girded....
>
> [S]o when He had washed their feet, and taken His garments, and reclined at the table again, He said to them, "Do you know what I have done to you? You call Me Teacher and Lord; and you are right, for so I am. If I then, the Lord and the Teacher, washed your feet, you also ought to wash one another's feet. For I gave you an example that you also should do as I did to you. Truly, truly, I say to you, a slave is not greater than his master; neither is one who is sent greater than the one who sent him. If you know these things, you are blessed if you do them." (John 13:4-5,12-17)

Jesus had planned and arranged to serve his disciples a Passover meal that would symbolize the significance of his own sacrifice for them. He gently washed and dried their feet—a job only the lowliest slaves were required to do. He blessed the food and passed it to them and led them in worship. His words of encouragement and love during this time are some of the tenderest words found in Scripture.

One of the last memories the disciples had of their Lord was of his ministering gently and humbly to them. I imagine that years later, when they realized just what Jesus had done by willingly dying on the cross, they must have looked back to that last supper with even more astonishment than they felt at the time. The Savior of the world had chosen to spend the night before his great sacrifice ministering to them—gently touching them, feeding them, cleaning them, and ministering to their deepest needs, so that they might truly know and feel their valued relationship to him. No wonder all of his disciples were willing in the coming years to give their lives for him. Not only had he *told* them that whoever wanted to be first must be a servant to all, but he had also *shown* them personally what servant leadership was all about. They had experienced the depth of his sacrificial love firsthand and had been changed by it.

This kind of servant leadership is the model that Jesus gave to us for all areas of our lives, including our roles as mothers. He reached the minds, hearts, and lives of his disciples not just by telling them what to do but by serving them in love—an example that contrasts starkly to the common view of what leadership is all about.

Since the beginning of time, societies have tended to operate on the notion that being in authority gives one the right and even the responsibility to command others, to order others about, and to lord over them. Jesus commented on this very subject in Matthew 20:25-28. He observed that the Gentiles—pagans, non-Jews, those who did not know God—tended to lord it over their subjects. Then he instructed his disciples in the approach he would later model for them: "It is not so among you, but whoever wishes to become great among you shall be your servant" (verse 26).

Surely this commandment applies to parental authority as well. I have often met well-intentioned parents who think they must be harsh and demanding to their young children in order to secure their obedience and good behavior and to build their characters. Too often, I'm afraid, they fall into the trap of simply lording it over their children rather than truly reaching their hearts.

I'm not saying that obedience and behavior and character aren't important. In fact, I think that teaching our children these qualities is essential. I believe, however, that Jesus showed us plainly the most effective way to do this: by *modeling* obedience and right behavior and good character. And this requires us to do what Jesus did for the disciples—to lead our children not only by telling them what to do, but by showing them.

When we choose to graciously overlook our children's messes and accidents, we are teaching them to be patient and forgiving with the mistakes of others. When we react sensitively, thoughtfully, and patiently to them, we are helping to instill these qualities in their lives. As they benefit from our unconditional love, they learn to extend it to others as well. As they watch us extend hospitality, care for others, and pray for them, they learn to make service a part of life. And as they observe us searching Scripture, spending time with the Lord, and making faith-based decisions, they learn these things as well. Modeling loving service to our children gives them something to emulate in their own lives.

Again, this doesn't mean we will ask nothing of our children or do everything for them. It doesn't mean we won't tell them what is right. It certainly doesn't mean we won't discipline them or require proper behavior from them. Jesus, after all, asked a lot of his disciples. He ultimately asked them to be willing to die for his cause! It is important to remember, though, that they first saw him give up his life for them. And that, I believe, is the model that he intends us mothers to follow.

CHOOSING TO LAY DOWN OUR LIVES

What does it mean to practice servant leadership as a mother? I believe it starts out with a choice. I have to choose to serve Christ by giving my time and energy to my children—not just when I feel like it but when they need me. This means I often must sacrifice my own needs and desires for the purpose of giving my children what they need and modeling for them the depths of Christ's love.

For me, choosing servanthood has meant sitting quietly on a child's bed, listening to her sorrows and loneliness, encouraging her, administering love— when I would rather have had some time to myself. It has meant being exhausted from caring for three children under six, yet still getting up in the middle of the night to soothe the pain of an ear infection—without complaining about how tired I am. It has meant making the effort to plan an outing—a picnic lunch, a drive to the mountains, a favorite book on tape—when we moved to a new area and my children felt friendless, even though I had a million other things to do.

Choosing to be a servant-mother means willingly giving up myself, my expectations, and my time to the task of mothering—and choosing to believe that doing so is the best use of my time at that moment. It means that, by faith,

I have already made a decision to make myself available in the routine tasks and myriad interruptions of daily life because I believe it is God's will for me to serve my family through them. Making this choice ahead of time means I will expect problems and needs to arise and be ready to deal with them in peace instead of impatience and resentment.

A Scripture passage that has been an anchor to me in learning to make these choices is John 15:13. Jesus said, "Greater love has no one than this, that one lay down his life for his friends." He had left his throne in heaven to humbly serve us on this earth. He gave me an example to follow. He gave his life so that others might live.

More than anything else, being a mother has helped me to understand this verse. I used to travel on airplanes, wear lovely clothes, speak in prominent places, enjoy fine cuisine in the various cities in which I ministered. I used to love having long teatimes and conversations with friends and colleagues and a sufficient salary to spend on my whims and pleasures.

Now most of the time I stay home. I spend a great deal of time doing things that will need to be done over and over again—washing clothes, cooking meals, cleaning messes, correcting attitudes, teaching, and training—over and over and over again. I don't have much extra money to spend on my desires because, with four children, most of my money is tied up in jeans, tennis shoes, Legos, dolls, piano lessons, doctor's appointments, and birthday presents. I have given up my personal rights to the priority of addressing my children's needs first.

But what is my sacrifice compared to the one Jesus made? I have often asked myself, How was Jesus able to make the choice to sacrifice his own life for us? How could Jesus leave the glory and the perfect fellowship he enjoyed with his Father and all the angels in heaven to come to earth and humble himself to serve the very human beings who would eventually desert him in his hour of need?

The answer to that question is my answer as well. Jesus was able to choose sacrifice and servanthood because of his deep love—and because he was looking to eternity! He knew that his life would, for all time, redeem all of creation and bring us back to himself. He understood the cost when he said, "Greater love has no one than this, that one lay down his life for his friends." But he also knew what laying down his life would accomplish in the eternal scheme of things.

When we choose to sacrifice our own goals and desires to serve our children, we, too, are furthering his eternal work. We know that, through our labor and love, over time he will faithfully build our children into a righteous heritage. But for this to happen, we must willingly lay down our lives. To have sufficient energy for the task, we must make the choice to embrace motherhood whole-heartedly.

When I had my last child, Joy, at almost forty-two, the diapers, sleepless nights, and naps started all over again. I realized I would be ready for retirement by the time she was ready to move on to her own life! And yet somewhere, over the years, the Lord convicted me that the future was not where real life began. Each day was God's perfect will for me. There would be no wasted years of "just taking care of the needs of my young children." On the contrary, these years would be among the most important of my life.

When I separated my squabbling toddlers and gently told them, "God wants you to learn to share and be kind; use your words and hands for gentleness and love, not for anger and selfishness," I was training them in righteousness. When I encouraged my older children to keep trying with their math or their English or their piano lessons, I was teaching them perseverance and helping to shape their minds. When I switched on the vacuum cleaner for yet another cleanup or kept after my forgetful teenagers to do their chores, I was teaching the importance of domestic order and personal responsibility.

In the end, what could be a better use of my time? And yet so many mothers fall into the trap of resenting the intrusions that children make on their time.

SERVING WITHOUT RESENTMENT

Recently, while getting a haircut, I began talking to a young mom about her children. I was taken aback by the resentment in her voice when she described her relationship with her children. She told me that her nine-year-old daughter, whose birthday was that month, had come to her and asked how they were going to celebrate.

The mother said, "I told my daughter, 'I know what *I'm* going to do! I'm going to go out to dinner with your father to celebrate that we are halfway through having you in our home. Only nine years to go, and then I'll be free of you!'"

She went on to explain, "I was my father's daughter, my husband's wife, and now my children's mother. I'm sick of people owning my life. I'm ready for my own time and my own life. I tell my daughter all the time that I'm tired of taking care of her and that she is an awful child."

She went on to say, "I told my children [ages nine, ten, and twelve] that if they would just stay home and let me work all summer, I would take them to an amusement park for a day!"

I have no desire to judge that obviously unhappy mother. Who knows what kind of pressures and pain in her life led her to such harsh pronouncements about her children? But I have often wondered what scars her resentment will leave on her children. How could they help but feel unloved and unwanted?

A day of fun can hardly replace a whole summer of days when a child has no one to talk to about her dreams, to comfort her in her small pains, to admire a pretty painting, to correct her immature behavior, or to have time to take her and her friends to the park. This mom clearly saw motherhood as a heavy weight and a burden. Instead of serving her children, she verbally abused them. Instead of giving them herself, she appeased her conscience by buying them off with one day of frenzied spending. But she herself was already picking the fruit of her own lack of servanthood: "My kids are awful."

The truth this mother had yet to accept is that children, by definition, take up our time. They're *supposed* to do that; it's the way God made them. But if we don't recognize or accept that fact—as that mother in the hair salon didn't and as many mothers today don't—we're bound to make things difficult for ourselves and our children.

I made a decision in my heart years ago, as I began to understand this principle, that God did not want me to resent my children for taking up my time. Neither did he want me to make them feel guilty for the sacrifices I had made on their behalf. I was called to give up my rights simply out of my love for Jesus. If I have had struggles and complaints over the years for these issues in my own life, they have been between me and the Lord, not between me and my children.

SERVING WITH OUR TIME

I had years of time as a single woman when I was ruler over most of my minutes. I decided when I would eat, sleep, vacation, work, or meet someone for lunch. I decided these issues according to my needs and desires.

But once I had children, as any mother will understand, my time was never my own again! Children simply don't fit into neat little time packages.

"Today Mommy has one hour to give to you for your needs—whatever you want! During this hour, I am willing to feed you, play with you, read books to you, correct your rude and selfish attitudes, clean up your messes, or attend to your ear infection and asthma attack. But you must understand that when this hour is over, I will have to leave you to yourself. You see, I have clothes to wash, food to buy and prepare, bills to pay, friends to meet, places to travel, books to read and write, movies to watch, work to accomplish, etc."

Ridiculous, isn't it? But practically speaking, I believe many women assume they should be able to do that with their children. As we have seen in earlier chapters, many aspects of our culture seem to be based on the idea that children should fit into neat little time slots. When we realize and accept that serving our children means giving them whatever time they need, whenever they need it, we will be far less likely to fall into the kind of bitterness and resentment I saw in the woman at the hair salon.

I regret the time I wasted in the early years of my children's lives because I didn't have a realistic understanding of what motherhood would cost me in this regard. I did enjoy being with them—usually. But I also tended to chafe at the demands these little ones made on my time and energy. I would become irritated or frazzled by their whining or clinging to me or crying. Sometimes it seemed that my children purposely thwarted my plans.

Another thing I tended to resent about being a mother was the time I had to devote to jobs that would soon need to be done again. Messes were constantly made, cleaned up, then made again. Clothes were worn, dirtied, and washed in an endless cycle. Dishes had to be done and redone at least three or four times a day when my children were small. Now, as teenagers, they seem to eat without a break.

Just as I would get one child down for a nap, another would wake up—and just as I was desperately hoping for a cup of tea all by myself. If I planned to trade children with a friend so I could have time alone, one of my children would get sick so I would have to give up my respite. A fun date with Clay would have to be cancelled. Much-needed sleep would be interrupted by a night feeding or a bad dream or an asthma attack.

My children always seemed to need me and want to be around me. They were always taking up my time. Instead of seeing that this is what children are made to do, for years I resisted their demands on my time. Often I served my children joyfully and enjoyed the memorable moments of their growing-up years. But sometimes I struggled irrationally with their demands and then felt guilty for struggling. Instead of understanding that this was normal and that how I handled it would make a world of difference in their lives, I often fought against it. In doing so, I'm afraid I lost many beautiful opportunities to be a servant leader in our home.

Thank goodness for the grace of God and for second chances! Six years passed between my third child, Nathan, and my fourth child, Joy. I had had three miscarriages and didn't think I would ever have another baby. By the time Joy came, I had lived through the early youth of my other three children and had seen that they really did grow up quickly. Finally, by experience, I understood that the dependent stage of early childhood was only for a season. I could see how important it was to enjoy each day and treasure these moments of early life with my children, because the years did pass quickly. How I wished I could take back all the impatient words I had said, all the guilt I had imposed on my older children just because they were acting their age and taking up my time. Fortunately, they remember mostly the good times and not my immature responses to their normal behavior.

I was much more patient with the interruptions that Joy brought to my life because I realized that I might never have this opportunity again. I cherished our time alone while she nursed. I enjoyed (and still do!) the sweet moments when she would crawl into bed with me and snuggle close. Having made my peace (mostly) with the reality that giving my children time is a part of serving them, I was able to relax and open myself to the joys of being with them.

These days I have no baby in the house. Instead, I have an exuberant seven-year-old and three teenagers. And these beloved children still take up all of my time, but in different ways. Yet since I know that this is a necessary sacrifice, a part of my service to them and to God, it is easier to bear—partly because I have made the choice to embrace the task of mothering, partly because I have come to terms with the natural demands children make on my time, but mostly because my attitude has changed.

SERVING WITH A GODLY ATTITUDE

Attitude, I have found, makes all the difference when it comes to serving our children. Serving with joy in the midst of messes and difficulty can only be done when we walk in the power of the Holy Spirit. When we are joyful and see each minute with our children as an opportunity to worship God through our service of him, our children sense our joy and feel secure and happy.

A couple of years ago our entire family had just returned home from a conference for a thousand women. (Our children have been part of our ministry from the beginning, and we try to take them with us whenever possible.) Clay immediately turned around to fly to another conference in California, but the children and I had to face the task of reestablishing our household routine.

All our suitcases were full of dirty laundry. The cupboards were bare, the house needed to be cleaned, phone calls needed to be answered. And for me, on top of those normal responsibilities was a sense of frustration and inadequacy that had been accumulating for several weeks.

We had gotten off our devotional schedule. Nathan really needed me to spend time with him on his math and spelling. Joel needed encouragement and accountability with his guitar and piano practice and needed me to attend to a problem with one of his instructors. Joy needed more personal time and time just to play or read with Mom. And Sarah needed advice and guidance on a book proposal. In addition, all of the kids were feeling lonely since our recent move. We had visited fourteen churches and still couldn't find a fit!

In that moment, as I took in the temporary chaos of my home and my life, it all seemed too much. Tears began to flow—a rare display for me in front of my children! I began to share my feelings of depression and despair, and they began to cry as well.

In the middle of our emotional crisis, Joel said, "Mom, when you are happy and content and easygoing with life, even if it's not all perfect, we feel good. We don't need everything to be perfect; we just want you to be happy. But when you start feeling like a failure and overwhelmed with life, it makes us feel guilty, as though it's our fault and that we haven't done enough. We feel like we have disappointed you!"

In a flash, I realized Joel was right. My children didn't need me to be on top of all my chores or even to be perfect in taking care of all of their needs. What they needed was for me to be content and patient with life. They needed me, as a mature Christian, to walk by faith that God was in control, allowing his Spirit to give me peace and joy in the midst of life's inevitable ups and downs. In a sense, they were looking to me as a barometer of how our lives were faring.

This is one of the best ways I can be a servant leader to my children. When I model patience in the midst of difficulty, joy in the midst of messes, contentment in the midst of lack, then I provide them a pattern for their own lives. They will learn that my joy is not circumstantial but real because I have an endless source of strength through the power of the Holy Spirit in my life.

This doesn't mean that I was wrong to feel exhausted or overwhelmed. It doesn't mean I always have to wear a cheerful mask in front of my children or hide my feelings. Feelings, after all, are just part of being human, and emotional ups and downs are a biological reality for most women. I certainly don't want my children to get the message that they should never admit feeling down or discouraged.

At the same time, we mothers need to recognize what a powerful effect our attitude has on our children. Laying down our lives for them can indeed mean giving up, for their sakes, our right to wallow in our negative feelings. And choosing the path of servant leadership certainly means making the effort to respond in faith to our circumstances and our feelings, turning to the Lord for help in maintaining a hopeful attitude. The beauty of such an effort, of course, is that it has the power to lift us up even as it sustains our children's spirits.

After I had had a good night's sleep and all of us had a day to get things back in order at home, I felt totally different about my children and about life. I was reminded again that my service to God is not just in what I do, but in what I choose to believe in my heart and how I learn to live out those beliefs through my attitudes and words and actions in my day-to-day life.

THE REWARDS OF SERVANTHOOD

Now that my children are growing up, I love seeing their emerging personalities. They are interesting people, and so far they have embraced with passion the messages and values of our hearts. I am so thankful that I learned the secret of servant leadership early in my relationship with them.

I have never been a perfect mom or accomplished all my goals or kept a perfect home. Yet through my commitment of servanthood to my children, the Lord has allowed us to build a relationship that includes strong bonds of security and love.

Late one evening after speaking to some moms, I returned to my hotel room. Just as I was ready to fall into bed, I discovered a lovely card that fifteen-year-old Joel, my introverted mysterious child, had left for me in my suitcase. It read:

> You are my friend of friends. You are the first one I want to tell when something happens to me, the one whose voice I want to hear when I am feeling sad. You are the one who knows me, the one I count on not only to listen but to really understand. You are my friend of friends, and I love you with my heart of hearts!

He signed my card with this inscription:

> I just wanted to write you a little note and tell you that I love you so much. I really appreciate all that you have been to me lately, my friend and comforter, my teacher; and especially I appreciate you being a good mother to me! Love you lots, Joel

Joel's card brought a smile to my face and served my heart with happiness for the rest of the evening. In that moment I was granted the gift of knowing that my choice to serve my children was truly a fruitful one.

From time to time we get these little glimpses of the ways the Holy Spirit is working in the hearts of our children. We see that our great effort indeed matters, and these moments are truly a gift of grace, because there are many winters in the lives of our children when we cannot see the fruit of our efforts. We still live in a fallen world, and this means that no matter how well we do our job as parents, our children can make poor choices or fail, sometimes with difficult consequences. Maturity comes only after many seasons of training and instruction in wise living.

I truly believe that God will cause all things to work together for good for those—especially mothers—who are called according to his purpose (Romans

8:28, paraphrased). Through the eventual faithfulness of his disciples, who also had once betrayed him, Jesus was able to reach the whole world. As we wait patiently for the fruit of our faith and service in the lives of our children to be revealed, we will see God's faithfulness. In the meantime, we can know that our choice to love our children and serve them with a whole heart is the right one.

FOR THOUGHT AND REFLECTION

Something to Think About...

"Weary to the bone" describes how I felt. Six weeks of battling asthma with Joy in the middle of the night had left me exhausted. Sarah, too, had been diagnosed with a possibly serious disease and faced more doctor's appointments. Clay had had to work out of town four days each week for two months. Our home was showing signs of stress, and piles of miscellaneous stuff accumulated all over the house.

"Quickly take the unfolded laundry and extra stuff to my bedroom," I pleaded with the kids. "My women's Bible study starts in a half-hour, and I need to make the living room presentable. I'll deal with the bedroom later." Everyone hurried around to tame this tornado of messes—or at least to transfer it. Then they all disappeared into my bedroom to watch a movie. "I can't think about this or deal with it now or I'll get depressed," I told myself as I closed the door to my now-cluttered bedroom.

Three hours later I said good-bye to the last woman. Sighing, I walked down the hallway to my bedroom to cope with the mess. I opened the door with dread, then gasped at what I saw. The room was sparkling clean, my sheets were turned down, and a vanilla candle flickered on my bedside table. Even my closet was immaculate. I sank down on the couch in my bedroom. Until that moment I hadn't realized just how discouraged I had been or how much I needed to feel loved and cared for.

A beautiful note sat atop my pillow.

Sweet Mama,

You have served us so generously in so many ways. I wanted to serve you and help you with your room. I love you so much. Sweet dreams!

Sarah

Often our children, like me, don't even know that they need us to serve them, and often they don't seem to notice what we do for them. Yet if we faithfully plant seeds of love and care in their hearts, in due time we will indeed reap a harvest in kind.

1. *Matthew 20:25-28.* What are the two leadership styles that Jesus describes? Which leadership style do you prefer? What heart attitude does servant leadership require? How does this apply to mothers?

2. *John 15:12-13.* Jesus spoke these words to his disciples after he had washed their feet and eaten the Passover meal with them. What was Jesus' commandment? How does this verse represent Jesus' life? What does it mean for mothers to lay down their lives? What are the possible sacrifices that must be made?

3. *Philippians 2:14-15.* According to this verse, what are we to avoid in our lives? What effect does choosing not to grumble and complain have on our children? What heart change must take place for this to happen?

4. *Luke 1:38.* What was Mary's response to the angel when he announced God's plan for her to be the mother of the Savior? Why does this reflect one of the reasons that God chose her to bear his Son? What did it cost Mary throughout her life to be available to God? How does this principle apply to your life?

Something to Try...

During times when our family life seems too busy or too stressful, I sometimes plan a "foot washing" experience for my family to show them my love and appreciation. A few weeks ago, for instance, I climbed out of bed early one morning. The stars were still in the sky when I slipped out the door and drove to the grocery store to buy some fresh cream-cheese croissants and chocolate-covered doughnuts. I sneaked back into the house before anyone had stirred (except Clay, who had already gone to work). I placed the pastries on a pretty china platter, poured cold milk into a pitcher, lit some candles and a fire in the fireplace, and turned on a melodic CD. I quickly placed a card of encouragement on the coffee table for each person. Then I gently awakened the kids and invited them to a little morning celebration. We all had a fun time of talking, eating, and praying together before the day began. "Let's do this again!" was everyone's request!

- Plan your own foot-washing time with your kids. Choose a favorite or special treat. Make sure that all conversation is positive. This should be a time of encouragement, not a time of lecture.
- Make a list of some things your children like you to do with them but aren't necessarily fun for you—playing a board game on the floor with a young child, going outside to throw a ball, sitting down with a child to read his or her creative story or to look at an artistic creation, and so on. Commit to saying yes to their requests instead of no, knowing that if you invest in what is important to them, they will be open to believing in what is important to you.

CHAPTER 5

The Discipling Mother

Reaching Children's Hearts for Christ

The beginning of wisdom is: Acquire wisdom;
And with all your acquiring, get understanding.

PROVERBS 4:7

The car was packed to the gills. Six people and their "must have" items—swimsuits, CD players, board games, favorite blankets, magazines, and lots and lots of snacks—competed for space in the crowded interior. One item we all agreed on as a necessity, however, was a rousing book on tape.

Every year when we started our ascent up the steep, winding roads to our favorite mountain town, we began a new book together. The only break we ever allowed in the narrative was a stop at an authentic A&W Root Beer drive-in along the way, where we would all indulge in big, cold Frosties (root beer swirled with ice cream). Our pick for this trip was *God's Smuggler*, the thrilling autobiography of Brother Andrew, a Dutch factory worker who helped open up communist Eastern Europe to Christian missions. We all listened in rapt attention as the British narrator began to unwind for us the details of Brother Andrew's story.

We learned about his early life—how the upheaval and heartbreak of World War II in Holland created questions and needs in the young man's heart. How he joined the army and how the death and devastation he witnessed while fighting in a brutal Dutch-Indonesian war led him to discover his own deep need for Christ.

As the story unfolded, we saw Brother Andrew learning to listen to the still, small voice of the Lord through his time of studying the Bible and in prayer. We saw him visiting Poland at the close of World War II, when the Soviet Union began to take over the country, and feeling compelled to visit a communist rally for thousands of young students. Though young and with few resources, Andrew dreamed that somehow God would use him to reach the millions of people behind the Iron Curtain for Christ.

Then the excitement really began as Andrew smuggled Bibles and Christian literature into Eastern Europe. Miracle after miracle took place as this young Dutchman trusted God for the impossible. Over and over again, God proved faithful through incredible, providential, and personal answers to prayers. And through it all, our family listened wide-eyed to this book that reads like a spy novel.

As we approached our destination, Clay reached to turn the tape off. "Dad!" all the kids cried at once, "Don't turn it off! We want to see what happens!"

As we talked about the tape later that evening, Joel said, "I would love for my life to be like that. I would love to see miraculous answers to prayers and see God use me in a special way. I hope my life will be like that someday! We as a family need to pray like he did!"

I felt a thrill in my heart as I heard Joel voicing his desire to be used by God. In his eyes and voice I could detect the early signs of a heart totally committed to God and his purposes. This is what I had always longed to see in my kids. It is my central goal as a mother.

I don't just want my kids to be moral. I don't just want them to know all of the biblical rules for behavior. I don't just want them to make it through my home with good grades, no drug addiction, and no premarital sex.

I want them to leave my home with a hunger and passion to know God personally and to be used by him to accomplish great things for his kingdom. I want them to personally hear God's voice and have his Spirit's gentle touch and impression on their hearts as they read the Scriptures and struggle with the issues of their lives.

That's what God wants for our children as well. Whatever else we give our children as they grow, he wants us to pass along an eternal vision and purpose as well as a passion for Christ. If we are wise, we will keep this goal ever before us— to keep us focused on what really matters, on the ultimate purpose of our activity as parents.

Often our lives are so overrun with small tasks that we get caught up in checking off the lists of things that need to be done and lose sight of the big picture. From there, we too easily fall into the trap of judging ourselves and our children by external standards of success and cultural priorities rather than by what really matters to God. We may even envy the success of others whom we feel may measure up better than we do.

I found myself doing that recently when Joy and I recently attended a mother-daughter tea at the home of a lovely, accomplished Christian friend. I was tempted all that afternoon to compare the shortcomings of our own family with the apparent strengths of the family at hand.

As I walked through the front door with its welcoming wreath, I observed a lovely environment with perfectly placed knickknacks from all over the world. But all I could think was, *How does she keep her house so beautiful with all of these children around? Six is a lot of kids to keep under control!*

The food for the tea was decoratively arranged on beautiful china dishes, but I was thinking, *She sure went to a lot of trouble for us. I need to try harder to do special things in my home!*

The food was served by the immaculately clad children of our hostess. *(I've got to get some new shirts for the kids; ours all look stained and faded!)* Each child appeared to be quite gracious. *(Boy, do I need to go home and work on my kids' manners!)* Each boy had a perfect haircut, and each hair was in place. *(I hope they don't see my boys' hair, especially not their fingernails!)* The mothers present discussed what their children had been doing. This child was head of the soccer team; the other child was almost fluent in French and German at age fourteen! Another had won a ballet competition. Yet another was teaching piano classes at age fifteen and making hundreds of dollars each month! *(I've got a long way to go with my children! I'd better get to work!)*

The mother who hosted the tea party, in reality, was just a sweet woman who wanted to make her friends feel special. And I admit I've exaggerated my response just a bit to make a point—though I really did wonder where that mother went for her boys' haircuts! But this is typical of some of the conversations that sometimes go on in my mind. It is so easy to get caught up in petty comparisons and unimportant issues and lose sight of what we are really aiming for as parents!

Someone once observed, "Christians are like people who are trying to straighten the picture on the wall while the house is burning down!" Isn't that what we as mothers are tempted to do—to waste our energies trying to meet external standards while our children's deep spiritual needs go unmet and unnoticed?

A BIBLICAL VIEW OF WHAT'S IMPORTANT

Jeremiah 9 gives us a different view of life that can help us refocus the priorities of our lives and our parenting efforts:

> "Let not a wise man boast of his wisdom, and let not the mighty man boast of his might, let not a rich man boast of his riches, but let him who boasts boast of this, that he understands and knows Me, that I am the LORD who exercises lovingkindness, justice, and righteousness on earth; for I delight in these things," declares the LORD. (verses 23-24)

Though this passage was written twenty-six hundred years ago, it is still applicable to us today. Our culture still seeks success through these three areas—the intellect; power and status; and riches. As mothers, we will be tempted to measure our success by the performance of our children in these areas as well.

For instance, we may find ourselves wondering how our children measure up intellectually and how we can help them achieve more in this area. *What do I need to do to help my child get into the best schools and colleges? How can I help them get good SAT scores? How can I give my child academic advantages? What degrees will they be able to earn? What kinds of skills can I give them that will help them to excel as writers, artists, sports figures, or musicians? What experiences will enhance their lives?*

Questions of social status may haunt us as well. *How can I give my children the edge that will help them succeed? What trophies can they win? What can I do to help them achieve high-status positions—cheerleader? class president? sportsman of the year? How successful is our business? How many people do we employ? What status value do our neighborhood, car, clothes, church position have to give our children a good self-image?*

And who of us is immune to questions of measuring up financially? Perhaps we compare our family income to that of our children's friends' families. Or we borrow money to buy toys or clothes that we think will make our children happy. What kinds of clothes are right? What kinds of lessons can we afford? How big a house can we buy? Should we invest in a playground? in computer equipment? What kind of job should I get to be sure my kids have all of the advantages and I can buy whatever experiences or possessions they might want or I might want for them?

There is constant pressure in our culture to place an inordinate amount of energy in seeking these things—just as there was in Jeremiah's day. And helping our children develop in these areas may indeed be worthy goals to consider in light of our children's training. There's nothing wrong with wanting them to live up to their intellectual potential, to learn manners and leadership skills, or to learn how to take care of themselves financially. In a future chapter we'll talk about how we can help our children improve in these areas.

At the same time, we must constantly keep in mind that, in God's eyes, the issues of intellectual prowess, social success, and financial development are peripheral at best. The most important goal of parenting, as Jeremiah 9 clearly indicates, is not to raise smart children, socially gracious children, or financially savvy children. And that's a good thing, because a lot of these factors are more or less out of our control.

The reality is that no matter how we try to control these external factors, each of us will fall short. No matter how we try to control life, we cannot make it behave. And pursuing only these worldly goals has a diminishing effect on us as mothers as well as on our children. Comparing ourselves to others and all they have will almost inevitably cause us to focus on the shortcomings of our families instead of progressing in truly important areas.

It may well be that our children are not academically gifted, athletically brilliant, or socially inclined. It may be that our marriage is conflicted or broken and cannot provide the stability we might wish for. Our finances might be in a mess, or our income may be insufficient to provide the material possessions our children want. Or perhaps we feel that we don't have a supermom personality and have a hard time just holding together normal life.

If we focus on intellect, social status, or wealth, it's almost certain that we will eventually feel we don't quite measure up. How comforting it is, then, to realize that the goals God has called us to as parents are accomplishable.

Any parent in any station of life has the ability to reach his or her child's heart for Christ and his purposes. All that God requires from any of us is a desire to serve him and a trust that he can make up the difference for the things we lack. The Lord would have us know that he is the one ultimately in charge of our children. He will use our willingness and our efforts, then fill in the gaps of our inadequacies, to prepare their hearts for what he has in mind.

A PLAN FOR SHAPING HEARTS

The fact that the word *heart* appears more than eight hundred times in any Bible translation should tell us something about how important our children's hearts are to God. The first great commandment given in Deuteronomy (and quoted later by Jesus) is "You shall love the LORD your God with all your heart and with all your soul and with all your might" (6:5; also Luke 10:27).

The book of 1 Samuel (16:7) reminds us that while human beings tend to focus on outward appearance—for instance, status, degrees, cars, houses, SAT scores—the Lord cares most about the state of the heart. Second Chronicles says that God searches throughout the whole earth to support those whose hearts are completely his (16:9). And Jesus repeatedly urged his listeners to live with pure, unhypocritical, God-centered hearts.

These biblical passages, of course, are not just talking about *heart* in the narrow sense of a blood-pumping organ or even the center of emotions. *Heart* in the biblical sense is a much deeper, more meaningful word. The vast majority of the eight hundred occurrences of the word in the Bible refers to the mental, emotional core of a person. In a sense, the biblical *heart* of a person is the core of that person's being—who she really is inside. The word *heart* encompasses her inner thoughts, her true feelings, her motivations, the very seat of personhood.

No wonder the Bible puts so much emphasis on the *heart,* because God cares most about who we are inside! We may be able to perform all sorts of skills and athletic feats. Our manners may be impeccable and our intellects imposing, but God will judge us all—including our children—by what is in our hearts, our innermost beings. And because this is true of our children as well, it simply makes sense that our primary job as parents is to focus on developing their hearts—their passions, loyalties, convictions, and commitments.

Doing this job well has powerful implications not only for our present family life but for the future as well. If families today would focus first on accomplishing God's purposes and developing godly hearts, then society would be filled with righteous people in the next generation. This means that our leaders would be righteous, our government would be righteous, our newspapers would be righteous, our movies and media would be righteous—all areas of life would be affected, because our culture would be filled with righteous people who are committed to God's purposes. Coming up with a plan to reach our children's hearts, then, is crucial not only for the future of our children but for our entire society.

When Jesus lived on this earth, he spent the majority of his ministry teaching his disciples, to whom he would entrust the task of reaching the whole world with the gospel. As I have studied his life, I have found a plan for my own parenting. Like him, I have a goal to love and train my children so they will be equipped to reach the world and their families and friends with the message of Christ after I am gone. This is what they were born to do—to truly love God and glorify him and follow him. Thus my goals for parenting must reflect my purpose. Several simple aspects of Jesus' life with his disciples have given me a simple plan for my own home.

BEING "WITH" OUR CHILDREN

Over and over again in the Gospels, we read that the disciples were "with" Jesus. Our Lord developed the hearts of his followers by spending time with them—instructing them, advising them, modeling right behavior. He spoke with them one-on-one and in small groups. He included them in his ministry and in his daily life. But what he almost never did with his disciples was to sign them up for activities and programs!

In contemporary society, we tend to value activity, and this is certainly true for most Christians I know. We don't want our children to miss out on anything. We take them to church on Sunday, to AWANA or some such Bible memory class, and perhaps to a Sunday night meeting or youth meeting. Making sure our children attend Vacation Bible School and special meetings is a must!

We are on the go for God. We are busy doing many activities and going to this meeting and that seminar. Yet all of the *going* in the world will not make us or our children spiritually deep or alive. It is only by *coming* to the living God and developing intimacy with him that we will really draw near in our hearts to Christ. What many in our culture don't understand—and many more forget—is that a relationship with Christ is best taught through a long-term personal relationship with someone who knows the Master, not through activities organized around lots of people in impersonal and distracting instructional situations.

Even as I write this, my daughters have just returned from a day at a local Vacation Bible School. My youngest, Joy, was one of the "VBS-ers." My older daughter, Sarah, and a friend were helping with the program.

I had a cool summer lunch waiting for my hot and worn-out troops when they returned from their first morning of VBS. While they ate, the older girls chattered on with their observations of the opening events. Evidently it had started with a couple of hundred noisy kids crowding around until the person in charge yelled above the crowd, "EVERYONE LISTEN! Have your children stand in lines according to their ages!" Immediately diligent parents began dragging their children toward the right lines. One five-year-old had thrown a screaming fit because he didn't want to stand in line. Others hadn't wanted to leave their mothers and protested loudly. Finally the crowd organized, and the children were assembled in their appropriate groups. But the rest of the morning had been fraught with ups and downs and lots of energy expended through the wiggles, giggles, and antics of lively little bodies.

What was Joy's take on her VBS experience? When I asked how the day went, she immediately replied, "Oh, it was pretty good, but I got slapped in the face by the girl in front of me. I also got a neat cupcake that I ate the frosting off of and a neat little truck that runs by balloon power."

"Well, what did you learn, Joy?"

"That Jesus is real powerful and can do almost anything. We got to yell, 'That's so cool' when anyone said, 'God can do anything.' I think my group yelled the loudest! Also, Mommy, did you know that a polar bear weighs fifteen hundred pounds and will stalk a human being for two hundred miles?"

My older ones agreed that the morning had offered a fun free-for-all for most of the kids there. Then Sarah said thoughtfully, "Mom, if that is the only exposure some kids got to the teachings of Christ, they would indeed have a shallow foundation. It was all pretty lightweight and almost meaningless. It's a good thing you spend time alone with Joy teaching her about the Bible."

Understand that I'm not down on Vacation Bible Schools in particular or children's activities in general. I'm sure over the years that many children have become believers through Sunday school, afternoon clubs, VBS, and youth groups. In my observation, however, many of these experiences are more like day camps than true discipleship tools. They entertain the kids, and the best of them offer some valuable biblical training as well. Yet I know that the real work of digging deep wells in my children's hearts with Scripture, a biblical world-view, issues of prayer and faith, and Christian convictions is a job for which God will hold Clay and me responsible, not the volunteers at church. And this is a task that is best accomplished day in and day out with our focused attention on each child's heart.

Jesus didn't meet with his disciples once a week for Bible study and then say, "I'll see you next week!" He gave his disciples his whole life. He lived with them, slept with them, traveled with them, and lived out a life of godly maturity before their eyes. Having the personality of the God who created the universe living with them every moment for three years gave them an understanding of his ways that nothing else could do. They observed him in the private times of friendship and eating and sharing and being exhausted and buying and preparing food as well as in pubic ministry—teaching, healing, worshiping, confronting, encouraging. There was perfect integrity between the words he spoke and the life he lived. Thus his disciples could learn what righteousness looked like in all situations.

In the same way, our children will learn righteousness best by seeing it lived out in every possible way in our lives, moment by moment, in the context of normal life. As we teach our children to do unto others as we would have them do unto us, they need to see it lived out in our lives so that they will know what it means. When a child breaks a favorite vase and we extend forgiveness and patience, then he will have heard he needs to learn patience and he will have seen it modeled in real life. The first principle of reaching our children, then, is that we have to make the time to be with them. And we need to be diligent to practice what we preach!

I have realized that one of God's purposes for my children is to be his tool for disciplining me to make me more holy! I do not have to be a perfect mom— just an authentic believer. From interacting with my children, I have seen my own selfishness and my lack of patience more clearly than ever before! I have blown it many times with my children, but even these mistakes have helped me to mature and depend on God more than I would have without my parenting responsibilities.

As I walk honestly before God, with my children watching, they will learn how to have a real relationship with him as well. As they see me apologize to them and pray in front of them to ask for God's forgiveness in my own life, my children will learn that God is a God of grace who forgives me and guides me.

My worshiping him in gratitude for a beautiful sunset or a rainbow gives them a pattern for their own spontaneous worship.

As my children see me in the deep waters of life, being tested to my core and still holding on to my Lord and choosing to believe the best, this observation will prepare them for their own trials, which will surely come. They will know that he will guide and forgive them as they lead an imperfect but devoted life before a loving Father who has always met their mother's needs!

Instructing Our Children

The second principle of reaching children's hearts that we can observe in Jesus' life is that of intentional instruction. Jesus talked to his disciples about the Scriptures and their meaning, he talked to them of God and his ways and laws, and he talked to them of the future. In their time together, he covered every possible subject from faith to humility to prejudice to forgiveness, adultery, murder, love, food, and morality.

Our children, too, need consistent, systematic instruction and teaching about God's Word and ways. They cannot be expected to know the truth or how to behave and how to think until they learn, preferably from us, what the Bible says that truth is.

Teaching the whole Bible to children can sound like a daunting task. But when we think about sharing it in bite-sized pieces, as Jesus did with his disciples, then it becomes possible. Teaching the Word to our children, though, requires that we be students of the Word so that we will have something to share.

How should we teach our children? Jesus employed many methods of instruction in his teaching, but one of the most common and effective was storytelling. This particular method, I've found, is one that children especially love. From the time my children were very young, I told them the wonderful stories of the Old Testament about how great people trusted God. I would also read, as dramatically as possible, from various Bible storybooks that retold the familiar accounts in simple, arresting language. Our family particularly likes Catherine F. Vos's *The Child's Story Bible*, which reads like literature and gives us a dynamic way to learn the history and stories of the Bible.

Another helpful instructional tool for teaching young children is memorization. They also need to learn the rules of life and understand the basics of morality. Children have a tremendous capacity to memorize, and they love to commit scriptures to memory. The Ten Commandments, Psalm 23, the greatest commandments in Luke 10:27, 1 Corinthians 13, the first ten verses of the Sermon on the Mount, and Genesis 1 are wonderful passages we can plant in children's minds at an early age that will build a foundation for them.

When children are older, of course, they need to learn how to study the Bible for themselves. We provided ours with age-appropriate study guides and other tools to help them better understand the Word. We have found that sharing with them from our own quiet times and praying with them regularly has helped our older children apply all that they have been storing up since their early years.

Family devotions can be another useful device for teaching not only the text of the Bible but also the importance of spending time with God on a regular basis. This instructional tool, however, like all the others, needs to be introduced gradually and in a way that is appropriate to the ages of the children involved.

I remember a time many years ago when Clay and I decided to start having daily family devotions. We first attempted to do this at mealtimes and quickly learned that teaching toddlers can be very frustrating if we expect them to behave like adults. Just when we would begin, one child would spill his milk or another would interrupt or another would have a reason to cry. I remember thinking, *Why do I even try? They aren't getting anything out of this!*

Over a period of time, though, I began to find other ways of establishing devotional times that really got through to our children. They loved it when I sang them songs in the rocking chair before we put them to bed at night and shared with them a dramatic story beginning with their names: "Sarah, imagine what you would do if a giant came to attack our country and you were the only one who could rescue us! Well, that happened to a little boy named David many years ago!" If I cuddled up my children on our couch and had grapes or cheese and crackers to eat, they would pay rapt attention while I read Bible stories and showed them picture books. Often I would give them markers and paper and let them draw while I read.

Little by little we accustomed our children to sitting still and listening and even participating in family devotions. This became a familiar time to them because we did it day after day; it was simply a part of their lives.

One important thing that Clay and I learned as we struggled to instruct our children in spiritual matters was that our attitude makes a huge difference. If we want our children to enjoy participating in devotions and to learn God's Word joyfully, then they must sense that these are important to us personally. They must feel that we love our Lord and are excited to share him with them. Even as we give instruction, we must also model what we are teaching. When it comes to reaching hearts for Christ, we cannot just tell our children what to do. We have to lead the way.

TRAINING OUR CHILDREN

Proverbs 22:6 says,

> Train up a child in the way he should go,
> Even when he is old he will not depart from it.

This verse succinctly states the durable value of *training* our children as well as instructing them. Teaching our children what they should know is not complete without *training* them to live out what they know.

What is the difference between instruction and training? Training is the practical application of a learned truth to actual life. Training involves advising our children on the appropriate application of Scripture and giving them opportunities to act out what they are learning. It also means taking the initiative with our children to correct their immature or sinful behavior and require them to do what is right.

It is not enough to know the truth; we must learn to walk in truth. As we lead our children with the principles of God's wisdom found throughout Scripture, we are helping them to establish pathways of righteousness in their hearts. When they are older, chances are they will tend to think and act according to those pathways they learned at home during the early years.

When our children were still very small, Clay and I designed our own training tool for the children: "Twenty-Four Family Ways." (I have included them in the back of this book as appendix B.) This basic set of family rules clearly spells out the biblical principles that our family follows. For instance, Way Five says, "We love one another, treating others with kindness, gentleness, and respect."

We even developed a devotional for our family so that each way would be discussed and a corresponding Bible verse would be repeated five days in a row.

Instructing our children about these Twenty-Four Ways came first. But training came in when we began using the list as a tool for guiding everyday behavior. If one child hit another or spoke rudely or took away a toy, we would say, "In our home we love one another and treat each other with respect. You may not talk to your sister that way. Please apologize to her. What is our family way?"

Over the years our children heard such references hundreds of times. I'm sure there were times when they didn't want to hear another word about our family ways! At the same time, they gradually moved closer to behaving according to godly principles.

Training often requires that we take the time to interact with our children about their attitudes or actions—even if that sometimes means confrontation. And confrontation, I've noticed, is something that many parents avoid. I have often seen that parents are willing to buy their children many things and provide them with many experiences, but they tend to back away from conflict because it is unpleasant. But unless we take the initiative to gently and lovingly confront our children's sin and selfishness, they will not learn to be mature adults. We need to be willing to risk unpleasantness with our children in the interest of their growth in righteousness.

And, yes, we are talking about discipline here! Hebrews 12:11 clearly states, "All discipline for the moment seems not to be joyful, but sorrowful; yet to those who have been trained by it, afterwards it yields the peaceful fruit of righteousness." The fruit in the heart of a disciplined child is the peaceful fruit of righteousness. The wise mother takes the time to correct her children over and over again so they can experience the peace and freedom of knowing how to govern their lives in such a way as to be mature, wise, and at peace with God. Though it takes time, patience, and courage to change the course of our children's ways, the result of wisdom in their lives is a satisfying reward both for them and for us.

Whenever we discipline our children, however, it's important to keep our overall goal in mind. The purpose of training our children is not to force them to do what we want. The purpose is not to produce guilt or shame but to free our children to enjoy the fruit of mature living. This means that training should always be exercised in gentleness, along with love and patience.

A verse that often goes through my own mind in this regard is Proverbs 15:1: "A gentle answer turns away wrath." I seek to reach my children's hearts through gentleness and understanding while still holding up the ideal of excellence. How can they learn to honor me if I do not speak to them honorably?

Clay and I have purposely trained our children in relationships, work habits, integrity, leadership, manners, thinking skills, proper self-image, service—the list goes on and on. We believe that children, who were made to reflect God's image to the world, will flourish when called by a parent to learn the ways of excellence in every area of life. We envision the outcome we desire in our children's lives so that we can sense how to train them. I have observed in my children's lives that the fruit of training is confidence, security, and peace.

This goes for all children. But some lend themselves more easily to training than others. Acknowledging this truth can bring some comfort to parents who are struggling to guide a difficult child.

My third child, sweet Nathan, has a very strong personality—he's a lot like his mother! When Nathan was two years old, we flew from California to Texas to visit Nana, Clay's mom. We stopped at a restaurant on the way home to Nana's house. While we were there, Nathan decided he had just had it! He threw a chicken leg across the table, lay down on the floor, and had a screaming tantrum.

I was paying the bill at the cashier's counter while Clay was attempting to wrestle Nathan down. The cashier said, "What that boy needs is a *strong* hand!"

It was true. I wondered many times if we were making progress with this energetic "wild child." Now, at thirteen years old, our Nathan is a charmer. We can see God's purposes in giving Nathan his personality. He is fun, encouraging, creative, and spunky, and Clay and I consider him one of our best friends and companions. However, it took many moments of training to bring out the good that was already in his heart and to help him learn to use self-control.

GUARDING OUR CHILDREN'S INFLUENCES

Proverbs 13:20 says,

He who walks with wise men will be wise,
But the companion of fools will suffer harm.

A similar verse is 1 Corinthians 15:33: "Bad company corrupts good morals." And both of these passages point to a final principle a wise mother will follow in reaching her children's hearts for Christ. While our children are young, we need to monitor carefully the people and ideas to which they are exposed.

When we go to the trouble of instructing our children in righteousness and training their character, then as wise mothers, we must see that the people who are models for our children—their parents, friends, teachers, peers, even heroes in history—are those who undergird what we are teaching instead of undermining it.

We just planted six young aspen trees in our yard. The professional who planted the trees bound each sapling to a strong pole that was placed deep in the ground. He commented that they were too young and weak to grow straight in the midst of the wind, rain, and snow without a guide to support them while they were establishing their roots.

Similarly, our young children need protection and guidance from outside forces that would threaten their future growth. Our children need us to help them have the gift of a pure mind, free not only from the violence, immorality, and pornography that is so prevalent in our society but also from the cynicism and hopelessness that pull at so many. They need time to grow their roots in love, innocence, kindness, truth, morality, and trust. When they are strong and tall, then they will be able to withstand and battle the forces of life, but not until they have been established first in their root—or heart—systems!

What does this mean in practical terms? Children tend to take in all information as truth. Guarding our children's influences, therefore, would certainly include keeping close tabs on their media exposure—television, movies, even books. A wise mother will do very careful research before allowing her children access to most popular entertainment.

Guarding our children means close monitoring of the people in authority over our kids—teachers, coaches, the parents of friends, and even church leaders. Before I let my children spend time with other adults, I want to know a lot about those people's characters, beliefs, and attitudes. And there may well be times when I need to make the uncomfortable decision to remove my child from another person's influence.

My children's peers, too, can have a strong influence—and children can definitely be immature, unwise, and lacking in righteousness. I have gone to great lengths to have many of our children's activities in our home so I can supervise their heart attachments as well as know what is going on in their lives. I have also tried to give my children sheltered and protected time at home during which they can become attached to their siblings and parents. Choosing to spend lots of family time together has given my children a close relationship with their siblings. Time together in our home, practicing our standards, has underlined these principles in their daily lives.

Proverbs 4:23 instructs us to "watch over your heart with all diligence, for from it flow the springs of life." When I realized that my children's hearts were also the springs from which their lives flowed, I pictured Clay and me as guards standing in front of their hearts to protect them from anything that could soil or poison the waters.

In this area of parenting, as in so many other areas, I have had to do a balancing act. If I protect my children from every evil that exists in the world, then I run the risk of keeping them weak and unable to stand strong in a sinful world. I also run the risk of cultivating pharisaical attitudes of "We are better than everyone else" because of the laws that we keep in our home. Yet if I want to protect them from the degradation of the cultural norm that does not value purity and innocence in the life of a child, then I do what is necessary to make the standards in our home righteous and holy, regardless of what others do.

I have noticed that all of us would love to have a formula for producing godly kids. "Just tell me exactly which rules to follow, and I will do it to the letter!" is the desire of our hearts. And yet parenting, just like every other area of the Christian life, is to be done by faith in the power of the Holy Spirit. I find myself constantly coming to the Lord and seeking his counsel about many issues in my children's lives. In the end, I must follow what I think are biblical principles, apply them to my life, and step out in faith, which means I must study the Word regularly!

Even when we do our best to protect our children, we will fail at some points. Yet vigilance will provide us the best opportunity to give our children a foundation of a godly moral character on which to build on the rest of their lives. One of the best gifts we can give our children as they go from our homes into young adulthood is a pure conscience and, if possible, a mind with no scars or regrets.

At the same time, because our desire is to prepare our children to reach out to the world as Jesus did, we provide lots of opportunities to have compassion on those less fortunate than we are—even those who live by different standards. As our children see us reaching out to different kinds of people, we hope our standards will become theirs. And we try to monitor this exposure carefully and to be as involved as possible with the process.

We once had a neighbor whose nine-year-old child was left by herself in the summers while her mother worked and the man with whom they were living was out of town. We would invite this sweet child over to share some of our summer treats and play in the backyard, and we tried to develop a relationship with her. She shared with us that she had been watching R-rated movies with her mom since she was a small child. She had bizarre ideas about God and life in general and was in acute need of nurture and love. By bringing her into our home, my children developed a heart for her and began to pray for her each night.

One of the things I try to remember in guarding our children's influences is that exposing them to positive influences is just as important as avoiding negative ones. We have sought and encouraged relationships with righteous older people and mentors who can encourage our children according to our goals. Having missionaries over for dinner, leading small-group Bible studies in our home where children and parents are welcome, taking our children to hear concerts where mature Christians share their testimonies, and going to hear a great speaker are some of the ways we have provided that exposure.

Now that our three older children are teens, we are beginning to see the positive outcome of our careful program of protection and positive exposure. Protecting them from harmful influences has not produced in them a superior attitude toward others or a lack of social skills. Instead, our children have compassion for kids their age who have had lots of trouble in their lives. They are also more secure and have stronger self-images, because they are deeply rooted in the faith and values we have taught them systematically over the years.

Giving our children a grounding in wisdom principles has prepared them to apply their own opinions to the situations of life. In our rousing family discussions about movies, music, cultural standards, and how to remain godly in a fallen world, we see they are beginning to apply truth and understanding to the situations and relationships that life is presenting to them. As our children gradually move out from under the protective umbrella of our home, I am confident they will have the strength they need, not only to confront and resist the elements of the outside world that could lead their hearts astray, but to reach out in love and to win other hearts for Christ.

And this, of course, is the beauty of parenting according to God's plan and making his goals our goals. Giving our children a solid foundation of truth upon which to build their lives provides us with the opportunity to influence our heritage for generations to come. It is not just our children who will benefit, but our grandchildren and the wider world as well. As our children catch a vision of righteousness in their own hearts, they will perpetuate truth wherever they go. Our wise mothering, in other words, is a way of providing our grandchildren, our great-grandchildren, and our entire society with secure homes, loving parents, and most of all, with enduring hearts for Christ.

FOR THOUGHT AND REFLECTION

Something to Think About...

A favorite place to visit with my children in Austria was the ruins of an old castle high on the mountains in a hamlet called Durnstein. Richard the Lionhearted was supposedly held prisoner in this strong fortress. His faithful servant Blondell, the legend goes, strolled through the countryside singing songs that Richard knew, hoping that the prince would hear a familiar tune from his cell and somehow signal his whereabouts to Blondell and be rescued. It worked, according to the story. Richard answered the singing entreaty with the chorus to the song he heard and was rescued.

This world in which we live is like a fortress of darkness in which our souls are imprisoned. Yet we are called by the Lord to sing the songs of redemption and freedom to our children so that when they hear our voice and respond to his songs, they may be rescued from darkness. In our homes the Holy Spirit will teach our children the songs of truth that may be instruments of redemption for others wherever they go for the rest of their lives.

1. *Jeremiah 9:23-24.* What does the Lord want us to teach our children to boast about? What are the worldly treasures that God says are not worthy of him? How do the priorities of your life show the importance of nurturing a heart for God? How do you need to adjust your priorities?

2. *1 Corinthians 15:33.* What corrupts good morals in our children? To what does "bad company" refer? Why should we be careful about the companions of our children when they are young and vulnerable? Compare this to Matthew 9:9-13. What are some specific ways you can balance protection of your children with the need to teach them Christlike compassion?

3. *Hebrews 12:10-11.* Why, according to these verses, does God discipline us? Is good discipline always pleasant? What is the fruit of training? If God so disciplines us, what does this say about our parenting responsibilities?

4. *Proverbs 29:15.* According to this verse, what gives a child wisdom? What does "gets his own way" mean? In what specific ways might a selfish child bring shame to his mother? What does this verse imply about the mother's responsibility?

Something to Try...

Intervening in my children's lives to train their hearts and words and attitudes is often wearying. It is rewarding, however, when my children come to understand the importance of their own training.

We had visited a children's museum one afternoon, and just about the time we were to leave, we noticed a rather large five-year-old boy. His parents called him to come so they could go home. But the little boy started screaming and yelling and pounding his parents. After quite a scene, the parents dragged the boy away, all the while fending off his blows and trying to ignore his ear-piercing screams.

My children stared at this rowdy in wild-eyed amazement! It was a perfect opportunity to affirm them for their own obedience to me. "I'm so grateful that you kids have learned to honor me when I ask you to do something. It is so pleasant to see children control their spirits and choose to be pleasant." Even though their obedience to me was not always perfect, it was a perfect object lesson in which to affirm them so they could see why it is important to give honor and desire to do so. They were indeed appalled at the little boy's behavior and have revisited that story for years!

- Seek opportunities to affirm your little ones for efforts made to obey you. All of us need encouragement.
- Plan the best time to have devotions or prayer and Bible reading *with* your kids. Make it convenient for you. Plan for a month at a time. If you get off track, just start back again as soon as possible so it can become a family habit.
- Take your children with you before the throne of God so they can learn how to pray to God as their heavenly Father. Help them to be comfortable and familiar in pouring out their hearts before the Lord and learning to listen to the counsel of his Word.

CHAPTER 6

The Teaching Mother

Training Children's Minds to Think Biblically

From childhood you have known the sacred
writings which are able to give you the wisdom
that leads to salvation through faith
which is in Christ Jesus.

2 TIMOTHY 3:15

Being opinionated and having something to say seems to be a Clarkson heritage. One never knows when some innocent comment might incite a rousing discussion in which every family member feels compelled to participate.

This particular Sunday evening was no exception. All the troops had just returned from a meeting and were congregating in the kitchen to prepare their own snack dinners. The boys opted for cereal—no messes or pots and pans to wash! The girls opted for a more elaborate meal—nachos. As everyone munched on his or her concoction, someone innocently asked whether we thought a certain Disney cartoon was evolutionary or creationist or neutral in its story line.

You would have thought we were discussing the deity of Christ!

Immediately vastly differing opinions began to fly in all directions. For some reason this discussion followed gender lines. The boys thought the movie reflected an evolutionary mind-set and cited the comparisons of humans to animals. The girls fought for the concept that innocent words may have been mistaken as evolutionary but were intended as a joke. Dad piped in with his two cents' worth, and the topic heated up. I finally said, "I don't know if it really matters. Besides, I need to put Joy to bed! It's late!"

As I picked up Joy and started downstairs toward her bedroom, the other four followed hard on my heels. "Mom, you and Dad are always telling us we need to evaluate the world-view of authors and producers and performers." This was a perfect invitation for Dad to throw in a few more cents. The discussion continued to heat up along party lines, and each voice got louder. The tension of feeling misunderstood began to change the pitch of the voices.

By this time I had four-year-old Joy standing on her bed, putting her gown on over her head, with the rest of us still fulfilling our obligation to announce our opinion to the world.

Joy suddenly dug her heels into the bed and stood as tall as she could with her hands punched firmly out, as though to stop an oncoming truck.

She said loudly and firmly, like a drill sergeant, "EVERYONE STOP! TAKE A DEEP BREATH AND THINK ABOUT JESUS!"

Her directive sent everyone rolling on the floor in laughter, and finally the discussion came to a close.

This story depicts our everyday lives—opinions stated, issues debated, topics taught and learned, questions asked, books and experts quoted, and heartfelt convictions passionately shared while washing dishes, eating meals, or sitting around the living room drinking tea. And even though they may occasionally get out of hand, these discussions, perhaps more than any other family activity, have shaped our children's lives for the better.

Why are such discussions so important? Because they do exactly what Joy said. They teach our children to think about Jesus—and to think biblically about every aspect of their lives! They are part of an ongoing process of sharpening minds, focusing thoughts, and allowing biblical truth to shape our mental processes as well as fill our hearts.

Scripture is filled with directives that show us how important our minds are to God. The book of Deuteronomy tells us that we are supposed to love the Lord our God with all of our minds as well as with our hearts and our strength—and Jesus later affirmed this directive as the greatest commandment. Loving God with our mind means we purpose to fill our minds—and our children's minds— with wisdom, truth, and righteousness.

"Taking every thought captive to the obedience of Christ" (2 Corinthians 10:5) is another directive given in Scripture. This indicates that following Jesus is supposed to dramatically influence the way we think. And the apostle Paul advises us what we are to think about: whatever is true, honorable, right, pure, lovely, and of good repute (Philippians 4:8).

WHAT WE THINK—AND WHAT WE ARE

Perhaps the most telling scripture about the importance of loving Christ with our minds is found in the book of Proverbs, which boldly states that as a person "thinks within himself, so he is" (23:7). That, in a nutshell, is why it's so important to train our children's minds to think biblically—because their thought processes and their beliefs will, in the long run, determine the kind of people they will be.

Everyone has a philosophy of life, whether he or she knows it or not. We all base our actions on what we believe. What we think about creation, life, God, marriage, our jobs, and eternity determines both what we do and what we become. If our philosophy is not based on truth, then our whole life will be a lie—or worse.

Ephesians 4 contains a sobering description of the consequences of such faulty thinking on both individuals and society. Those who don't focus their minds on the Lord are described as confused and unstable—"tossed here and there by waves, and carried about by every wind of doctrine, by the trickery of men, by craftiness in deceitful scheming" (verse 14)—and as ignorant and deceived—"in the futility of their mind, being darkened in their understanding, excluded from the life of God, because of the ignorance that is in them, because of the hardness of their heart" (verses 17-18). As a result, "they, having become callous, have given themselves over to sensuality, for the practice of every kind of impurity with greediness" (verse 19).

But just as faulty thinking leads to painful consequences, right thinking leads to the kind of lives we want for our children. "Speaking the truth in love, we are to grow up in all aspects into Him, who is the head, even Christ," says verse 15. And verses 23-24 tell us that we are to be renewed "in the spirit of your mind, and put on the new self, which in the likeness of God has been created in righteousness and holiness of the truth."

This passage seems to indicate both the dangers that children are likely to encounter and the remedy that lies in training their minds. As mothers, we need to protect our children from all of the godless philosophies that lead so many astray. We can help them learn to withstand the gusty danger from the winds of doctrine that will indeed blow their way.

But doing this effectively requires far more than just indoctrinating our children with Christian platitudes. We teach our children how to think and reason in their own minds so that they may be able, when mature, to discern what is true and what is false. It is our job to train them to understand "righteousness and holiness of the truth" in their everyday lives. We will not always be there to think for them, so we teach them to think for themselves according to biblical convictions.

When I was in college in the seventies, I was buffeted by a great many winds of doctrine. Though I had grown up in a Christian home, the ideas and lifestyles I encountered during that turbulent era challenged just about everything I had been taught. During that time I had to ask the question "What is truth?" I struggled through many doubts about the relevancy of Scripture and its authority and was forced to reexamine whether the Bible was really true for me. I worked through these issues by reading a variety of books and spending hours listening to tapes and attending Bible studies. Sometimes I found that many people who called themselves Christians had never taken the time to think about these issues.

After a year of intense questioning, I came to the conclusion that there was ample evidence to satisfy my heart's need to affirm the relevance, truth, and authority of Scripture. This confidence, followed by my commitment of faith, has since provided me with a dependable anchor to steady my ship of faith through many storms of life.

Now my children are growing up in a world in which the concept of truth is challenged, where it's widely assumed that there is no absolute truth. In this atmosphere of relativity, I have found that my children look to Clay and me and our confidence in the authority of Scripture to give them an anchor for their own faith.

Our task is to train ourselves and our children to think clearly, truthfully, and biblically about Jesus and the world. We want to help them develop a Christian world-view based on the truth of Scripture, our personal trust and application of Scripture to our own lives, and our testimony of God's faithfulness to us. This task requires us to understand the scope of the biblical knowledge our children need and to develop a plan for helping them acquire it. In addition, we help them understand biblical principles and guidelines and learn how to apply them in everyday life.

As Clay and I pondered our own plan, we came up with five major areas in which we wanted to train our children's minds: biblical literacy, morality and laws, theology, wisdom, and faith.

SCRIPTURE: TEACHING BIBLICAL LITERACY

In ministering over the last thirty years, I have often observed that many people wonder why God allowed a certain thing to happen to them. I have seen God blamed for many things. Yet, as I probe these people, I often find they have virtually no knowledge of Scripture.

Jesus promised in the Sermon on the Mount that if we built our lives on the foundation of his words, our lives would be stable, like a house on a rock. Though winds and storms come our way, we will not fall, if we have "been founded upon the rock" (Matthew 7:25).

It's just common sense that in order to think biblically, a person needs to know the Bible. That's probably the most basic aspect of training our children. They cannot find biblical answers or comfort in the midst of difficulties if they do not know God's Word. How can they live life well if they don't have a good understanding of life's ultimate instruction book?

Studying the Old Testament stories shows us how God interacted with man firsthand—providing us with pictures of the origins of life, man's struggle against sin, and God's willingness to love, bless, and guide those whose hearts are open to him. Abraham's faith leads him to trust God with his most valuable treasure, his son, despite a seemingly impossible request. The story of Moses shows God's power to save his people, even against the pressure of a wealthy and powerful culture that disdains his power. Ruth shows God's reward to those who are faithful. Job teaches that there is a spiritual battle raging in heaven in which we can have a part when we trust God. The story of David and Goliath teaches that through God's strength we can face giants. The prophetic writings of Isaiah, Jeremiah, and others show both the dire consequences of turning from God and God's patient willingness to bring his people back to him.

The New Testament, of course, tells the thrilling story of God's final redemption of his people through the life, death, and resurrection of his Son. It also provides a practical understanding of how to live the Christian life. Through the teachings and examples of Jesus, we learn about the kingdom of God—both what it requires of us and how we can be part of it. The Sermon on the Mount teaches the humility of Christ's way and spells out biblical priorities. The miracles described in the Gospels show the Lord's compassion and power. The Last Supper shows the servant leadership of Jesus as well as his loving desire to comfort his friends and send them help.

The letters of Paul, Peter, John, and others teach us how to live in communion with God's people and how to pursue ministry. Revelation reminds us of the inevitability of judgment but also the glorious hope of Christ's second coming and ultimate triumph. And so on and so on. The Bible, quite simply, is the richest treasure we can offer our children, the most valuable tool for shaping their thinking.

Just as I had to settle in my mind the reliability of Scripture, however, my children need to work through this issue on their own (with our guidance and input) so that their faith can be their own. If they become convinced of the authenticity of Scripture, then they will have reason to obey its principles. However, if they just mimic me or Clay in what they say they believe, they will not have a deep-seated, authentic faith. At some point of crisis, their faith would easily give way to doubt.

So, too, parents must come to their own conclusions about the authority of Scripture, its historical reliability, and its application to life before they can lead their children in these issues. Because I was not taught the Bible in depth as a child, I often have not had the specific answers to my children's questions. Knowing the Bible inside and out requires a lifetime of study. Yet their questions have motivated me to search the Scriptures even more thoroughly and to learn along with them.

Second Timothy 3:16-17 reminds us that Scripture is "inspired by God and profitable for teaching, for reproof, for correction, for training in righteousness; that the man of God may be adequate, equipped for every good work." If Scripture was inspired by God himself, then I desired to help our children see the importance of understanding the truth of Scripture and learning to obey its principles as faithfully as possible.

Psalm 119:160 tells us, "The sum of Thy word is truth, and every one of Thy righteous ordinances is everlasting." This means that all ordinances and principles of God's Word were written to apply to all generations at all times. In training our children to think biblically, then, we use Scripture to illuminate Scripture. When addressing contemporary cultural issues (creation versus evolution, biblical views of women, divorce, marriage, sexuality), we turn to Scripture to come up with universal answers that will provide a foundation of truth.

Though there are a variety of interpretations to various scriptures, in order to give our children integrity in their education of the Bible, we seek to give them the tools to study Scripture for themselves. This way they will learn to base their convictions on biblical principles and develop confidence in their faith.

When our children were very young, we began to teach them Scripture by reading Bible stories to them. Once a week we would have a special family devotional time in which we would act out the stories or try to bring the stories to life in an interesting way.

One such evening I made flat bread and flavored it with honey. Then I soaked some boneless chicken thighs in teriyaki sauce and baked them. I spread out tan towels (to look like dirt) in front of the living-room fireplace and scattered little pieces of chicken and bread all over them.

A little later in another room I read the story of the Israelites in the wilderness to the kids. I asked them, "How would so many adults and children ever find the food to eat on such a long journey? There were no grocery stores in the wilderness." After they attempted to answer the question, finally an insightful child said, "They'd have to pray to God for a miracle!" At that point I gave them all baskets and led them into the living room. They gasped as they saw the towels on the floor and began to collect the food as though they were hunting Easter eggs.

"What is this, Mommy?"

"Quail and manna," I replied.

Then as they munched their unusual dinner, I finished reading the story. For years after that they remembered the story whenever we as a family needed God to provide us with a miracle!

Often, however, we didn't have time to go to such lengths to teach a story. So we followed a simple formula Clay had picked up at seminary. The acronym ARTS helped us remember what to do:

A—Ask a simple question about the passage to spark interest before reading the story. For example, I might ask, "What is the greatest treasure in all of the world that you would like to own? What would you give to have the treasure?" before reading the story about the pearl of great price.

R—Read the passage enthusiastically and with interest.

T—Talk about the passage. Sometimes I give a little background on the story. Or I might ask the children what the story meant, how the people in the story acted, or what God was trying to communicate.

S—Supplication. Close the time by praying together. Often the prayers will relate to the passage: "Lord, help us be more compassionate to others, as the good Samaritan was."

This little formula got us through years of short devotions. As the children began to mature and needed more substance, we began to offer them incentives for reading through the Bible for themselves. We would promise a special date for an ice cream cone or dinner with Mom or Dad when they had read through the Old Testament or New Testament. We memorized passages of Scripture together by repeating the words out loud each morning at breakfast.

Next we began to show the kids how to use the concordance in their Bibles to study topics that were relevant to their own lives. For instance, when they were caught in immature arguments, I would have them look for three verses that addressed the issue of how to speak to each other or the dangers of an uncontrolled tongue. Then I would have them write a paragraph about how these verses applied to the situation with their offended brother or sister. By learning to search through the Bible for themselves, they became familiar with using it to give instruction for their life questions and issues.

Now that they are older and have begun to ask deeper questions, we have passed books and magazines their way as a point of discussion. When our kids reached junior-high age, we had them read a book by Larry Richards called *It Couldn't Just Happen*, which explains how the world gives its own evidence of a Creator. We sometimes read this book's short chapters aloud and discussed issues one at a time. Because our children had a taste for C. S. Lewis from our many readings of The Chronicles of Narnia, it also seemed appropriate for us to introduce them to *Mere Christianity*, Lewis's treatise on the importance of our faith.

Helping our children become biblically literate has been a systematic, step-by-step process. As we helped them first become familiar with Scripture, then learn to apply it to their own lives, and finally grapple with deeper issues by reading commentaries and thinking through ideas that were more sophisticated, we have also had the joy of watching their faith mature—and their understanding of God's Word grow broader and deeper.

CHRISTIAN LAW AND MORALITY:
TEACHING RIGHT AND WRONG

Understanding basic morality is also fundamental to teaching children to think biblically. Before they can ever make right decisions, they need to understand what the Bible says about right and wrong.

Concrete principles provide the early foundations for their understanding of biblical morality. Young children think concretely. They understand the idea of following rules—and I have found they respond well to being taught the Bible's "rules" about how to act.

The Ten Commandments, for example, provide concrete principles for children to understand. "Do not lie. Do not steal. Do not murder." These essential truths can be learned by very young children.

As we teach our children these concrete principles, we have opportunities morning, noon, and evening to help them understand how to apply them. When a child cheats at a game, for instance, we have an opportunity to remind them about not stealing. We can point out that there are many ways to steal— winning a game by cheating takes away another person's opportunity to compete fairly for a prize. Cheating a store owner by not giving back the change he overpaid us is actually stealing from the store. We instruct in principle and then expand on their understanding through daily discussion and example.

Jesus also taught principles of right and wrong in simple, concrete ways that are easy for children to grasp and apply. His Sermon on the Mount instructions to treat others the same way you want them to treat you (Luke 6:31; Matthew 7:12) has to be one of the main training points of toddlerhood! I can't begin to count how many times I have separated squabbling little ones with gentle but pointed reminders that they should not snatch toys or hit—because they wouldn't like it if someone did that to them...and "Jesus tells us to treat others the way we want to be treated."

I have learned over the years that training our children to think biblically about right and wrong often involves teaching the same principles over and over and over again, trusting that someday, in God's own timing, they will get it.

I remember a time when Joy was about three years old and she and I were lying in bed together. She had been watching her favorite video—a tape of *The Promise*, in which she had participated as a baby. The play depicted Jesus' crucifixion, and watching Jesus die always made her sad. Her viewing that night prompted the question: "Why did Jesus have to die?"

I quickly groped for an explanation simple enough for a three-year-old. I explained to her that each of us has sin in our hearts, which separates us from Jesus. I said that sin causes us to think mainly about our own needs and causes us to fuss or hit our brothers or to say no to Mom and Dad when we don't want to obey. Sin is the sickness in our hearts that causes us to want to do bad things.

As I was about to go on with my grand explanation, Joy turned to me and said, "Well, Mommy, I've never sinned before, and you have never sinned, so there's no problem. Let's just not talk about it anymore!"

All of us have times when we're resistant to truth, and that includes children. Faithful, repetitive teaching of the biblical principles of right and wrong—plus a gentle but firm insistence that the children *act* on those principles—is what helps to build familiar pathways in their minds so that when they are mature, they will have a reliable basis for making decisions about what is right and what is wrong.

A friend of mine taught her children a saying when they were young: "Right is always right even if no one is doing it! Wrong is always wrong even if everyone is doing it." This little saying has helped my children in a number of peer-related situations to make the right decision, even though it meant going against the flow of the crowd.

As children mature, of course, our teachings about right and wrong need to move beyond the simple to more complex issues. Clay and I have always tried to engage our growing children in what-if scenarios about situations they may have to face and choices they may have to make. Real-life choices often don't fall into simple black-and-white, right-or-wrong categories, and we want our children to be equipped to respond wisely and biblically to these situations.

In addition to the biblical content about right and wrong, it's important to teach the biblical reality that there *is* right and wrong. This may seem obvious, but in many circles, even Christian ones, the biblical concepts of right and wrong are rapidly being replaced by what is usually referred to as "tolerance." But that perfectly good word for patience and forbearance has been turned into a buzzword for moral relativity—the belief that no one religion, morality, or belief system is better than any other.

An overemphasis on tolerance can mean we are fearful of taking a stand on any moral issue, such as divorce, adultery, fornication, or even some crimes. We can reach the point—and some Christians have reached it already—when we'd rather tolerate evil than make anyone feel different or uncomfortable.

Don't misunderstand me here. I'm not saying we should not be patient with one another or tolerant of one another's imperfections. I'm talking about something completely different—an exaggerated tolerance that ignores the reality of sin and denies that there is any right or wrong.

Galatians 6:7-8 is very clear on this point: "Do not be deceived, God is not mocked; for whatever a man sows, this he will also reap. For the one who sows to his own flesh shall from the flesh reap corruption, but the one who sows to the Spirit shall from the Spirit reap eternal life." In other words, there are consequences to sin, and we must teach our children this moral principle if we want to protect them and provide them with the best chance at emotional, spiritual, and mental health. To fail to teach them biblical morality will take them away from the protection of God's Word.

In teaching biblical morality, of course, we also need to teach the reality of what happens when we fall short of God's standards. Children need to know the painful consequences of sin, but they also need to know the reality of God's grace and forgiveness. They need to know that all of us fall short of God's glory and that God has provided a remedy for these failures—not an easy out, but a costly and precious chance for redemption.

This is especially important for parents to keep in mind because some of us let guilt over our own moral failures hold us back from teaching biblical morality to our children. Parents who were sexually active before marriage may be hesitant to press issues of sexual morality to their teenagers. Parents who dabbled in drugs or engaged in petty theft or vandalism may feel like hypocrites for forbidding their children to do the same or disciplining them if they do.

It's crucial, however, that we not allow our sins to keep us from teaching the holy standards God has in mind for his children. In spite of our own failures, we can try to protect our children from repeating our mistakes. To do this, however, we need to take seriously both our *own* need for redemption and the reality of God's forgiveness.

Repenting of past sins and accepting Christ's redemption means that we can put our past behind us and move forward to what Christ has given us through his life, death, and resurrection. In Christ we can become new creatures, as stated in 2 Corinthians 5:17: "If any man is in Christ, he is a new creature; the old things passed away; behold, new things have come."

I have seen Christ redeem and heal and free so many who have felt trapped by their sins. After one of my speaking engagements, a woman in her fifties came to me in private. She had had an abortion at a young age. She eventually became a Christian, married, and was committed to having a godly influence on her children. Until that evening she had felt guilty because of her past decision to terminate her pregnancy. She said, "I feel that now I am free from guilt and can be a worthy wife and mother. No longer do I have to live under a cloud of condemnation that makes me insecure in my relationships."

Whether we actually share our past sins and shortcomings with our children is a purely personal matter. It depends on the nature of the sin, the personality of the child, and the quality of the parent-child relationship. Some children may benefit from discovering their parents weren't perfect or from hearing about hard lessons their parents had to learn. Other children may be better off not knowing. What to tell children about our past is a matter for much prayer and for personal discretion and wisdom based on Scripture.

The thing to remember is that all of us sinners are precious to God. Those of us who are divorced for unbiblical reasons, or who have committed adultery, or who have lived with someone outside of wedlock are precious to him. So are those of us who have lied or gossiped or neglected the poor or engaged in other forms of more socially acceptable sin. But it is only as we understand God's laws, repenting of our waywardness and accepting God's forgiveness for our past, that any of us can experience the wholeness that God designed for us. It is only as we seek his ideals that we can best experience his fullest blessings. This is what our children need to understand so they will know how to behave in a culture opposed to God's design for morality.

THEOLOGY: TEACHING THE KNOWLEDGE OF GOD

Every one of us, whether we know it or not, has a personal theology. The word *theology* basically means "the study of God" and is often used to refer to a specific academic discipline. But *theology* in a broader sense refers to an understanding of who God is and what he is like—and how our children think in that regard will determine the scope of their Christian life. The degree to which they comprehend the holiness, sovereignty, omniscience, omnipotence, and redemptive love of our heavenly Father will determine the depth of their faith and devotion to him.

The Christian life, after all, is not merely a list of dos and don'ts. It is a faith in and a relationship with the real and living God who created the universe. In order to understand God so that we can know what the Christian life is all about, we must understand who he is. And that means we need to develop—and help our children develop—a sound biblical theology.

When I was in college, I longed to find someone who had an authentic faith. I thought that if someone really knew the living God who created the universe, surely his life would be visibly different. By God's grace, I met many such people. They lived as though God had called them specially to himself to accomplish great things for him during their short lives.

Now my own eighteen-year-old is looking for the same thing. She said to me recently, "Mom, it seems to me that those who really know God should be more loving, more deeply driven with enthusiasm about their purpose in life, more unselfish and sacrificial and more gracious than those who don't believe—more creative and more excellent in every way. Shouldn't knowing God change them forever? But most Christians don't seem the least bit moved by the 'wonderfulness' of God. I would die if the lack of enthusiasm I see in most people is what defined the living God!"

My children long to give their hearts not to a list of rules but to a living, loving, vibrant Person—a God who is truly worthy of praise and their life's devotion. They will encounter that God in the pages of Scripture, but they will come to know him even more intimately in the lives of those who love him. In a sense, I give my children their best theological education by seeking to really know and love God in my own life and living my life out before my children. Children will read our lives as the most important book they will ever know. How important it is that we allow our hearts to be confronted by his reality daily so that they may see his reality in our lives.

From the time our children were very young, Clay and I have tried to model the importance of knowing God intimately and worshiping him in a worthy manner. Kneeling in prayer as a family and trusting him for our needs has been one way for us to show the reality of God lived out personally. Rather than use lofty formal language to address God or use our prayer time to give him a shopping list of what we want him to do, we address him as someone with whom we have a close, trusting, respectful relationship.

Since the Bible is in essence God's self-portrait for his people, the Bible has been our most important source for instilling in our children a sound theology. As they read scriptures like Psalm 139 and 145, they are memorizing word pictures of God's magnitude that will be in their minds forever. Studying the life of Christ with us gives them even more insight into God's personality and character. Jesus himself told us that "he who has seen Me has seen the Father" (John 14:9). And Hebrews 1:3 reminds us that Jesus "is the radiance of [God's] glory and the exact representation of His nature, and upholds all things by the word of His power." Jesus was an exact picture of God on earth—so getting to know him through the pages of Scripture is one of the best ways of sharpening a child's understanding of who God is and what he is like.

WISDOM: TEACHING GOD'S POINT OF VIEW

The word *wisdom* refers to both practical insight or knowledge and discernment about how to make decisions. In the biblical sense, being wise means understanding God's point of view about daily life and the whole scope of the universe and learning to live and act according to his perspective. In one sense, this wisdom cannot be taught; it is something that grows with maturity and experience. At the same time, the Bible offers a collection of basic principles for living that point the way to God's wisdom, and these wisdom principles are well worth teaching to our children.

God generously gives us a list of advantages for all who would seek wisdom and be wise. Proverbs 3:13-18 says,

> How blessed is the man who finds wisdom,
> And the man who gains understanding.
> For its profit is better than the profit of silver,
> And its gain than fine gold.
> She [wisdom] is more precious than jewels;
> And nothing you desire compares with her.
> Long life is in her right hand;
> In her left hand are riches and honor.

Her ways are pleasant ways,
And all her paths are peace.
She is a tree of life to those who take hold of her,
And happy are all who hold her fast.

A great treasury of biblical wisdom principles is found in the book of Proverbs. There our children can learn "the fear of man [peer pressure?] brings a snare" (29:25), that it's good to work hard (chapter 6), and that they should trust in God and not in their own understanding (3:5). The wisdom of Proverbs is infinitely practical and specific; it warns of the danger of unbridled passion and the desire for instant gratification. It teaches our children ways to cultivate good relationships by avoiding quarrels, respecting elders, practicing forgiveness, and learning to be humble.

Even as God had Solomon write this book as a picture of a father writing to his son so that his son would have confidence on the path of life, so it is a picture to us of God's desire to instruct us and give us guidance in the path of life. God desires us to be more than academic theologians who can think great thoughts about him. He desires to make his wisdom principles a fundamental part of our thinking so we can apply them to our lives in a realistic way. As we teach our children to act wisely and think about the biblical approach to living, we help them develop the character and integrity that will serve as a foundation for their decisions.

But Proverbs is not the only place in the Bible where wisdom principles may be found. The entire Bible, in a sense, is a wisdom manual—given to us to help us understand God's point of view and live accordingly. God's wisdom principles in the Bible give us glimpses into eternity and his purposes ("I go to prepare a place for you"—John 14:2). This gives us an advantage in this life over others who don't know God and his purposes, because of the hope that we have in our future with him. Other passages provide us with an understanding of the patience we need to wait for God's timing ("And we know that God causes all things to work together for good to those who love God, to those who are called according to His purpose"—Romans 8:28).

Many principles of God's wisdom as set forth in the Bible are basic common sense. They would seem logical to almost anyone, Christian or non-Christian. But at the heart of the gospel is a series of wisdom principles that are completely counterintuitive, even preposterous or scandalous in the world's eyes. These wisdom principles point to spiritual realities that actually contradict the wisdom of the world. Losing ourselves to find ourselves? Going last to be first? Leading by serving? Dying in order to live. These life-changing paradoxes speak of a wisdom much deeper and more powerful than the world can understand. As the apostle Paul explained,

> Has not God made foolish the wisdom of the world? For since in the wisdom of God the world through its wisdom did not come to know God, God was well-pleased through the foolishness of the message preached to save those who believe. For indeed Jews ask for signs, and Greeks search for wisdom; but we preach Christ crucified, to Jews a stumbling block, and to Gentiles foolishness, but to those who are the called, both Jews and Greeks, Christ the power of God and the wisdom of God. Because the foolishness of God is wiser than men, and the weakness of God is stronger than men. (1 Corinthians 1:20-25)

The fundamental wisdom of Christ's gospel, in other words, relies on the kind of truths that must be lived by faith, not common sense. If we are to convey this wisdom to our children, what we really need to pass along to them is a living faith in a person, not a principle—the Lord who is ultimately the source of all wisdom.

FAITH: TEACHING TRUST IN GOD'S REALITY AND RELIABILITY

When we lived in Colorado, each summer our whole family would sleep under the stars in our sleeping bags out on the deck. Since we lived outside of the city, there seemed to be an endless number of stars, and the great expanse of the heavens confronted our souls with our own smallness.

One evening when the skies were particularly clear, Joy snuggled up against me and said, "Mama, the sky and the stars are so, so big that I know God's brain must be a lot bigger than mine if he could make all of them. I don't have to know as much as he does. I can just be glad he is so smart."

In her own way, Joy was defining faith—and doing a pretty good job of it.

Hebrews 11:1 tells us that "faith is the assurance of things hoped for, the conviction of things not seen." And this is the last area in which we must train our children to think biblically. From the beginning of time, God has desired that we live not just by what we can see and hold and touch but by faith in the presence and reality of God and his kingdom.

Children tend to come by that kind of faith easily. They are accustomed to trusting in things they don't understand, and they have never developed an exaggerated dependence on their own intellects. But as children grow—and especially as they encounter a culture that either discourages faith altogether or encourages a vague, unbiblical "spirituality"—they need a firm understanding of faith and how it works.

When we know God's moral laws, understand basic biblical theology, and have a grasp of the wisdom principles of Scripture, then we have a foundational basis upon which to act in faith. Faith is not a matter of mindlessly believing in God. It is believing him because of the soundness of the foundation he provides for our lives. We receive Christ by faith. We put aside guilt and the accusations of Satan by faith. We see God do miracles by faith. Our belief that God is accomplishing what we cannot presently see is the essence of following Christ. And this, in essence, is what our children need to understand about faith.

Faith is not necessarily an absence of doubt. It's certainly not a matter of checking our minds at the door and refusing to think. Rather, it is a commitment of our wills to trust God with our lives, based on the inherent value of his moral law, an understanding of his wonderful attributes, the magnitude of his domain and creation, and the astuteness of his wisdom. It is a personal decision we make based on our trust in the validity of these things—not a feeling that we drum up. This faith will lead us through the dark times when there is no feeling and through the ecstatic times when God seems to be very close.

When God commanded us to worship him with our whole mind, he was giving honor to the intelligence with which we are blessed. The older I get, the more amazed I am at the unity of Scripture, as well as the comprehensive nature of God—and the stronger my faith grows. The most intelligent and reasonable thought I can ever have always leads me to a reverence toward God. My faith in him has grown through my understanding of his life, his ways, and his wisdom. I have more reason to trust him because I am more aware of his power and his excellence.

TALKING ABOUT GOD

Helping our children think biblically requires that we live shoulder to shoulder with them in all the phases of their lives so we can pass on God's point of view. Though I have mentioned Deuteronomy 6:6-9 in other chapters, it is well worth quoting here:

> These words, which I am commanding you today, shall be on your heart;
> and you shall teach them diligently to your sons and shall talk of them
> when you sit in your house and when you walk by the way and when
> you lie down and when you rise up. And you shall bind them as a sign
> on your hand and they shall be as frontals on your forehead. And you
> shall write them on the doorposts of your house and on your gates.

The truth of God's Word—about God's reality, about wisdom, about faith—is to be spoken of constantly in our homes. Talking, talking, talking to our children all the time about everything has been, for Clay and me, the most important way in which we have passed on our faith to them. This constant talking and instructing is what was modeled by Jesus while he lived with his disciples and prepared them to be leaders of the faith when he went to heaven. It is significant to me that, in recording the last evening he spent with Jesus, John took four chapters to record all that Jesus said to them. He talked and talked and talked to them.

God desires to communicate to us and to our children through words and ideas, and he wants us to communicate with each other as well. He wants us not only to think about Jesus but to obey him and to speak of him often in our homes. Passing on his truth to our children requires that his wisdom and perspective, his life and history, his laws and love, his stories and his ways always be ready on our tongues. This does not mean we spiritualize everything that happens to us, but it does mean that speaking of God and his reality with the children he has entrusted to our care is as natural as the air around us.

So the next time your child asks a question or wants to discuss the philosophy of a Disney movie, see it as a steppingstone to a strong mind and a growing faith. Talk, talk, and talk some more—about Scripture, about theology, about wisdom—and you will be on the road to a rock-solid foundation for a faith that will not be shaken.

FOR THOUGHT AND REFLECTION

Something to Think About...

Sometimes during wakeful moments in the middle of the night, I find myself worrying or fretting about a child, our finances, or some personal difficulty. When this happens, I try to take advantage of the rare quiet in my home to seek God and his Word on these matters.

This happened recently when one of my children awakened me out of a deep sleep with symptoms of a twenty-four-hour flu. When I finally got my sweet one back to sleep, I was wide awake. So I pulled out my Bible and began to read.

It happened to fall open to the great passage in Deuteronomy 6:5-9 about the importance of parents' talking to their children morning, noon, and night about God's Word. It's a passage I've read a hundred times. What struck me now, though, was the first part of God's commandment—that his words were to be on the hearts of the parents first so that they would have something to teach to their children!

If my mind is not filled with God's principles, then how can I ever pass them on to my children? Training in the area of thinking must be my own goal before I look at the training of my children. I must say, however, that much of my own learning has taken place alongside them; as I studied the Bible with my children, I learned just as much as they did! They never suspected, and they imputed wisdom to me that I didn't previously have!

1. *Matthew 22:37-38.* What does it mean to love God "with all our mind"? How do we honor him with our mind? What are the different areas of our mind in which we can choose to honor him?

2. *Philippians 4:8.* What adjectives are used in this verse to describe the kinds of things we are to think about? What does it mean to "dwell" on these things? What things does this verse imply that we are not to dwell on?

3. *2 Corinthians 10:5.* This passage shows us how to actively fight for righteousness in our inner thoughts. What does this passage say we are to

destroy? What is an example of "speculations...raised up against the knowledge of God"? What does it mean to take thoughts captive to the obedience of Christ? How would you do this in a real-life situation?

4. *Psalm 119:160* and *2 Timothy 3:16-17.* According to the verse from Psalms, where do we find truth? How long is God's Word relevant to us? How does 2 Timothy 3:16-17 relate to this verse? For what is God's Word useful? How can you make a plan to systematically begin teaching truth to your children?

Something to Try...

When my children were young, we found recordings of Scripture songs to be a gentle way to encourage them to go to sleep at night. The music on the tapes we collected was as soothing as a lullaby, and in that relaxed setting the Scriptures really had a chance to settle into their hearts. I have been amazed at how many times my little ones have applied verses they learned from tapes at bedtime. The combination of music and quoted Scripture is a wonderful tool for teaching children gently and effectively.

- Build a small amount into your budget for Christian resources—books, devotionals, tapes, and CDs—you can use with your kids. Ask your friends and your church staff for recommendations, browse your local Christian bookstore, or shop online for excellent materials. The resource list at the back of this book will give you some ideas as well.
- Challenge your older children to memorize sizable sections of Scripture. Promise a one-time ten-dollar prize to any child who can memorize a chapter of your choosing in one week. (Some great possibilities include Psalm 139; 145; Philippians 1; the Sermon on the Mount in Matthew 5-7; or Romans 8.) Such challenges have given my children great pride in their ability to do so much so quickly!

PART THREE

A MOTHER'S HEART for HER CHILDREN

CHAPTER 7

Strong Friend

Building Loving Relationships with Our Children

But we proved to be gentle among you,
as a nursing mother tenderly cares
for her own children.

1 THESSALONIANS 2:7

One more time I gently held the chip in place as I tried to repair the spout on my ceramic Austrian teapot. The traces of glue already there reminded me that my efforts would probably be in vain. As I gently cradled my slightly scarred but greatly loved teapot, memories came flooding back of the many special occasions on which this pot had served our family so generously.

Candles were always a must to establish the specialness of our family's Sunday afternoon tea parties. So was soft instrumental music, specifically selected to give a lovely and relaxing ambiance to our time together. Irresistible desserts and spicy treats satisfied our palates just as enticing stories from the very best in children's literature captured our imaginations. (Reading aloud was always a special part of our family teas.) Countless times that old teapot filled our cups as the joy of being together filled our hearts.

So many memories were connected to that old teapot. I remembered a peacefully festive Christmas breakfast in Vienna when Sarah and Joel were just babies. Three friends from Taiwan, Austria, and America joined us for a joyful celebration of our Savior's birth. There was Sarah's five-year-old birthday "tea" when she and her friends dressed in frills and acted like grown-up ladies—not to mention all the birthday breakfasts with tea and cinnamon rolls and pajama-clad children watching with sparkling eyes to see what surprises would unfold. And there were bittersweet memories, too, like the tea we shared with a dear friend who had just learned that her brother had died. That teatime turned into a sad but beautiful hour of shared prayer and comfort.

As I placed the big pot back on the shelf, all those warm remembrances and many more warmed my heart—conversations shared, tears shed, books read, birthdays celebrated, Scripture discussed, and friendships deepened. It might be an old, cracked teapot, but it held so many precious, irreplaceable memories. And through the years it had been an invaluable tool in our home for nurturing the intimate relationships that are the heart of our mission as a family.

Because people will last through eternity, relationships have eternal significance. The relationships we make and cultivate and nurture will also sustain us throughout all of life's seasons. The quality of our relationships help determine the level of friendship we can enjoy, the depth of intimacy we can share, the success of our marriages, our ability to work with and influence other people, and even our ability to relate to God. Often our most basic sense of well-being stems from our connectedness and sense of being unconditionally loved by the significant people in our lives. When that sense of love and connection are missing, depression and insecurity result, and the search begins to find someone to fill in the lonely times.

God designed the family to be the stabilizing structure in our culture in which to build those vital relationships and also to teach the art of true intimacy. In the context of family, children learn how to be themselves, how to live peacefully with others, how to give and receive affection, how to care for each other. They develop both the personal security and the relational skills that are necessary to attach themselves to another person, as well as the wisdom to choose healthy attachments over unhealthy ones. When children have a safe haven—a place to be protected from the storms of life; a place to be emotionally, mentally, and spiritually encouraged; a place where they enjoy the time and attention from the important people in their lives—and time in which to mature, then they will have a good opportunity to become emotionally healthy and flourishing human beings.

THE RELATIONSHIPS WE REAP

Galatians 6:7 tells us plainly that we reap what we sow—and I believe this is especially true of family relationships. If I sow affection, commitment, and encouragement into the lives of my children, chances are I will reap deep, close relationships with them that will last for a lifetime. If I don't make our relationships a priority, I risk reaping the consequences of a broken, scarred, or distant relationship.

My daughter Sarah shared with us at dinner one night that her friends who spend most of their time with their peers tend to communicate negatively about the guidance their parents want to give them. She expertly mimicked their complaints: "My parents insist that I can't drive my car because I don't have insurance! But it's *my* car! My baby-sitting job is so close I won't get into any trouble! It's so unfair!"

Sarah said, "Mom, I see it all of the time. The kids who aren't close to their parents act as though their parents' rules are unreasonable and even as though their parents have no right to tell them no. They think they should be able to make all of their own decisions."

The problem with these kids, as Sarah sees it, is not just her friends' attitude but the fact that these kids' parents haven't done what it takes to maintain a close relationship with them. Though children are rightly told to honor their parents, it is certainly easier to honor those parents who have shown honor to their own children by doing what it takes to build a relationship.

The hunger for love, affirmation, attention, and acceptance is a deep drive that will search for fulfillment until it finds it. A child's first attachment is meant to be with its mother, so lots of loving touches and caresses from her make a difference in the child's future intellect, emotional stability, and sense of well-being. Time and affectionate attention from a father and significant others is crucial as well.

However, if a child's need for such attachment is not met in the home, he will tend to look for it from his peers or anywhere else he can find it. In order to fit in with those willing to give him time, the child will tend to adapt his values and morals to whatever is required. At the same time, a child who does not learn to make healthy attachments and maintain healthy relationships in her family may have a hard time developing intimate bonds with anyone in the future.

As a mother, I have the ability to provide the love, acceptance, and attention my children need to grow up secure and able to develop mature relationships. I also have the opportunity to model mature love, commitment, forgiveness, accountability, grace, and encouragement for my children. The home is an ideal environment in which children can experience the growth of a mature relationship where give-and-take are learned in the context of real life. And this ideally includes an understanding of the true power of God's love.

How to develop strong relationships with our children deserves the focus of a whole book, but the following five principles can serve as a helpful guide for mothers who want to nurture strong relationships within their families.

RELATIONSHIP PRINCIPLE #1: TIME AND AVAILABILITY

Several years ago I thought I was providing my children with some wonderful opportunities. One of them was involved in a renowned boys' choir, and two were taking tennis lessons. We all participated in a professional musical production. Clay was attending a father-son club with the boys, and I had begun a mother-daughter Bible study with the girls. Reading and discussing some excellent books about history and about missionaries in Eastern Europe was a regular family event before bedtime. And the list went on and on! The entire family was constantly on the run, and for the most part we were enjoying our busy, hectic life.

Nine-year-old Nathan, however, was showing signs of stress and emotional struggle. He was having a hard time being obedient and having difficulty getting along with one of his friends. So one evening I invited him into my bedroom to talk. He joined me on the couch where I had been reading and laid his head on my lap. Then he looked up at me with resigned eyes and said, "You know this isn't going to last long!"

Sure enough, over the course of the next hour, the phone rang six times. Each of the other children bounded into the room needing me for some "important" task. Clay stuck his head in to ask me about an article that needed writing. The dinner dishes were unwashed, Joy needed an asthma treatment, and bedtime for everyone was approaching quickly.

To Nathan's surprise, however, as each person interrupted, I said, "I will be with you as soon as I can, but I have something important to do right now. I don't want to talk to anyone on the phone. Sarah, you do Joy's asthma treatment. Joel, you start cleaning the kitchen. And please don't interrupt me again."

Each time I said it, Nathan looked at me with big, doubtful eyes. But he relaxed more and more as the hour went on. I began to scratch his back and gently massage his head. And then, eventually, he began to talk.

Nathan shared with me his hurt feelings and insecurity regarding a couple of his friends. One in particular had been bullying him lately. He spoke to me about feeling lonely. He shared some secrets. I had the opportunity to talk with him, to share some verses with him, and to pray with him.

As I tucked Nathan into bed later that night, he said, "You know, Mom, when you spend time with me and talk to me and encourage me, I want to do the right things and be what Jesus wants me to be. But when I'm lonely or having a hard time, and you don't spend time with me, I'm really tempted to want to do wrong!"

Well, that's my Nathan! He has always been a child who holds me accountable for spending time alone with my children. His words reminded me once again that all the activities that keep us so busy and involved are nice but not necessary. What *was* necessary was taking time to build my relationship with my son. No activity can replace the heart-to-heart process of sharing emotions, truth, training, and prayer.

A lot has been written during the past fifty years about the time we spend with our children. There has been a lot of discussion pitting quality time against quantity time, debating whether small amounts of focused, loving attention are worth more than hours of mere presence. The problem with this debate, of course, is that children need *both*. Developing deep relationships with our children and teaching them how to relate to others require time in both quantity and quality. We need to be available to provide love and care when our children need it, not just when our schedule permits.

Yesterday Clay and I were talking to some friends. One shared that his junior-high years had been disastrous. He explained, "My mom went to work when I was in junior high. Before then, she was home when I came in from school, and we were quite close. But without her at home, I had lots of time on my hands, no one to give input, and I happened to be with lots of wild kids. There was nothing to stop me from doing the very things that emotionally scarred my life."

The point here is not that women who work are automatically not there for their kids—or that the children of working women will inevitably go astray. Stay-at-home moms, too, can be overly busy and emotionally unavailable to their kids. But it's hard to get around the reality that deep relationships, especially with children, rarely happen on a predictable schedule. When children have a need for love or consolation or guidance, they need it *right then*. Very small children, especially, have little ability to put their needs on hold until a more convenient time. But even older, more mature children have a hard time fitting their relationship needs into a few set hours each day. The junior-high and high-school years, when peer pressure is so strong and temptations have such far-reaching consequences, are a crucial time to be available to our children.

In fact, I find that maintaining relationships with teenagers, who often veer wildly between dependence and independence, often requires around-the-clock availability, a sensitivity to those reachable moments when their spirits are open to us. My teenagers have such a desire to talk at length and demand my full attention, yet it has to be at a time that they find convenient within their own full schedules. So I try to make myself available when they desire my time. With four children still living at home—and three teenagers at that—there seems to be a constant demand for talk time and attention. Yet I am grateful they seek out Clay or me, so I don't complain!

Whatever the age, my children develop better when they know I will make our time together a priority. As they grow, it is certainly appropriate for them to learn to wait, to sometimes defer to the needs of others. But even then, knowing that the most important people in their lives are committed to spending time with them helps them to feel secure enough to wait their turn.

It's important to realize that spending time with kids means so much more than just getting the parenting job done. Sometimes it's easy for busy parents to forget this. We become so focused on training our children, correcting them, teaching them responsibility, and providing them with enriching activities that we forget how important it is just to be around them.

Helping our children build godly character is indeed essential and requires years of diligence. Simply being with them, enjoying their company, playing whatever game they choose for us to play (even another round of Candyland!) matters most to our children and best fosters a loving relationship with them. This commitment to them will build bridges of love and intimacy far more effectively than one more correction or assigned chore.

This should hardly be a surprise. After all, it's the way all close relationships develop. People grow close not through monitoring one another's behavior but by working together, playing together, talking together, celebrating together, weeping together. Relationships develop when people are there for each other—and that's as true for parents and children as it is for anyone else.

I recently received a letter from a mom who had wisely applied the principle of choosing to spend time with her child over focusing on his behavior. Her letter grabbed the attention of my heart and reminded me again of the importance of making time for building a relationship with our children. She wrote:

Dear Sally,

I wanted to share with you how God has used you in my life. Our oldest son, aged sixteen, was going through a hard time in his life. He rebelled against us in many ways. At some point in the fall, I was reminded of your seminar and pulled out my notes. The words you spoke took root and grew and bore fruit this year by God's grace. I heeded your advice and committed to spending personal time with him as he rebelled. I prayed for ideas, did things differently, and prayed for understanding of my dear son.

I was able to let go of the "academics" with my son and his need to do well in school and simply focus on my relationship with him. I wanted him to know that I loved him and accepted him, no matter what, and that God loved him. As a result we spent many happy hours together talking in the kitchen, going on "dates" fishing and to the movies. By the end of the year, we hadn't accomplished much academically, but we had a great relationship.

Two weeks ago, my precious son unexpectedly died in his sleep and went to be with Jesus. (He apparently had an undetected heart problem.) In the first hours after his death, I cried out in joy over the gift God had given to me in this year together. Despite the challenges, heartaches, frustrations, tears, and endless prayers, he knew how much I loved him, and I knew how much he loved me. I had been given a very precious gift of time spent with my son (sixteen wonderful years!) and I could honestly say I had no regrets.

As I read this letter, the Lord reminded me again how important it is to focus on relational time as well as on activity or discipline. All three are important, but relationship has the highest priority, because it is the foundation upon which the rest of our life with our children will stand.

RELATIONSHIP PRINCIPLE #2:
ACCEPTANCE AND UNCONDITIONAL LOVE

My children and I loved trips to the zoo when they were little. We were always amazed at the diversity of animals, and each child had his or her favorites. The monkey cage with the furry, skinny creatures climbing, scratching, and looking back at us through the windows was a favorite with Joy. The sleek, mysterious panther was more Joel's style. The gentle, cuddly koalas appealed to Sarah. And Nathan loved to go to the underwater tank to observe the freshwater fish, especially the huge wide-mouthed varieties he loved to imitate. We always left the zoo amazed at the Lord's artistry and sense of humor in creating so many different kinds of critters!

As I look at my four children, I see as much diversity as we saw at the zoo (and sometimes my home feels like a zoo!). No two of them are alike. Two of my children are extreme introverts; two are extreme extroverts. My children have all grown up with the same standards and rules in the same home, and Clay and I have shared with all of them the same values and tastes. I am amazed, however, at how different each child is in looks, metabolism, personality, preferences, sin habits, and communicating. It would be so much easier if they were at least somewhat alike so I would know how to deal consistently with them.

Added to this mix, of course, is the reality that all four of these very different people are very different from Clay and me! I always assumed that if a child came from my body, surely he or she would be something like me. And of course they all resemble us in one way or another. But there have been times with each of my children, some more than others, when I have felt totally mystified. Sometimes I have felt embarrassed by their behavior and even frustrated and annoyed by their personalities and weaknesses. There have even been occasions when I wondered if God made a mistake by sending me these particular children! I have often felt inadequate to train their characters and reach their hearts.

In building meaningful relationships with my children, however, I must learn to accept unconditionally the person God made each of them to be—even with personality traits that differ from mine or that make me uncomfortable. I need to accept the "warts" and irritating characteristics that may never change. I have to love my children with a mature commitment that reaches past my feelings for them, which can change from circumstance to circumstance.

At times I think I have the most precious children ever born. Other times I feel that my children came from outer space. However, my commitment to love them unconditionally doesn't change, because it is not governed by my feelings of the moment.

It is this basic acceptance that provides children with the opportunity to mature. A child who can go to her mother or father and reveal her inner heart and still feel accepted will feel secure enough to take risks and grow. If that child senses she might be rejected because of her performance—or, worse, because of her thoughts or feelings—then she will wonder if she can ever live up to her parents' standards. She will look for acceptance elsewhere or give up entirely on the idea that she is lovable. When children feel that pleasing their parents is impossible, they often reject the values and beliefs of their parents.

Offering love and acceptance to children is not always easy, even when we love our children deeply. Sometimes it's tricky to reconcile our duty to train and discipline our children with our need to accept them unconditionally. One thing that has helped me immensely in this regard is the realization that my children are still immature. This may sound obvious, but it's something many parents forget. We often have unrealistic expectations of our little ones living in our adult-oriented culture. When our children fail to meet our expectations, they are doomed to disappoint us and to challenge our own feelings about loving our children unconditionally. I have observed that many parents, out of a desire to train their children properly, resort to guilt and nagging, which causes their children to feel guilty anytime they fall short of their parents' expectations. We must realize, though, that children's misbehavior often comes from simple immaturity or a lack of training.

I once dined with a group of leaders who I had noticed were very strict with their children. My children were at the dinner as well, but they were seated at the other end of a long banquet table. After about forty-five minutes, little Joy could take no more separation from me. She called out in a loud voice, "Hey, Mom! Look what I can do! If I poke my french fry real hard with a straw, I can pick it up and eat it without even touching it with my hand!"

All heads turned toward Joy, and then they all looked back at me to see how I was going to discipline my child for this interruption! I was tempted to say, "Joy, you know better than that! We don't eat french fries with a straw!" As I pondered the situation, I realized Joy was not being rebellious or disobedient. She was just being immature, which is normal for a four-year-old. She needed my understanding and support in front of all of these people, not public correction and humiliation. A good poke in the ribs and a comment from a friend sitting next to me confirmed my dawning realization. "Don't you dare correct Joy in front of all of these people!"

Other times when our children misbehave by throwing tantrums and crying out of control, it is because we have exhausted them. Children need regular food, sleep, and a familiar environment in which they can relax, explore, and refresh themselves. Too much time in an unfamiliar or overstimulating environment can frazzle a child's nerves, and often the only way he has to show his physical and emotional frustration is to cry. Instead of discipline, what he may really need is a nap or some cheese and crackers or a quiet time on Mom's lap.

I have been in superstores and have seen a young child or infant left to cry uncontrollably while the mother looks disgusted and keeps pushing her cart. An experienced mother can see that the child needs to be held and attended to. But some parents apparently have other things to do and are unable or unwilling to give the child what is needed.

Accepting our children means we must understand that they will inevitably disappoint us in many ways—just as we will inevitably fall short as parents and need to fall back on our heavenly Father's unconditional love. Because they are human, children are sinful and selfish. Because they are immature and inexperienced, they will make mistakes and sometimes annoy or embarrass us. Because each is unique, their personalities may sometimes grate against ours, or we may have difficulty understanding them. But loving them unconditionally means that we are committed to giving them what they need!

There are so many more stages of childhood to live through than I expected when I first became a parent. I knew the twos and the teens were supposed to be challenging, but I wasn't prepared for the many other seasons in which my children would test my sanity. There are periods when children are clingy and want to stick close to Mom and Dad. There are times of independence and testing their wings. And because children develop differently when it comes to milestones such as social relationships, potty training, reading or scholastic prowess, and athletic abilities, it's easy for parents to fall into comparisons or frustration.

God designed it, though, so that children should feel totally accepted in their own home, just as we are totally accepted by him. Mothers, in fact, have the privilege of instilling in children a deep experience of God by modeling his unconditional love and acceptance.

Every child should feel that there is no greater champion for his causes than his mother. The best person to confide in, to receive sympathy and affirmation from, should be the mom who gave the child life.

One of the times when the need for unconditional love is crucial is the teen years. Teenagers live through this high-hormone period as though everything in their lives is under a magnifying glass. Everything feels bigger than it really is— emotional highs and lows, successes and failures, and especially pimples!

One of my teens asked me this week, "Mom, do you think I'm always going to be this bad, or is there hope that someday I'll return to my senses? Sometimes I feel so confused about stuff. The tiniest thing, like someone leaving the drawers open in the bathroom can drive me absolutely nuts! Some days I want to be mature, and other days I just want to be left alone to be totally irresponsible!" Teens have a tremendous need for unconditional love, because they have such a difficult time loving themselves!

We would never expect a monkey to act like a butterfly or a buffalo to behave like a mouse. Why then is it so hard for us to trust God with the design of our children and allow them to be who God made them to be? He created them all differently, and each one reflects this design uniquely. By accepting each child as he or she is, we are not only affirming the excellence of God's perfect design in the lives of our children but helping them to grow in knowledge of their heavenly Father's perfect love.

RELATIONSHIP PRINCIPLE #3:
AFFIRMATION AND ENCOURAGEMENT

Throughout Jesus' ministry, he constantly used words of encouragement to affirm those around him. "I've never seen such great faith in all of Israel" to a Roman soldier. "You are the rock upon which I will build my church!" to Peter, in spite of the fact that he knew Peter would fail him. "A man in whom there is no guile!" to reach the heart of Nathanael. "Mary has chosen the good part!" to the friend who put aside her duties in order to sit at his feet to listen to him.

We all need that kind of encouragement in our lives. Sometimes I feel I can never receive too much! When one of my children says, "Mom, you are such a great cook! Thanks for this meal," I am much more likely to want to cook another meal. If all I get is complaints, my motivation drops immediately! And this is doubly true for children.

I once read a popular child-training book that warned readers not to affirm their children too much, lest they come to depend on the affirmation. The author also cautioned that verbal encouragement is essentially flattery and could cause children to be vain.

Well, I didn't believe it then, and I don't believe it now! I believe most children are acutely aware of their limitations and their failures. While they often need correction for their mistakes and even confrontation for their sinful selfishness, they also need recognition for their real efforts and accomplishments and positive reminders of who they can be with God's help.

"I really appreciate your helping me today! I don't know what I would do without my strong boy!" "What a great job you did on making the table beautiful! God has made you so artistic!" Such encouragement is food for the soul that gives them hope for their future maturity in spite of present failure, immaturity, or weakness.

This is not to say that we must praise our children indiscriminately. Effective encouragement requires thoughtfulness and effort. Words of affirmation should be both positive and true, based on a careful, loving, and specific observation of a child's strengths and efforts. Even gentle words of correction, if balanced with affirmation of a child's potential and efforts, can be encouraging, but thoughtless criticism merely stings a child's soul.

Encouragement gives all of us the impetus to keep going, to keep trying to live up to our ideals. I thrive on encouragement and often long for a kind word in the midst of the hard work and long hours we invest in reaching out to other parents. Over the years Clay and I have pioneered numerous ministry situations and have given a lot of our lives, energy, and love to many people. We have noticed that while people are often quick to tell us what we have done wrong, only a few will take the time to thank us and encourage us to keep going. They are the ones who have strengthened us in our commitment to serve the Lord.

The thoughtless critics, on the other hand, are the ones who tempt us to quit. We call them the "rice is too spicy" people.

Back when we held our very first mothers' conference for 150 women, we gave out a questionnaire. We had poured our hearts into that conference—thoughtful speakers, beautiful decorations, lovely music, a nice facility. We asked the participants to give us helpful feedback on how we could better meet their spiritual and emotional needs. We received many wonderful comments from the sweet moms who attended, including some honest criticism leavened with praise. One questionnaire, however, was blank except for the words "The rice was too spicy!" The comment was irrelevant, nonconstructive, and only a matter of taste. It discouraged us and did nothing to help improve the conference.

I am committed not to be a "rice is too spicy" person for my children. Instead I limit my negative comments to those issues that are relevant to their heart and character issues. Even then I try to keep my voice gentle and my wording constructive. And I seek to make more encouraging comments to our children than negative in order to keep their emotional reservoirs filled with the joy and motivation that comes from knowing they're loved and appreciated.

In particular, I try not to criticize my children for what they cannot help. Toddlers should not be made to feel guilty for being afraid of the dark or being whiny when tired. Boys do not need to be made to feel guilty for being wiggly and noisy. Girls should not be shamed for giggling or talking too much. (For that matter, noisy girls or talkative boys should not be shamed for these natural tendencies.) God made children the way they are, and it's not fair to criticize them simply for being themselves. As we gently accept their limitations and encourage them to fulfill the beauty reflected in their sweet lives, they will grow closer and closer to the people they were meant to be.

Even better, as we accept and encourage our children, we will teach them to be encouraging in their own relationships. Children who are constantly criticized will tend to be negative and critical in their relationships with others. When children feel appreciated and encouraged, they become encouragers themselves, sources of life and hope in an often discouraging world.

RELATIONSHIP PRINCIPLE #4: GRACE

One day, when my children were young, I was more frustrated than usual with the chronic messes around the house. I said to Clay, "It seems like our training makes no difference in the lives of these children! How many times am I going to have to tell them to pick up after themselves?"

Clay gently responded, "Honey, how old were you when you quit sinning? That's how old they will be when they learn to obey us perfectly!"

As I thought about his statement (after I cooled down!), it made sense. All of us are sinful and will blow our own standards and God's again and again and again. Because of this sinful nature, we also have a sense of our own inadequacy—and an intense need to be loved and forgiven and trusted despite it all. This kind of unmerited favor is available to all of us from our heavenly Father. But children also desperately need this from their parents.

Jesus continually built up his disciples and served them even though he knew they would all leave him in his time of greatest need. After his resurrection, after every one of the disciples had let him down, Jesus not only forgave their shortcomings, he trusted them with his Great Commission. He extended them the grace to grow into the strong, mature apostles he knew they could be.

And this, in turn, is what our children need from us—the grace to grow. If we make them think that we expect perfection, then eventually they may give up trying to please us, because they know they will always fail, or they may spend their whole lives feeling guilty for their failures. I know many teenagers who have rebelled and run away from home when strict authoritarianism was the constant standard.

Obviously it's important to hold our children to high standards. They need structure and discipline in their lives. But they also need grace for their failures, just as you and I need grace. If we are consistent in guiding our children in the right direction, and extend grace to them to be immature on the way to maturity, then we will have the best chance of maintaining both our standards and a close relationship with our children.

When Nathan was nine years old, he came in one day and gave me an unexpected hug. "Mom, sometimes knowing that you believe in me and my dreams keeps me from doing wrong and makes me try a little harder to do right. I love you, Mama!" As he ran off, I wondered what spiritual battle he had just won, but I was thankful for the hug!

RELATIONSHIP PRINCIPLE #5: RELATIONSHIP TRAINING

Finally, in building relationships with our children, we need to consciously train them in the skills and attitudes that will enable them to sustain positive relationships. A person can only experience true intimacy when his heart has been deepened and exercised in real love and commitment. Consequently, an important part of deeply loving our children is training them to deeply love themselves and others. We train them by helping them to confront their own sin and selfishness and to replace these attitudes with patient and generous love. This provides them with something to give in a meaningful relationship and seals their ability to be the best they can be.

Relational training involves teaching our children the value of honor—giving worth to another person out of the dignity of our own heart. It often involves learning to reach out to others in practical, thoughtful ways and teaching them to be good friends. I have often said to my children, "It is natural to be selfish, but it is supernatural to be kind and loving. It is only when we allow the Lord Jesus to speak with our words and use our hands and our voice to give his love to others that we can really know how to be close to others."

This kind of relational training fits naturally into the course of a day. "Sarah, let's surprise the boys with some cookies and hot chocolate!" As we mix the batter and talk about how much I appreciate her help, Sarah learns how to give away her love. The result (over many sessions of cookie baking) is increased maturity in her own ability to relate to others.

Every day offers countless opportunities to teach thoughtfulness and compassion: "Boys, let's make the girls a card and surprise them with a teatime." Or, "Let's take cookies and a card to the family who just moved in!" Or, "I bet Mrs. Brown could use a visit from you kids. She's so sad that her little dog has died, and she's told me how much she enjoys your visits." Or, "It was so nice of the Roses to take you guys to that movie. Let's have a sleepover for their kids next weekend."

Teaching children to be content is another, perhaps more surprising, aspect of relationship training. I tend to think my children should be happy most of the time in our home, especially after I have put so much effort into meeting their needs. Yet they often act out their selfish and sinful behavior toward me and their siblings, and that can mean whining, complaining, or just being sullen. When this happens, it's easy to fall into the trap of assuming it is our responsibility to make our children happy—and feeling guilty if our children don't get what they want. Our children's bad attitudes can sometimes make us feel that we have failed in our relationship with them. But if we give in to these temptations and feelings, we could very well be training our children to be self-ish in their future relationships.

Instead of feeling that I need to make my children happy, I am trying to focus on teaching them patience and contentment. I want them to learn, even in this materialistic culture, that they cannot have everything they want. Training my children to practice self-control over their sometimes negative and self-ish feelings helps them to become more sensitive in considering the needs of others. My biggest concern is not for them to be happy, but for them to under-stand how—and why—to be content and to accept their circumstances as from God's hand.

Learning to be content and patient with what God has provided in my life has been a constant issue for me as an adult. I hope that if my children learn this before they leave my home, they will be able to adjust to adult life more easily and establish healthier relationships.

Children naturally know how to feel love, and they appreciate the good feel-ings that come from helping others. Yet, without training, they usually don't know how to take the initiative to express love or to receive it graciously. They need help to learn how to reach beyond their own needs and desires, to take the initiative in helping others, to express verbal appreciation, to give thoughtfully and listen attentively, and to be loving even when they don't feel loving. When we model that kind of love for them, show them what to do, and then see that they do it, we are preparing them for more fulfilling lives as husbands, wives, parents, and friends. In the process, as a bonus, we are most likely creating strong friendships for ourselves.

Soon after the evening in which I gave my time, back scratching, and ear to Nathan, I received a surprise myself. I came into my bedroom at the end of the day and found the room had been straightened, my covers had been turned down, and on my pillow was a card. "Thanks, Mom, for making time. I love you. Your son, Nathan."

Life as a mom is a constant roller coaster of events and activities. But the little moments of love and sharing are the greatest rewards a mom can receive; they give us something to revisit with joy for the rest of our lives.

I have not loved my children perfectly over the years. I have made many mistakes. Yet as I have followed the principles of availability, acceptance, encouragement, grace, and relational training, I have felt the satisfaction of seeing my children grow into the kinds of friends I would pick to be my closest companions. I believe I have secured friendships that will not wane but will grow closer over time.

God must have known we moms would need strong friendships as we grew older. Surely that's one reason why he created families. Friendship is the natural fruit of time invested in each other.

FOR THOUGHT AND REFLECTION

Something to Think About...

Fussing, complaining, and whining are three of my least favorite things in life—especially when they come from my children. I have little patience with verbal harshness and unreasonable selfishness. So when my usually self-controlled teenage daughter marched into my room one day with a BIG attitude, I was really annoyed. In fact, I was just about to launch into a lecture when the Holy Spirit put a check on my spirit.

Instead of scolding Sarah, I asked her to sit down with me for a cup of tea. I lit a candle and served her out of a pretty china cup. All of a sudden the tears started streaming down her eyes. "Mom, I feel so unlovable. I don't know what has happened to me! Something has taken over my body! All I seem to be able to do is get mad or cry!"

Suddenly I remembered what it was like to cope with hormones and the awkwardness of being a teenager. "Honey, I want you to know I love you a lot," I told my daughter, "just as you are. I'm so glad we are friends!"

"Really, Mom? I was afraid you and Daddy might be upset with me, but inside I need your love more than ever. I already feel bad about my attitude. Thanks for not lecturing me!"

Once more, by the grace of God, a battle had been avoided...and a precious relationship had been nurtured.

1. *Ephesians 4:1-3.* What adjectives in this verse describe the kind of love we are to give one another as believers? What might it mean in practical terms to show "patience" or "forbearance" to one another? (The words in verse 2 might vary according to the translation you are using.) Why do we, as sinners, need people in our lives who can "bear with us"? How can we, as mothers, preserve the unity of the Spirit in the bond of peace?

2. *1 Peter 4:8.* In what specific ways can love cover a multitude of sins? What is there about Peter's relationship with Jesus that helped him learn this lesson (see Matthew 16:21-23; 26:69-75)? Why do our children sometimes need for us to overlook some of their sins and shortcomings?

3. *Proverbs 15:1.* What, according to this verse, turns away wrath? What stirs up anger? What does it mean, in practical terms, to discipline with a spirit of gentleness? How can we avoid stirring up anger and still give our children the firmness they need?

4. *Hebrews 10:24-25.* According to these verses, how do we stimulate one another to love and good deeds? Why must we consider (plan or think about) how to do this? In what kinds of situations does your child most need encouragement? In what ways can you help by considering his or her needs?

Something to Try...

Over the years I have made personal memory books for my children—small scrapbooks with pictures of their favorite memories: birthday parties, fun moments with our dog (a favorite with all of them!), proud displays of milestones such as pulled teeth, or silly times with their friends and with the rest of us. I want them to have tangible evidence over the years that I loved them and believed in them. Joy's comment about her most recent book was, "I really am pretty cute, aren't I?"

- Make a list of tangible ways you can show your children your love—a surprise picnic in front of the fireplace, an "I Love You" card under their pillow, a back-scratching or a foot rub, or even a long-stemmed rose for a romantically inclined teenage girl. Try to pick items that would speak to each child's spirit. Then make a commitment to act on at least one item from your list for each child in the next few weeks.

❧ Mark your calendar for one-on-one time with each of your kids this month—an early morning restaurant breakfast, an ice cream date, a walk or run, or just a quiet cup of hot chocolate alone in your bedroom. I have found that it is when I am alone with my children that they are more likely to share what is in their hearts and allow their friendship with me to blossom.

CHAPTER 8

Gardener of Souls

Cultivating and Enriching Our Children's Lives

By wisdom a house is built,
And by understanding it is established;
And by knowledge the rooms are filled
With all precious and pleasant riches.

PROVERBS 24:3-4

During the years that I lived in Vienna, I loved to take walks in the rose gardens of the beautiful eighteenth-century Belvedere Palace, home of the Hapsburgs who ruled the Hungarian Empire. The roses grew prolifically in exquisite shades of pink, red, yellow, gold, and white. The formal layout of the rose beds and walkways was peaceful and soothing. The fragrance from all those flowers was absolutely intoxicating. These gardens were truly works of art.

Many thousands of people have enjoyed the beauty of these gardens over the centuries. And no reasonable person would ever have suggested that they just grew on their own! Those glorious, fragrant gardens resulted from more than two hundred years of careful planning and tending.

Generation after generation of gardeners at the Belvedere Palace worked on the plans for the walkways and rose beds, choosing just the right colors and varieties to suit each section. Year after year they loosened the ground around those bushes and carefully picked out the weeds and harmful insects. Decade after decade they judiciously pruned the plants to encourage growth, built trellises to support and display the climbing varieties, and moved plants as necessary to make sure each rosebush received the optimal amount of sunlight and shadow. And century after century they paid careful attention to the state of the soil, enriching it with organic matter and applying fertilizer at just the right time.

The gardening I've done since those Vienna years has made me more appreciative of those generations of Belvedere gardeners. What I've learned through my very basic efforts is that a garden without a plan and careful attention will probably grow *something*. Sometimes it will even show patches of beauty, but it's not likely to grow into the peaceful, productive place I want it to be.

If our gardens need cultivating to grow well, our children need that attention much more. Seeds of excellence and grace must be planted and tended. The weeds of selfishness and bad attitudes must be plucked. The plot must be protected so that the wild storms and prevailing winds of culture will not damage the fruit. In addition, wise food for thought and the finest of art, music, literature, hospitality, and creativity must be fed to fertilize the soul so that the child may grow fruitful and productive.

Children do not accidentally become mature adults of strong character, great faith, gracious relational skills, effective leadership qualities, and sharp intellects. God's design includes the presence of a hands-on gardener, a mother, to tend and cultivate their hearts, souls, minds, and relationships. As a garden cannot flourish without a gardener, neither can a child reach his or her potential without someone committed to careful cultivation. Just as a garden without a gardener will eventually go to seed and be covered over with weeds and debris, a child whose growth is unsupervised or left to chance will likely grow wild and undisciplined or stunted and unfruitful.

Seeing myself as a gardener is helpful to me as I think of my mission as a mother. After all, I want more for my children than just getting them to adulthood. I want them to thrive. I want them to grow up confident and civilized. I want them prepared to live as abundantly as possible. In order for that to happen, I need to do a little intentional "gardening."

There is such a vast potential of spiritual, emotional, and intellectual aptitude hidden in each of my children's personalities. Becoming a gardener of each of them is like planting and tending the unique flowers and plants suited to the soil and climate of each child's heart and mind. To neglect this kind of cultivation can only have negative consequences in their lives.

I know a lovely woman who has often talked to me about this idea. She always had her physical and emotional needs met as a child but had received little in the way of enrichment. "I was greatly loved by my large extended family," she told me. "I was clothed, bathed, and protected. Yet, now that I have gotten out into the world, I feel regret that my parents didn't take the time to give me some real skills and build my confidence in areas that would have served me the rest of my life. I know my parents did the best they could. But I still wish I had taken music lessons or been taught how to host a dinner party or been exposed to great thinkers or even been taught how to dress in a feminine or becoming way. I was left as somewhat of a blank slate—uncultivated and underdeveloped. Just about everything I have learned has been slowly, as an adult, by trial and error. I can't help but think I could have gone so much further in life if I had received better training and instruction from my parents."

There are so many ways to cultivate the lives of our children. Each family brings up their children differently according to their personalities, convictions, abilities, and passions. But intentional nurturing, like gardening, requires a plan. Some of the "gardening" efforts Clay and I concentrated on were teaching real skills to our children, arranging life experiences for them, instilling graciousness and good manners, and whetting their intellectual appetites by exposing them to excellence in art, music, and literature.

CULTIVATING REAL SKILLS

Helping our children to develop skills that will serve them the rest of their lives has always seemed important to us. Having observed people in many different settings, we realized that those who felt competent in at least one or two areas seemed to have an edge in life. The confidence they gained from knowing what to do in one area carried over into other areas, including the ability to reach out and serve others. Having observed this, we were determined to give our children this kind of confidence by providing sufficient instruction and practice for them to perform certain tasks well.

One set of skills involved hospitality. Actually, this was a skill I had learned as a child. I was brought up in a hospitable home that my parents opened for a variety of occasions. We would host dinners for up to one hundred people, including brunches, luncheons, buffets, and barbecues. When I graduated from high school, my mother served tea in our backyard for sixty-five young women. And we were not a wealthy family with servants—just a normal family who loved an open home.

Because hospitality was a priority in my family, all of us children were involved in entertaining our guests. We were given assignments—mowing the lawn, decorating, cooking, cleaning, and welcoming guests—and we were each carefully taught by our parents to do things right. By the time I was a teenager, I was a pro at welcoming people, answering the door, serving the guests, and making sure their needs were met.

As a result of this early training, serving others in my home has always felt easy and natural to me. And the skills and confidence I learned from my parents has served me well in reaching out to others in ministry. This was especially true when we lived overseas and hosted international guests, which opened many doors to sharing the gospel. My children grew up entertaining all kinds of people, from diplomats and professionals to refugees and homeless people.

This was a specific nurturing goal for our family. We wanted our children to grow up comfortable in the presence of kings as well as paupers. Passing on our skills at serving others was foundational to our overall goal of training our children to reach others with the message of our Lord. The results were well worth it, though it did take time and energy to teach our children how to be hospitable.

When we were young parents, Clay and I realized that we would have limited financial resources and limited time in which to pass on any skills that required lessons. We reasoned that we would be a lot more likely to support and back our children if we chose areas of interest that were our own and fit into the life of our family. So we mapped out these areas, including areas in which all of us could participate so we wouldn't be going in a thousand different directions.

Music was a common love and talent for Clay and me. So we decided to provide the children with a basic knowledge and experience in music, and we would encourage each child to pursue specialized instruction in the musical area of his choice. Each child started with piano lessons and had the opportunity to be in choirs, sing at home, and perform from time to time with Clay and me. We now have a pianist (Sarah), a guitarist (Joel), and a beginning violinist (Nathan). Joy is still getting exposure to music and will decide in a few years what her specialty will be.

Communication skills defined another area of experience and strength we decided to pass on to our children. Since both of us are writers and performers, we wanted to share with them the importance of ideas and how to communicate those ideas in writing or through music, drama, or public speaking. For three years, as a family, we acted and sang in a professional dramatic musical production called *The Promise*. We all had parts in the play, which featured Friday and Saturday night performances five months out of the year. All of our children view their experience in *The Promise* as the time they became confident speaking and singing in front of crowds.

Our speaking and writing ministry has provided us with yet another opportunity to teach our children practical skills. Helping out in the home office of Whole Heart Ministries has taught all of our children basic office skills—answering phones, doing basic computer work, and fulfilling book orders. Greeting people at seminars and helping with the book tables have helped them acquire cash register experience and people skills.

Each of our children has benefited from the skills we have sought to build into their lives, although they have vastly differing personalities and interests and apply those skills in different ways. Since we started when they were young and participated in these areas together, each child seemed to adjust his or her personality to the training and to derive something slightly different from the experience.

Because families and children are so different, each family has a unique opportunity to define their own particular heritage of skills to be shared with children—skills the parents already possess and want to pass along, skills the parents value and are willing to hire a teacher for, or skills the parents agree to pay for because of special interest on a child's part. Learning to play sports, speak a foreign language, cook, farm, garden, work on cars (or drive them!), play an instrument, paint and draw, decorate, refinish furniture, do desktop publishing, sew or quilt, or build a home—these are just a few examples of skills that can enhance the lives of children.

Providing our children with real skills not only expands their interests and gives them confidence, but it also provides them with constructive ways to use their free time. Teaching skills has the added advantage of teaching them how to learn. That is, when we help our children acquire special skills, we are also preparing them mentally for acquiring additional skills on their own. As a bonus, developing skills together helps solidify family relationships.

CULTIVATING APPROPRIATE LIFE EXPERIENCES

Exposing children to many different life experiences—within the context of family relationships and parental teaching—is essential to broadening their understanding, their interests, and their compassion. If we want to train our children to help bring God's kingdom into the world, we need to prepare them by letting them come along with us as we reach out to others.

Because we lived overseas, Clay and I have a particular desire to help our children to be familiar with and comfortable in many different cultures. For Sarah and Joel, spending their early years in Austria certainly helped with this. Later, traveling to Russia to perform together in *The Promise* in the Kremlin Palace Theater gave our children firsthand exposure to life in a communist country. Adopting an international student from our local university helped our children develop patience and compassion for friends who had difficulty speaking English. Traveling with Clay and me to conferences all over the United States, Canada, and Europe has provided our children opportunities to interact with people of different cultures and economic and educational backgrounds as well as different spiritual and moral commitments.

Our personal travel, too, has done wonders to provide our children with wonderful experiences, expand their knowledge, and broaden their understanding. Several years ago a friend and I decided to take the kids on a trip to historical places in the United States so we could see firsthand the famous landmarks we had read about. Our trip took us to the South. Visiting Civil War battlefields, exploring historical homes, visiting a prominent space museum, and enjoying the white beaches of the Gulf of Mexico were highlights of this trip. Two moms and seven children had to learn how to pack a single Suburban with our gear and nine bodies, get along together, eat economically, and be civil to all the people we met!

That first trip went so well that we followed it up with a five-thousand-mile trip from Colorado to Boston. What an adventure! Exploring historical sites gave my children an interest in the people of history. We rode the elevator to the top of the great Gateway Arch in St. Louis, built to commemorate Lewis and Clark's great westward journey, which started from this gateway city. After visiting the first-rate museum below the arch, the children were eager to spend the next few travel days listening to a six-hour tape series about Lewis and Clark.

So many other experiences on that trip ignited their interest. After visiting the innovative Dana Thomas home in Springfield, Illinois, which was designed by Frank Lloyd Wright, Joel became interested in reading about the architect and trying his hand at designing homes. Visiting Louisa May Alcott's homestead and talking with New England lobstermen also captivated the children. One of the highlights of that trip was staying with four families who offered to serve as our hosts as we explored some of the sights. The friends we met, the jokes we shared, the meals we ate, and the prayers we prayed together—as well as the books on tape we listened to along the way—filled a well of memories to draw from for years to come!

The next venture was a jaunt to Washington, D.C., which we titled our political trip. This year we are considering a train trip from Nashville to Chicago to New York (to take in a few plays) and home again to Nashville.

The tradition of an annual road trip has greatly influenced our children. Spending time with each other away from the phone, television, and computer has not only broadened our horizons but has also helped us to develop more intimate relationships by drawing the cords of our hearts together with common memories.

I am well aware, of course, that many people's jobs and lifestyles are not compatible with this kind of traveling—although I would urge every family to try it just once! The sooner children learn to enjoy family travel—sitting in the car, listening to tapes, playing road games, singing, or simply talking—the easier such trips will be.

But even if long road trips are out of the question for your family, there are many other ways to provide valuable, broadening experiences for children. Taking short day trips to local historical sites, serving food in a homeless soup kitchen, attending a local production of *Les Misérables*, raising an animal to compete in a 4-H competition, picking apples at a farm and learning to make applesauce, camping, entering dance contests, volunteering at a library or a political office, or holding infants in intensive care are examples of enriching experiences that can be found close to home—and that the family can do together.

Planning and making time for such experiences is essential for giving our children tolerance and appreciation for others who are different from themselves. Experiences with a wide range of adults and children teach our children to relate to people as individuals and can even help break the hold of peer dependence. Seeking out such experiences also provides opportunities to discuss real-life issues within the context of a biblical world-view. And as a wonderful bonus, enjoying varied experiences together builds family cohesion and creates wonderful memories—something for parents and children to talk about for years to come.

CULTIVATING MANNERS AND GRACIOUSNESS

Our family's travel schedule has unearthed for us another area of cultivation that I believe is unintentionally neglected in many homes today. In our experience, meeting a child or young man or woman along the way who has been nurtured and trained in manners and simple graciousness—reaching out to others and helping them feel comfortable—has become a rare treat for us.

We feel special when new acquaintances ask us about our family and work, interact with us about their own lives, and graciously reach out to us. Such thoughtful people always refresh us on our tiring journeys. But many children today seem unable to extend themselves in this way. They have no confidence in meeting an adult, much less another child. Carrying on a conversation with such passive people is often all but impossible.

One of the worst consequences of televisions and computers is that, as a society, we have become inarticulate and ungracious people. Graciousness is not often modeled for our children. Yet, as mothers, we can train our children to be more thoughtful and responsive.

When we lived in Colorado, our home was close to the Air Force Academy. Since my nephew attended school there, we would often have a group of cadets over on the weekend for home-cooked meals and a real, warm bed. What a blessing it was to have a cadet offer to help in the kitchen, reach out to my six-year-old by playing a game or reading a book, or engage my older daughter in conversation.

A few of the boys we invited, however, were so shy they hardly interacted with us. When a guest did not take the initiative to say thank you or reach out when being served, my children sometimes resented the work such a weekend had cost them. They learned from these experiences how to serve unselfishly. At the same time, they developed strong opinions about how clearly the training and character of a person show up in real life.

On one such occasion, after a whole group had been fed and entertained and had departed, one of my boys said, "Mom, I thought you had to be the cream of the crop to get into the military academies. But even with these guys, you can observe their lack of character and training. Trying to be with some of them is like trying to have a conversation with a piece of Melba toast! But the ones who have been taught how to act are real fun to have in our home. Now I know why you keep trying to train us in this area."

In many situations at speaking engagements, I have been left to fend for myself. Often no one in the crowd talked to me or helped me—it just didn't occur to them. Consequently, I feel compelled to train my children to take the initiative in relationships so they will be more sensitive to the needs of others. I want them to develop the sensitivity to notice and the confidence to respond.

I'm not speaking of personality. Four out of six in our family are introverts. We are naturally shy. However, I have tried to train my children, out of common courtesy, to meet people and reach out to them. We are not perfect in our behavior, but I have seen a lot of progress. My teenage boys have even become comfortable at playing Legos with toddlers and entertaining girls older than themselves—situations that would normally make them feel uncomfortable. I don't want to insinuate that our family has reached perfection in this area; we still have a long way to go! Yet our specific goals and practical training steps for our children have definitely paid off for us.

I am convinced that mothers have a lot to do with the manners of their children. And, yes, I am really talking about yet another set of real-life skills. No child I know is naturally polite and thankful and prone to take the initiative. No child instinctively knows what to do in a social setting. And yet a child who doesn't know how to act with others will suffer socially the rest of his or her life! Job interviews, professional interactions, marriage and family relationships, and friendships are all enhanced by politeness and graciousness or suffer because of thoughtlessness and rudeness. Cultivating our children's manners and gracious attitudes not only makes them more pleasant to live with, but it also helps give our children a platform of confidence on which to build their future lives.

Committing to regular, specific training in manners and graciousness is all that it takes to build this kind of confidence. Before we have company for dinner, we instruct each child to think of one interesting question he or she can ask our guest. We train our children to take the initiative to help when they are in the home of another child. Helping our children write and send thank-you notes teaches them to extend thoughtfulness. Discussing with them ahead of time what we expect of them at a dinner or during a visit to someone else's home gives them a pattern to follow in their future behavior.

CULTIVATING APPETITES FOR EXCELLENCE

Walnut Springs, Texas, is a small town of just over seven hundred people. When we moved there in 1993 to start Whole Heart Ministries, we were surprised to discover that the nearest large grocery store was forty miles away! To help us pass the time on those long drives, we developed the habit of listening to stories on tape.

One of the stories that entertained us for hours was a twelve-tape set of *Oliver Twist*. Charles Dickens's classic is both thrilling and touching, and it held the attention of even my youngest children. As we listened, however, I often had to stop to explain a complicated idea or unfamiliar vocabulary word.

Reflecting on the fact that this author had very little education or training, I was amazed at his genius for writing and his articulate ability to make the 1800s come alive. I was also impressed by the high literary quality of this book, which was created for the average reader of his day. Dickens's work was both widely popular and widely understood. Today, despite his storytelling genius, many average readers find his writing hard to follow—if they have the patience to sit down and read it (or listen to it) at all. And yet my young children, with just a little help from me, were able to enjoy the wonderful storytelling of this truly great writer.

As I pondered this phenomenon, I observed that our brain capacity for ideas and words is the same today as in Dickens's day. Yet in this entertainment age, with so much time given to televisions and computers, our brains often tend to remain unstretched and unexercised in this regard. In Dickens's time there were no radios or televisions or computers. Instead of spending time passively receiving input from such devices, people spent hours reading, conversing, or simply thinking, with the result that the vocabulary level of the average person was considerably higher than that of most college graduates today.

As a result of these musings, I decided that, as much as possible, I would stretch my children's brains (and my own) so that they would have the opportunity to excel in their thinking skills. I determined to educate their taste by exposing them from an early age to the finest examples of the written word. Rather than dumbing down the material for my children, I would do what was necessary to help them keep up.

Thus began my campaign to select the best classical literature and children's stories for us to read aloud together or listen to together. I began to build a library for my children when they were quite young with books that inspired and under-girded God's purposes for their lives. I was always on the lookout for beautifully written and illustrated children's books that reflected moral excellence, family values, and a reverence for nature or God and that delighted the mind and heart. My children and I have enjoyed hundreds of these books together over the years. In the process, they have cultivated a taste for great literature.

We started out with simple books such as Frances Hodgson Burnett's *The Secret Garden* and Kenneth Grahame's *The Wind in the Willows* and advanced to longer books such as *Little Women* by Louisa May Alcott and *Freckles* by Gene Stratton Porter. We were surprised to find that Shakespeare captured the imaginations of even our very young children. When reading *Romeo and Juliet* out loud dramatically, the boys donned capes and wielded toy swords and played for hours with the ageless story of family feuds. "Mom, I didn't know that there were gangs in the old days, too! This story is just like the gangs of kids that fight today! I didn't know Shakespeare was so interesting!"

We didn't just read fiction though. Our reading journey encompassed history, creation science, nature studies, Christian history, and more. Biographies of great people who invested their lives significantly or made an impact on their culture were an important part of our collection. We loved learning about war heroes (George Washington, Francis Marion, Molly Pitcher, Clara Barton), inventors (Thomas Edison, Henry Ford, Galileo), artists (Michelangelo, Rembrandt), writers (C. S. Lewis, Charles Dickens, L. M. Montgomery, Robert Frost, Gene Stratton Porter, Louisa May Alcott), composers (Ludwig van Beethoven, Antonio Vivaldi, J. S. Bach, Wolfgang Amadeus Mozart), world leaders (Winston Churchill, the Russian czars, Napoleon, William Wallace, Robert the Bruce), and missionaries (Saint Patrick, Brother Andrew, Corrie Ten Boom, Hudson Taylor, Amy Carmichael).

Reading out loud to my children from these books became a family habit that still goes on today. Reading before naps and bedtime became a favorite habit. Giving my children a mandatory rest time when they were quite young gave me a retreat and built into their lives a habit of reading—those who didn't nap were allowed to read or look at picture books. Reading aloud at mealtimes from colorful books like James Herriot's stories for children intensified our sense of shared experiences and developed our children's appreciation for the beauty and humor and power of words.

As a person's palate is trained to enjoy the foods he has been accustomed to, our minds tend to prefer those things that were introduced to us at an early age. This is exactly what I was trying to do in exposing our children to quality literature from an early age. Even as I sought to give them appetites for nutritious food so they could be as healthy as possible, I wanted to feed their minds with mental food that would provide them with excellent thoughts but would also cultivate in them a love for what is excellent. Philippians 4:8 encouraged us in this principle: "Finally, brethren, whatever is true, whatever is honorable, whatever is right, whatever is pure, whatever is lovely, whatever is of good repute, if there is any excellence and if anything worthy of praise, dwell on these things."

Expanding this principle to include the best in art, music, toys, videos, movies, and computer games has helped Clay and me to determine how we would invest our money and what "things" would best serve our purposes. We want to fill our home with what is true, honorable, right, pure, lovely, of good repute, excellent, and worthy of praise. In the evenings, at dinnertime, for instance, we have always chosen quality instrumental music as a peaceful background for our time together—but also to teach our children to appreciate instrumental music. Our collection of dinner music ranges from Chopin piano nocturnes to original tunes played on a hammer dulcimer to traditional Scottish and Irish songs to lushly orchestrated hymn arrangements and first-rate movie soundtracks. For more focused times of listening, our family repertory includes choral masterworks, passionate symphonies, first-rate contemporary Christian music, and many other varieties of music.

Whenever possible, we have tried to take the children to concerts and other live performances. We have read biographies of composers—a learning experience for me as well as the kids. And as they have gained their own musical proficiency, we have made singing and playing good music together a part of our family experience.

A gratifying bonus of this deliberate exposure over the years is that our whole family has come to share common tastes in music. We each have our favorites, of course, and we don't see "ear to ear" on everything, but we have developed a kind of family repertory that we all enjoy.

Exposing our children to great art, too, has been part of our strategy to whet their appetites for excellence. Artists such as Michelangelo, Rembrandt, Monet, Jessie Wilcox Smith, Mort Künstler, Norman Rockwell, and Tasha Tudor have all been familiar people in our living room. We love to collect large-format books with reproductions of their works. Leaving such books on our coffee table and hearth has given us spare moments to soak in great art when just sitting in the living room. Small easels in different places around our home have held replicas of classical art as well as books opened to a favorite pictures. (My boys especially love battle scenes.) My children developed appetites and appreciation for these prints because they are natural fixtures in the décor of our home.

Whenever possible on our travels or in the towns where we've lived, we have tried to visit museums to see in person the pieces we have learned to love. But we try to keep in mind the attention span and interest of our children in doing this. Forcing children to stand for hours in museums when they feel bored can actually hinder their love of art, so we have tried to keep our visits short. We encourage our children to interact with what they see—whether it's copying a great painting from a book (a time-honored way for young artists to learn), playing around the bronzes in a child-friendly sculpture garden, or just sitting and discussing what we see.

This principle of exposure to excellence can apply to any area. Learning to cultivate in our children an appreciation for great thinkers and creative geniuses can apply to so many areas. And as we practice nurturing their minds, the natural result is that our own tastes are refined as well. Exploring the worlds of literature, art, and music with my children—and doing the research to discover what to explore with them—has certainly broadened my education in these areas, and I have relished the chance to learn along with them.

CULTIVATING YOUR OWN SPECIAL GARDEN

In a sense, gardens are like snowflakes—no two are alike. A formal rose garden will be completely different from a billowy English-style planting or a landscaped rock garden. And yet each garden, when carefully planned and tended, is a source of beauty and growth.

And that's certainly true of "family gardening." The way you tend to your children's lives will depend on your particular interests, skills, and convictions— as well as on the needs and personalities of each child. The overall benefit is that your children will blossom in mind, heart, and soul because you took the time not only to love and protect them but to cultivate their skills, experiences, relationships, and appetites.

Blessed are the children whose mothers garden in the soil of their souls. The fruit they bear will not only serve them in the future, but a whole generation will be beautified and enriched.

FOR THOUGHT AND REFLECTION

Something to Think About...

Years ago, when our family first lived in Nashville, I was baby-sitting the ten-year-old son of some friends for the weekend. Our family took this boy along as we went out shopping on a Saturday morning. When we stopped by the fast-food window to get some Mexican food, I placed a large order that included all our separate requests. When we arrived home, however, the taco that our young friend had ordered was not in the bag of food.

Immediately the young boy said, "Don't worry about my order, Mrs. Clarkson. Anything you have for me is fine. I just appreciate you getting us lunch." My less-than-perfect children marveled at this boy's wonderful attitude.

"Mom, I don't think we have ever met such a gracious person. He was so nice to all of us all day. He didn't complain once about being the only one who didn't get the right meal. His mom and dad must be good trainers!"

At the time I was grateful for this young man's good example to my kids, but I didn't think much about it. Ten years later we all took a trip to Nashville in preparation for moving to the area again. As my children were reviewing different places and people they remembered, the boys asked, "I wonder whatever happened to that real nice boy!"

"Who are you talking about?" I asked.

"You know, Mom, the boy who was nice to all of us kids and ate the wrong taco with a good attitude!"

How amazed this boy would be if he knew how that one small act of graciousness had helped him stand out in the memory of four children for ten years!

1. *Proverbs 22:15. Foolishness* is a synonym for *immaturity.* With this definition in mind, how would you rephrase this verse? What does this imply about the importance of cultivating or nurturing children?

2. *Proverbs 22:6.* What does "in the way he should go" mean? What does the word "train" mean to you? How long does training in the heart of a child last? What happens to the heart training of a child who has many conflicting cultural voices coming his way?

3. *Proverbs 24:5.* Why is a wise man strong? The word translated *wisdom* in Proverbs has the same meaning as "knowledge of life" or "skillful living." How does a person of knowledge or skill increase his power or influence? How can you provide a foundation for your child in the areas of wisdom, skill, and knowledge?

4. *Proverbs 22:29.* How does providing your children with real skills give him or her the opportunity to excel in life? What does this verse imply? How does this apply to motherhood?

Something to Try...

When my first three children were very young, Clay and I bought a family membership at the local children's museum. One or two Saturdays a month Clay would take the kids for a fun breakfast and then to the museum or nature center and spend most of the day. This gave me some coveted time alone and helped me maintain my sanity while it enriched the children's relationship with their father! These outings also developed my kids' taste for family field trips, which eventually became a fun staple in our life. Enriching our children's lives with various experiences enriches our lives as well.

❧ When your children are young, check out a simple book of manners from a library or buy one at a local bookstore. Take a few minutes a day to read aloud at least one or two specific points to your children. Take the time to practice some of these rules with them (how to make introductions, how to set a table, and so forth). Look for opportunities to affirm and encourage your children's efforts toward gracious social skills.

❧ Look at the Web site that lists the chamber of commerce in your town, or visit the chamber of commerce office for information. Look for information about places to visit, including museums and historical sites. Schedule a time to take your children (if age appropriate) to three of these places over the next three months. If your local opportunities are limited, look for information about nearby towns and cities and plan a weekend excursion.

❧ Go to the library and check out several oversized, beautiful books that show great works of art or reflect outstanding natural photography. Take them home and display them on a coffee table or stand them up on a shelf. Take the time to leisurely page through the books with your children, giving them a chance to point out their favorite pictures. Don't force them to sit still and be serious, but cultivate an inviting atmosphere and show interest in the books yourself.

PART FOUR

A MOTHER'S HEART *for* HER HOME

CHAPTER 9

Keeper of the Domain

Embracing God's Call to Home-Making

An excellent wife, who can find?
For her worth is far above jewels....
She looks well to the ways of her household,
And does not eat the bread of idleness.

PROVERBS 31:10,27

For six grueling weeks, our family had been on the road hosting Whole-Hearted Mother seminars. Though we had each been rewarded through the fellowship and excitement of ministering to two thousand moms, the effort had left all of us a bit depleted.

We had followed the last seminar with a fun reward. While Clay returned to the office to follow up on the seminars, the kids and I embarked on a ten-day historical field trip in the Washington, D.C., area. We toured Colonial Williamsburg, Richmond, and Washington, D.C., with side trips to George Washington's home at Mount Vernon and Thomas Jefferson's Monticello. On the way we visited with friends both old and new, rekindling some important relationships and building new ones.

Unforgettable memories were made on that trip. At a friend's farm Joy had loved seeing soft, fuzzy baby goats nestle against their mother just hours after birth, and she enjoyed milking a resistant nanny goat! I had especially liked Jefferson's innovative home with its tall ceilings and high windows and was captivated by his thought-provoking writing. Nathan reminisced about charming Williamsburg and "all the fun friends we played with," while Sarah loved the romance of the creaky but lovely antebellum home where we had eaten a delectable meal with kindred spirits. Joel especially enjoyed our friend Cheryl's sumptuous meals as well as Seth's tour of the veterinary clinic and the two special dogs that kept us company.

All of these events melted together in our minds like one very special holiday celebration. But as our trip drew to a close, what we really longed for was the comfort and familiarity of being home. When we rounded the last curve in the dirt road leading up to our mountain home, the excitement of the children's voices filled the air.

"I hope Penny [our beloved golden retriever] is in the yard waiting for us!"

"Oh look, it snowed on the mountains while we were gone."

"I can't wait to show Daddy my souvenirs—I bet he's been real lonely without us!"

"I'm going to brew a real strong cup of Yorkshire gold tea, light a candle, put on my Celtic CD, and curl up on my bed and stay for three days."

When we parked the car, fourteen-year-old Joel jumped out and ran inside. He bounded upstairs and called out in his manly young voice, "I love my bed the best! I love our dog the best! I love my tea and our fireplace and my reading chair and my books and music and our mountains and I may never, ever, leave home again!" This from the child who couldn't wait to fly to Washington for our adventure with friends.

We did indeed have a wonderful time, lots of excitement and precious fellowship with friends. Yet though our time away from home is like a holiday treat, special once in a while, the place our hearts really hungered for was home.

Home—it's such a beautiful word! It's the center of our lives, the place that holds us with invisible strings of love within its walls. Home is the place where the delectable smells and tastes of "my favorite food" linger; where the comfort and beauty of "my room" and "my bed" can be enjoyed; where "my dreams" are inspired and begin to grow; where bedtime routines, prayers, and blessings give comfort; where the intimacy of deep relationships—unconditional love, grace, forgiveness, encouragement, unselfishness, laughter, and memories—is shared with people who have made us a priority in their lives. It's where appetites for favorite music, movies, books, games, art, and traditions are shaped from infancy on up.

Home is a haven from a world that is swimming with challenges and difficulty. It is a school where one learns how precious life is intended to be. It provides the context of learning to know and love my Creator, the beauty of the world he made, and his Word, which guides me. And it is the environment where direction and purpose and values are passed from generation to generation, protecting and preserving all that is precious in life.

The task of building our homes into places of beauty and life that will feed the hearts, souls, and minds of our children is the most comprehensive task to which God has called us as mothers. We are called quite literally to be "home makers"—to plan and shape a home environment that provides our families with both a safe resting place and a launching pad for everything they do in the world.

What does that mean in practical terms? It seems that in the contemporary Christian world, there is a proliferation of simplistic how-to books. Readers snap up easy formulas about how to live the Christian life. Ten steps to creating a nurturing home environment (or twelve steps to having perfectly disciplined children, or seven steps to a perfect marriage) would surely make our lives easier!

Yet the more I study Scripture, the more I realize it doesn't provide simplistic formulas for successful living. Through the Word, God has indeed given us principles of wisdom that can guide our lives, including many that can guide us in shaping our home environments. But God leaves enormous room for personality, circumstances, creativity, resources, and culture to shape the specific decisions we make about our homes and the ways that we live in them. Each of us is called to make daily faith decisions that will determine the kind of environment that shapes our family's lives.

In this chapter I will share some ideas of how Clay and I have tried to build our home into a place where God is glorified and our children are trained to love and serve him. However, I would never hold up my home as the standard by which everyone should live. Each family will learn to develop its own distinct way of living out the principles of wisdom God has provided in his Word. Each home should be different and uniquely suited to meet the needs of the children and parents who live there.

A VISION FOR HOME

I have been in several exceptional homes that made a lasting impression on me and helped me to catch a vision of what I wanted my home to be like. My mother's home was the first and most important of these. She had a gift for using her home to cheer all sorts of people. Returning home after a semester of college caused me to realize how precious our home was to each of us kids. As I walked in the door, I saw she had posted little signs all over the house that said, "Mom and Dad love Sally!" "Welcome home!" "We missed you!" "Hurrah! Sally is home!" In each room every little decoration or picture seemed precious to me—a reminder of a holiday or day spent together or just a familiar object that said, "This is *our* house. Now I'm home!"

I would go to the kitchen and peek in all the cabinets and the refrigerator. Predictably, there would always be brownies or chocolate-chip cookies with pecans—my favorites. A brisket would be roasting in the oven, or some other delectable recipe I had grown to love would be prepared. I remember feeling loved and cared for upon returning home from far away because my mother had taken time to provide me with all the things that were special to me. Her preparations spoke to my heart about my worth to her and my father.

Another home that has really inspired me is that of my friend Phyllis, who shares my mother's gift for hospitality. She always prepares for her guests ahead of time—lighting a fire in the fireplace, placing glowing candles throughout the rooms, turning on soft music, placing a plate of hot muffins on the coffee table—so that they always enter a room anointed with comfort. More important, though, is the way this woman greets her visitors. When I walk in her door, she always looks into my eyes with an expression that says, "I am so happy to see you!" Her warm embrace and welcoming words always give me the feeling that I, above all others, am special to her. I know that Phyllis has to make a special effort to greet the many people who come in and out of her door this way. Her warm welcome is a reflection of the commitment in her heart.

As a young woman living in Poland during the communist regime of the late 1970s and early 1980s, I visited in homes that enhanced my understanding about what is important in a home and what really doesn't matter. The mothers there had very limited resources. Apartments were hard to come by and good food was scarce, so the homes were typically small and crowded and the meals very meager. One family I knew housed seven children in a four-room apartment!

Yet love was generously served each day from the minuscule kitchen of these tiny homes. A captivating passion for the Lord filled their crowded rooms, and the gospel was discussed and passed on each minute of the day. Hospitality was standard practice, and moral purity was modeled and taught. In the context of these homes, where the moms and dads sought wisdom every day in directing their homes for God's purposes, the children thrived. Now, as young adults, these children are living out a passion and love for God and his purposes.

In the past few years, I have also known families who are wealthy in the eyes of the world, and their homes reveal the same beauty as those Polish apartments. The physical details and material possessions and personality of the parents may differ, but the way life is lived in these homes is much the same—because they were built on similar visions. The daily work of training children, praying with them and reading God's Word, disciplining them in their attitudes, teaching them hospitality and generosity to others less fortunate are what have built the life in these homes.

What was the common denominator in these homes? It was the woman's commitment to make her home consistently welcoming, comfortable, and life giving. Each home was directed by the dreams of the mom, and her willingness to flesh it out every day helped her household to run as smoothly as possible.

That kind of home-making is not easy. Establishing and caring for a home is so much more than a decorating dilemma or an organizational challenge or even a call to love one's family! It is a commitment of heart, mind, and soul to the task of subduing (making productive) a very specific part of the earth—the domain of the home. It involves teaching minds and nurturing hearts and shaping souls, in addition to getting the rugs vacuumed and dinner on the table!

It's not a job for the fainthearted. To me, at times, this task has seemed almost overwhelming. But the example of so many lovely home-makers in my life has assured me it can be done with grace and panache. Every instance has helped me to develop a vision for my home as a lovely, gracious, life-giving place. This vision has kept me going through times of discouragement when my work seemed endless and thankless. It has helped me to keep my priorities straight and my budget focused. And because I knew what I was striving for, it has helped me to recognize the results when I saw them and give thanks to God for helping me shape my home according to his purposes.

What is this vision and sense of purpose that has shaped my efforts at home-making over the years? I want my home be a laboratory of life, a place where my children and husband may flourish and feel loved, encouraged, spiritually refreshed, and emotionally prepared to face the work God has for them in life. I want it to be a place where they can learn in safety yet be challenged to grow.

I also want my home to be the best place to be in the minds of my family.

Peace and acceptance, excellence and a passion for living, comfort and fun—I want all these qualities to come to my children's minds when they think about home. If I can succeed in creating a nurturing environment that speaks peace to their souls even as it helps them grow, I will feel that I have done my job as keeper of my domain.

CREATING A NURTURING ENVIRONMENT

When our family moved to Colorado, we purchased a lot and set about building our home. This provided a wonderful opportunity to shape a perfect environment for our family. We chose child-friendly, stain-resistant floor coverings and upholstery. An open floor plan in the entertainment areas accommodated many visitors, and yet the cozy furniture arrangement made the large rooms warm and conducive to our hot chocolate and reading times. We saved our pennies for a long time to purchase playground equipment suitable for big and little kids, with a giant pile of sand underneath for building tunnels and imaginary worlds. I insisted on a long breakfast bar in the kitchen, big enough for five stools, so the kids and I could work there together with clay, paints, or cookie dough.

What fun we had together in that beautiful home! And yet each of the fifteen other homes we have established in the life of our family—from tiny apartments to spacious suburban settings, from creaky old houses to bright newer ones, in a variety of cultural settings—has proved equally conducive to nurturing and welcoming our brood. Each place has offered a challenge of its own. But each, with a little work and planning, became an environment of beauty, warmth, and comfort that effectively served our needs and spoke a welcome to those who entered.

Over the years, as I strove to transform each of these living spaces into a home for my family, I discovered a few keys that determined whether the home was comfortable, peaceful, and conducive to the life of my family. In every subsequent home, as I put those principles to work, our new living space quickly began to feel like home.

One of the first things I have always considered was how to make the physical home a giving place—a source of rest, comfort, beauty, peace, and pleasure for those who live there as well as for those who visit. Having four children of various ages has meant that I considered these issues in special ways. For instance, I learned that when each person has his or her own comfortable place to sit in our living areas, we are more likely to enjoy being together as a family. So I have always tried to make comfortable seating a priority.

For our large family that means two large couches positioned in a cozy grouping and facing each other. These, along with some big overstuffed chairs and lots of pillows, provide enough space for all of us to curl up and read or to congregate for games or discussions.

All our furniture has been chosen with an eye to comfort and durability—equally accommodating to small, active bodies and lanky teenaged ones as well as slightly creaky older bones. I always look for durable carpets and upholstery that don't show stains and that clean well. Our life is so much more relaxed when I'm not worried about accidents and the children aren't worried about making messy mistakes.

Since sharing meals is a central part of our life and our family outreach, we always try to have a table that accommodates a crowd. Our oak table is plenty big to host another family for dinner. It has even accommodated eighteen people at a tea party for moms and girls! (Piano benches and picnic benches are also great for seating crowds.)

Making the house our own is another important element in establishing a nurturing environment. From the colors on the walls (warm and bright) to the books and magazines on the shelves, the treasures displayed on mantels and coffee tables, work spaces in our family room and kitchen, and even the music on the CD player and the lighting in our rooms, I have sought to make our home a place that reflects our values, personalities, pleasures, and pursuits while it provides us space to carry on the business of our lives. Our house is our home because it houses my teapot and teacups, Clay's laptop, Sarah's books, Joel's guitars, our family piano, Nathan's magic paraphernalia, and Joy's stuffed animals—all reflections of who we are and what we love.

I have also tried to make sure that each family member (including Clay and me) has a space to call their own. When a room had to be shared with a sibling, we made sure each child had his or her own bookshelf and desk to display personal treasures—pictures, a blanket or stuffed animal, and favorite toys or books. I have always tried to make sure that each person's bed is a cozy and inviting place to lounge, dream, and sleep. Setting aside personal space for each person not only gives my children a place to retreat and regroup, but it helps them to learn to take responsibility for caring for their own things.

There are so many creative and effective ways to make a home welcoming, inviting, and personal—and we will discuss more of these in the next chapter. Before I leave this idea, though, I want to focus on the one environmental element that makes the most difference in establishing a truly nurturing environment. It's one I've become especially aware of recently, during an especially difficult time for our family. Over the past few months, we have encountered challenges in every area of our lives, from health concerns to financial challenges to ministry problems to personal discouragement to the need for *another* cross-country move. Each of our children has been affected by the turbulent winds of these trials. And I have been tempted during this time to be introspective and self-doubting. Yet little by little, the Lord has helped me to focus on him and to tune my perspective to his point of view.

I remember one night close to Christmas when our dog was barking periodically and awakened me so often that finally, at three in the morning, I decided to get up. I spent some time with the Lord over a cup of tea. I listened to Christmas music and enjoyed some candlelight and tree lights, but still sleep did not come. I felt compelled by the Holy Spirit to go kneel at each of my children's bedsides and gently place my hand on their heads to pray for them. So I tiptoed into their rooms and very gently and lightly stroked their brow while they slept. I prayed silently for their needs, desires, future, and struggles. I finally returned to my room and was able to go back to sleep.

The next morning each child came to me at a separate time and told me how much it had meant to them to have a middle-of-the-night visitor. Sarah said, "Mom, I felt so loved and cared for—knowing you were there with me unexpectedly. I need a lot of love right now. Thanks so much!" Nathan said, "Mom, I wrote in my journal today about your visit to my room. I feel like I really have someone behind me who's committed to my dreams and aspirations." Quieter Joel said, "Thanks for being with me, Mom. It was so soothing to have you with me and not to feel alone." Joy said, "Mom, I had the best dream last night—that you were in my room loving me."

I realized again that the ultimate key to providing a nurturing environment in my home is me. The physical surroundings can make a big difference. In the end, though, what my children and husband need most from me is not a perfect home or perfect training or a perfectly spiritual role model or a wife without faults—but a mother and wife who is committed to doing whatever it takes to love them and make a home for them. They need to know that they are cherished by someone who is a champion for their cause, a cheerleader for their lives—someone they can always count on in the light and dark times of life. Accepting the responsibility of being the overseer of my domain with all of the heart and energy and faith I can muster is what nurtures my family best and provides my children with the sense of security and stability they need. My attitude is ultimately what makes our house a peaceful haven. And because I can only accomplish this by leaning on the Lord, it is my relationship with him that ultimately will provide a nurturing environment for the people I love.

A (SOMEWHAT) ORGANIZED HOUSEHOLD

Most of us live under the heavy cloud of "house beautiful." We see it in those magazines at the grocery-store checkout, in the elaborately decorated homes and apartments on television—perfect furniture and décor, sparkling-clean floors and countertops and baseboards, fresh flowers in crystal vases, candles whose wicks are long and actually light each time, with perhaps a few toys placed "just so" to let us know that adorable—probably nonexistent—children add to the ambience of a certain house. But having four children in a home (or even one child) automatically means frequent messes, poorly completed chores, a few dozen socks lying on the floor at any given time, crumbs hiding in different corners throughout the house, and at least some dirty dishes, no matter how recently the kitchen has been cleaned.

Because the responsibilities of maintaining a home, especially a home with children, are so varied and unrelenting, the pressure to get it all together and keep it together is constant. Doing laundry, cleaning messes, cooking, washing dishes, shopping, organizing, keeping clutter under control—the tasks can be daunting. That's why effective home management is an important part of making a home into a nurturing environment.

A perfectly ordered home isn't necessarily a haven, but neither is a messy, chaotic one. Coming up with a plan for subduing the messy details of our domain is essential to maintaining a peaceful atmosphere, teaching children to take care of themselves, and simply keeping the work from overwhelming anyone.

Personality is also a factor to consider in the subduing of our domain. A mom with a "Martha" personality probably has some practical systems in place—though her children might feel that a clean house is more important to Mom than they are! If you are a mom who likes to influence the world and move people to action, it is possible that the pursuit of influencing your children and spending personal time with them leaves your schedule and home in a constant state of flux. There are many varieties of personalities and possibilities of home organization. Each of us simply has to find the combination of routines that suits our lifestyle and desires.

I tend to be artistic and visionary—in other words, organization is not my strong suit. I love developing the ambience in my home, but keeping everything under control has been a challenge for me. To begin with, I am not naturally detail oriented. And as the youngest child in my family, I spent most of my high-school years flitting from activity to activity with friends and never really prepared to be a wife and mother. I never developed the skills or vision for running a household efficiently. The reality of constant, repetitive chores has sometimes taxed my personality to the core. For every tea party that I prepare for my family and enjoy with them, there are dishes that need to be washed when it is over!

God, however, with his marvelous grace and sense of humor, gave me a husband whose nature is organization and orderliness. He is my "Adam," and he has helped me to define some simplifying strategies to subdue our domain. With his guidance, I learned that I needed a plan to successfully manage our home.

The material in the next few pages was originally contained in the book *Educating the WholeHearted Child,* which Clay wrote a number of years ago. I was listed as coauthor on the cover but only because I was the faithful nightly consultant for our work in progress!

The reason I make this point is that, stereotypically, many assume that women should naturally be better at organizing a home. In our case, Clay is much better suited to this task. All these years women have thanked me for helping and influencing them through my first book, when it was I who benefited from my husband's strengths. He helped me figure out how to run our home more efficiently! So I dedicate this portion to Clay.

The most important thing he taught me about home management is that it is essentially a stress-reduction system. My purpose in organizing my household is not to live up to some external value system but to make life easier and more peaceful for the whole family. I have learned that I can reduce the anxiety we feel by reducing the stressors, at the same time knowing that they will never totally go away—because, after all, stress is a part of life.

Learning to live with the tension of never getting all of our work done and still being content is a worthwhile attitudinal goal as we serve our children. At the same time, effective home management can do a lot to reduce the stress in our families. Once I began thinking of home management as stress reduction, I found it much easier to pinpoint the areas of my home life that needed attention and to come up with a plan for reducing the stress. The three primary and constant sources of stress in my home life have always been "stuff," information, and time.

MANAGING STUFF

Stuff consists of all those things that seem necessary to life but also seem to pile up to unmanageable levels. Stuff is what surrounds us, collects in the corners, and jumps on any open tabletop or counter. In our house it tends to multiply until it fills every room. In particularly busy times, our home can look like something exploded, leaving books, toys, socks and shoes, sports equipment, catalogs, pens (often out of ink) and pencils (unsharpened when you need them), Legos, papers, cups and mugs and glasses, coats and clothes, videos and CDs, and other assorted shrapnel (we call it a "stuff bomb") all over the place. If there are children in the home, their stuff will always give evidence of their existence. *House Beautiful* will inevitably become *House Reality.*

Even though a certain amount of stuff is inevitable in a household where people live, developing a system for handling the stuff on a regular basis has definitely cut down on stress levels in our household. Clay has helped me train our children to know that everything should have a place and should be returned to its place when it is not being used.

When we built our house in Colorado, we closed in a large closet under the stairs and installed wall-to-wall shelves. Narrow shelves on one side held several hundred videos side by side with the titles easily visible. When we lived overseas, my sweet mother-in-law taped many children's shows, nature shows, and concerts for us. Now all these videos have a home in this closet.

The other shelves are filled almost entirely with plastic boxes. We have purchased hundreds of these boxes over the years. We prefer the kind with tight-fitting lids that keep everything from spilling out when the box is dropped. Each box is labeled as to its contents: craft items, rubber stamps, colored pencils, paints, science magnets, Legos, and so forth.

The idea is that when a child wants to play with a certain item, he brings the appropriate box out. When he is through, he dumps the item back in the appropriate box and puts it back on its shelf. We even have a miscellaneous box for orphaned items that don't have a specific home. Even each puzzle is stored in its own large zippered plastic bag so that pieces don't get lost.

Even with organized and adequate storage, clutter quickly builds up in the rooms of my house. I can feel totally overwhelmed when the stuff bombs explode over the weekends (or any time), so setting aside a regular time to put away the stuff makes a big difference. In our house, we have tried to make a habit of having one time a day when everything is picked up and put away. For us, this time is just before dinner in the evenings.

It has taken years to develop this routine, and even now we are not always consistent about sticking to it, but making the daily pick-up times a family goal has helped a lot. This little bit of daily maintenance helps our home stay relatively clutter free, and everything can be picked up quickly when company comes. Even the children—none of whom shows any signs of Clay's organizational genes!—have become adept at getting the rooms straight within a relatively short time.

In addition to our daily maintenance, every few months we take a day off from our regular routines and "purge." Purging means going through the accumulation of stuff and cutting it down to manageable levels. This is when we decide what can be tossed, what can be given away, and what needs to be stored more efficiently. Purging means sorting through all the papers in a cluttered area and either filing them or throwing them away. It involves getting rid of outgrown clothes and toys and repairing or tossing broken items.

The best time to do this is after busy seasons or holidays, when all of our rooms tend to get stacked up with items. If I don't set aside a regular time to get rid of the cancerous growth of stuff, I find myself getting depressed. For my own emotional good, I've had to learn to keep the accumulation of stuff to manageable levels.

MANAGING INFORMATION

Information management is one of the hardest areas of home management for me. I have always had trouble keeping track of new addresses or e-mail addresses, bills, order forms, faxes, receipts, research articles and magazines, check registers and bank statements, catalogs and advertisements, letters, and other essential paper items.

To address this weakness, I bought a roll-top desk to hide the messy stacks of paper. My stress level definitely drops when I'm not constantly reminded of how far behind I am! But hiding the paper is obviously just a temporary measure. I developed systems for keeping all that information under control.

For me, one of the most helpful principles in organizing paperwork is to keep the system simple. I have a whole big drawer, for example, where I throw cards and notes from the kids and loved ones that I might want to keep or look at someday. They are not organized, but they do have a place they belong. Who knows, someday I might even get around to putting them into files or albums! But in the meantime, they're not crammed in miscellaneous places all over the house, and I can usually find one when I want it.

Most of my other organizational systems follow this simplifying mind-set. A large manila envelope holds all business receipts until I have time to organize them. One bookshelf is lined with metal magazine holders for my favorite magazines and the newsletters I want to keep.

Another important organizational principle is to deal with every item as it comes in, assigning it a place to belong, even if it's not perfectly organized. I try to throw away unsolicited magazines and catalogs the day I get them unless I am quite sure they contain some information pertinent to my life. Important information for future reading goes in one place, bills in another. Addresses and phone numbers go in an envelope in my desk so I can find them and copy them into our address book when I have time or when an older child is available.

Of course, I also need to set aside a regular time to deal with the papers underneath my roll-top desk. Most information, after all, is just a specialized kind of stuff, and the principles of storing and purging apply. Knowing I have a designated day in the future when I will deal with all my paper is critical to keeping my stress down.

Managing Time

The third area of home management is organizing our time. With six people in our home, the number of activities that are possible is almost innumerable. If we don't keep a close eye on those activities, the busyness could easily overwhelm us.

For us, organizing time has been less a matter of juggling a calendar and more a matter of carefully choosing activities and priorities. Because so many activities entice us, it is very easy to become overcommitted as a family. But 1 Thessalonians 4:11 tells us we should make it our ambition to lead a quiet life and attend to our own business, and this word of guidance has helped me tremendously as I have made choices about how we spend our time. If we didn't build quiet time, home time, and family time firmly into our schedule, our peace would quickly be eroded by other activities.

From the time our children were little, we began giving them a taste for those activities that Clay and I knew would be easy for us to support and enjoy together as a family. We also realized that for the children to be influenced primarily by us, they had to spend most of their time with us. This meant that we had to make personal choices that would make that possible. Saying no to many good individual activities gave us time that was better used as a family.

When we made the decision to try out for *The Promise,* for example, we knew this professional dramatic production would require many rehearsals and five months of performances. So we decided this activity would be all or nothing. Everyone had to be involved or none of us would. *The Promise* ended up being a wonderful family experience that we shared together—even baby Joy— for three years.

A difficult choice our family made was to avoid regular involvement in organized sports. Such activities can be highly beneficial, but they also require a huge commitment of family time—time we felt we just couldn't afford. We gave our children the choice of being involved in the local soccer league or traveling with Clay and me to our conferences. Our choice to be a traveling family instead of a sports family has been a good one for us, providing us with a wonderful heritage of memories. But the real choice we were making was to spend as much time as possible as a family sharing the same activities. Other families who have chosen to invest this time in sports together—like our friends who have spent years skiing together—derive a similar benefit.

Each family is different and will decide on different activities for a variety of reasons. Yet for children to develop a healthy attachment to home, there must be time built in for nurture, instruction, training, and just plain fun—together.

Managing time in a family setting involves sacrifices. We have to say no to some things—even good things—in order to make relationships and peace in our home a priority. For me, this has meant giving up some freedom, some preferences, and a great deal of sleep.

Instead of having a private office where I can contemplate life and design winsome books, for instance, I have had to beg, borrow, and steal quiet moments to write. I have often chosen to leave the house messy in order to have an afternoon to take my son out for a milkshake and some "talk time." Staying up all hours to talk with Sarah about all that is bothering her has been a regular investment of time. Making myself play Candyland with a bored six-year-old has sometimes had to take priority over my demanding to-do list to ensure that I build my relationship with her as securely as I attempted to do with my older children.

As we have learned to say no to some of our options in the interest of relationships and peace in our home, our reward has been the strong and deep relationships that were our goal all along. Our children enjoy being with their friends and have benefited greatly from carefully selected activities, lessons, and competitions, but these outside activities were always added after the basic priorities of home had been taken care of.

As our children have grown older, their interests have specialized, and this has given them a focus for their outside time. Their greater involvement outside the home is appropriate to their age though. I find it exciting to watch them spread their wings, knowing that their freedom and confidence is built on our firm foundation of family togetherness.

ESTABLISHING LIFE-GIVING ROUTINES AND TRADITIONS

One of the most helpful time- and life-management techniques Clay and I have developed over the years is the use of routine. Children thrive on routine. Daily and weekly routines provide children with a sense of belonging, a sense of confidence in knowing what to do and when to do it, a pride in their own home life and work, and a feeling of stability and constancy in a world that is rife with change. Routines also help parents because they avoid the need for constant and repetitive planning.

When our children were quite young, Clay and I used to go out once each week to plan the week's activities. As time went on, our routines became more ingrained, and we didn't have to spend nearly as much time on the details of running the home. Instead, we were free to concentrate on larger issues. We still routinely get together when we feel a need to plan holidays, set spiritual goals, map out trips, decide about outside lessons, or determine how we will spend our money on all of these things. This planning time is crucial to ensure that our plans agree with our overall goals. But we don't need to spend that time deciding how the grass will get cut and the laundry will be done or how we will handle mealtimes. Not having to reinvent the wheel every week saves us a considerable amount of work and worry.

Many of the routines we have developed over the years involve how our household is run. Chores are done the same way each day, week, and month of the year so that our children know what to do and when. Each child has a part of the kitchen to attend to—counters cleaned and cleared and the floor swept; dishes and pots and pans washed; dishes dried; and garbage taken out. Whoever cooks does not have to spend time cleaning the kitchen. Rooms are to be picked up at a certain time before dinner. Garbage day is always on Monday. My sons will definitely know how to be a help to their wives because home maintenance was a routine part of their daily lives.

Bedtime routines have also been important to our family. When our children were very young, I would nurse and rock the baby to sleep while Clay read to the older ones and put them to bed. Today, whenever possible, we gather for a family reading time before bedtime. For about fifteen minutes, Clay reads to all of us from any of a variety of books. He then prays for all of us. Everyone finishes his or her personal nighttime rituals, then I go to each child's room for a personal prayer. I see it as a time of blessing my children and reconciling all wrongs before we go to sleep.

Sometimes these bedtime routines are broken. These days, with three teenagers in the house, there are times when Mom or Dad go to sleep before the kids do! Yet the regularity of our basic routine has served to give our children a sense of closure to their day and peace of mind. Even today, it happens more often than not—and our older children seem to value it as much as our youngest one.

Mealtime routines have helped give stability to our days and have created time to talk together. Dinner is an appointment with each other that we keep at least five times each week. Whether we have a bowl of oatmeal or an elaborate feast, it is a time to share news about our day and enjoy one another's company. Devotions and prayer most mornings over breakfast give us time to pray together before going out into the demands that each day brings. Sunday afternoon teatime provides us all with a soothing break from the busyness of life. A weekly family night featuring pizza and a movie or other family activity provides regular family fun and builds relationships. Periodic private teas in my bedroom have secured my intimacy with each child's heart through many seasons of our life together. These routines vary, of course, depending on the ages of my children and our seasons of life.

Family routines, of course, easily become family traditions—those things that "we always do"—and such traditions are essential to maintaining a secure sense of family identity. They build a sense of belonging that all of us were meant to enjoy. In our house, holiday and birthday traditions are lived out year after year—unique ways of celebrating the important moments of life together— yielding a bountiful harvest of memories and providing a warm sense of family heritage. They provide us with identity as "the Clarksons."

Each family can develop its own identity through routines and traditions, both simple and complex, silly and profound. I know of a family who celebrated Christmas Eve for years by going out for hamburgers after church, and those Christmas Eve hamburgers became an annual event that each child in the family treasured. It is not the fanciness or complication factor that gives the definition of a family, but the joy shared and the memories made and the sense of belonging generated by a long history of being together.

ENSURING THE FUTURE

Even under the best of circumstances, the work of subduing the domain of the home often goes unappreciated. Children are often oblivious to the fact that they have an important person who is managing so many areas of the home in order to provide them with a stable life and a warm, nurturing home environment.

They rarely appreciate the work and toil and emotional drain that mothers are required to pay. Children who live in a stable, well-managed home tend to take that stability for granted.

Yet children who have such a "shepherd" in their homes to oversee, provide for, direct, and protect the life of the home will benefit profoundly. In addition, as mothers establish the work of the home with honor and dignity, our neighborhoods, towns, governments, and institutions will prosper by being filled with wholehearted, secure human beings who have been prepared to live for God's purposes. By embracing our call to home-making, we are ensuring that these life centers are thriving and well.

The strong and secure future we help to build for our children is laid by the hundreds of small deeds we do every day as we serve faithfully in our homes. Yet the great value of our service will be felt for generations to come and throughout eternity.

For Thought and Reflection

Something to Think About...

Our family sets aside one special day every year to remember the ways we have seen God's faithfulness over the years. We call it Family Day. After a special meal together, we bring out old picture albums and talk, reliving memories.

When we do this, the children never say, "I'm so thankful our home runs so smoothly." Yet their memories always center around our relationships with one another and the meaningful, creative things we do together. Dinners and discussions, reading by the fire, family walks—all mundane parts of life and yet precious anchors to those who need them.

1. *Proverbs 6:6-8.* What does this passage teach us about how we should manage our lives? Why is self-motivation so important to our task? What home-making task tends to overwhelm you the most? Take a minute to brainstorm some ways you can simplify your life to make this task easier.

2. *Proverbs 31:27-29.* What are some of the "ways" of your household that need attending? What are the results of being a good manager at home according to verses 28-29? In what areas can you reduce household-related stress?

3. *1 Thessalonians 4:11.* What does it mean to "make it your ambition to lead a quiet life"? In what ways do too many activities tend to take away from the peace and emotional connection of our homes?

4. *1 Peter 3:3-4.* How does a gentle and quiet spirit exhibit itself in real life? How does your own peacefulness of heart feed the souls of your children? What worries or issues are keeping your heart from trusting God? How can you seek to develop a more peaceful attitude in relationship with all those who live in your home?

Something to Try...

Recently, when paying a bill in an office, I was helped by a very pleasant and efficient young woman. As we waited for the receipt to print out, we began to talk. When I complimented her on her service, she told me, "My mom was one of those women who believed all of the children needed to be involved in the work of our household. I grew up cleaning house, cooking, helping with the laundry, and doing every other chore you can think of. But the overall result was that I became independent at a very early age. I knew that I could do almost any task if I was willing to work!"

Though relatively new with her company, this woman had advanced very quickly. She also had a higher level of confidence than many of the women who were older than she. How interesting to find that this competence and confidence was due, not to a degree or special academic training, but to learning how to be responsible at home!

- Make a list of the stressors in your home that most disturb you and pull at your spirit. (A chronically full sink? The daily grind of getting dinner on the table? Socks in the living room?) Pick one item from your list and brainstorm with your family ways to alleviate that pressure (paper plates during the day, periodic snack meals instead of full-fledged dinners, a special sock hamper for the living room?).

❧ From your brainstormed list, come up with a reasonable plan for resolving that one stress point and put it into action for the next six weeks. Notice I used the word *reasonable*. Making and implementing a home organization plan takes time. Strive for progress, not perfection.

❧ Plan a specific purging time during which you can dispose of unwanted items and clear out problem places. If you can devote the time, a week allocated to this project will do wonders. If you manage a week, schedule regular chunks of time for this activity and stick to your schedule until it's finished. Stock up on boxes or bins to sort toys and trinkets and labels to show children where to put things. If you have little ones who get in the way, have friends or grandparents keep them during this organizational period so that you can give undivided attention to your task. If your children are older, give them a job to do!

❧ Pick out three or four items to purchase that can help you feel like your home really speaks personally of you and the gifts you provide for your home environment. If you're the crafty type, consider a permanent craft or sewing corner with a usable workspace and storage. If music is important to you, create a music center in the living room where instruments and music can be displayed, organized, and played. Dream about ways to make your home reflect more of what you want your family to remember and enjoy in the environment you provide.

❧ You don't always have to go it alone. Save your pennies to hire someone—a neighborhood teenager? a retired friend?—to help you clean and organize your home from top to bottom. You could also trade off "organization days" with another mom and help each other.

CHAPTER 10

The Creative Mother

Opening Windows to God's Artistry and Greatness

The heavens are telling of the glory of God;
And their expanse is declaring
the work of His hands.

PSALM 19:1

What a thrill it was to be hiking together on the outskirts of my beloved Vienna with two of my best-loved companions—my daughter Sarah and my dear friend Gwen. A rush of the chilling autumn wind caused all of us to pull our coats a little tighter, but we delighted in the crispness of the air. The dramatic blues and purples of low-hanging clouds showed promise of a coming snow. The three of us laughed and chattered as we climbed the sloping, vineyard-covered hillside.

Gwen is famous for planning adventurous picnics for her friends, and this excursion was no exception. How special to be with her again in the country where we had met as missionaries in 1977. We wound our way toward our destination on tiny pathways between rows of grapevines recently stripped of fruit. With the harvest now complete, all that was left on the vines was a beautiful array of leaves in shades of crimson, gold, orange, and brown. The vibrant colors of the vineyards and the nearby trees lit up the whole hillside. We plucked a few of the brightest leaves to take home as a memento.

Gwennie suddenly announced, "Here we are at my secret garden!" She led us into a tiny clearing surrounded by a circle of trees and bushes—a private sanctuary for our special time together. A little park bench nestled up against the bushes on one side. There Gwen began to unpack our lunch and tell us the enchanting story of how she had discovered this private little place years before.

We feasted on egg-salad finger sandwiches, crusty Austrian *Semmels* (the famous kaiser rolls), smoked ham, Gouda cheese, and luscious apricots, then ended with fresh *krapfen* (pastries) purchased straight from the oven of a local bakery. A foil-wrapped chocolate followed by steaming Viennese coffee out of a thermos warmed us before we gathered the leftovers and headed back downhill.

Sarah was amused at the stories of long-ago memories Gwen and I shared as we made our way down the hillside toward Gwen's house. The brisk exercise in the cold fall air colored our cheeks a bright pink that shows in the photograph we took to remember our special day.

The picnic that my friend arranged for us that day was a whole (and wonderful) experience that ministered to me in many different ways. My physical needs were met through the invigorating exercise, the delectable food, and the restful afternoon. My appetite for beauty and my awareness of God's artistry in creation was fed by the colors and details of the beautiful hillside. The sounds of crisp leaves blowing in the wind and the noise of a few brave birds awakened poignant memories of other walks. I was mentally stimulated by Gwen's wonderful story, spiritually challenged by new convictions shared during our time together, and emotionally caressed by my friend's encouraging words and act of friendship. The many beautiful details of that day orchestrated an unforgettable experience. And the creativity that inspired Gwen to think of that autumn picnic stimulated my imagination, encouraging me to dream up similar adventures for my own brood.

That delightfully memorable afternoon with my friend is also a picture of what I consider a crucial part of the mission of motherhood: exposing our children to the power and majesty of our Creator God and encouraging them to respond with gratitude and their own creative efforts.

This, I have found, is a creative task in itself. It means taking all of the different elements given into our hands—our time, imagination, intelligence, emotions, spirituality, physical reality, relationships, circumstances—and devising moments for our families that help everyone experience the wonder and beauty of creation in a fresh way. It means acquainting all the children with the tangible evidence of God's nature, creativity, and character, as well as helping them to express their God-given creative nature.

RESPONDING TO GOD'S CREATIVE HANDIWORK

One of the best ways I can appeal to the yearnings for beauty and wonder that God has already placed in my children's hearts is to expose them to the many facets of God's artistry as expressed in what he made. The sheer splendor of his creation, from the tiniest plankton to the biggest whale, from microscopic crystals to soaring mountains, calls to the deepest part of our human nature. The beauty of the environment God designed for us to live in has the power to move us to tears and gives us a sense of joy and appreciation of life.

All of this God created for us to experience so that we could enjoy more fully the life that he prepared for us to know. He did not intend for these things to bring us fulfillment in themselves but to point beyond, to the Artist himself, in order to affirm his magnificence, his power, and his kindness and generosity in making our lives so full. He gave us a richly created world to help us know him better.

Creativity, after all, is one of the essential expressions of God's personality. He is the Master Designer who has the power to make something out of nothing and something fresh and new out of the ruins of something old. His inventiveness knows no boundaries. The beauty of his handiwork is unparalleled. His creativity is awesome and powerful as well as unbelievably beautiful—he is the God of exploding volcanoes and awe-inspiring storms as well as rainbows and sunsets. Even his means of creation are creative, for sometimes he creates directly and sometimes he lends his creative powers to his children and delights in their inventiveness.

Romans 1:20 demonstrates to us the great importance of observing and being surrounded by the beauty of God's creation: "For since the creation of the world His invisible attributes, His eternal power and divine nature, have been clearly seen, being understood through what has been made, so that they are without excuse." God made all that he made in all of his creation to demonstrate the reality of his existence and the vastness of his personality and the reality of his glory.

How important it is that, as mothers, we seek to expose our children to the evidence of God's artistry and power that is all around us. Our children are not just brains that need to be developed academically or trained to think right thoughts. Our children were designed by God to receive pleasure through their senses, their hearts, and their minds, because of all the wonderful things he made for us to enjoy—and also to come to know their Creator through the works of his hands.

Creation was a gift from God to Adam and Eve and to all of us. It was meant to be experienced and enjoyed and responded to with our own creativity. A wholehearted person is best ministered to through the mind, heart, tongue, skin, eyes, ears—as well as the heart and mind and soul. When our children experience the Lord's reality this way, then we become whole, healthy people. The wideness of our experience reflects the vastness of the interests of our omnipotent and omniscient God.

This is one of the most important foundations of all that draws us near to the reality of the existence of a God, the Master Designer who created this world to be a reflection of his glory. As I mirror his image in my life through the creative ways we live in our home and the ways I expose my children to what he has made, he will be more personal and real to them.

EXPERIENCING GOD'S CREATION
THROUGH OUR SENSES

What are some of the ways in which we can bring the creativity of our Master to bear in the lives and minds and hearts of our children? As we reflect on the way the Lord created the world, we see that he designed it to be a place that pleases our senses—which he, of course, created in the first place. He made a world full of amazing sights, sounds, smells, tastes, and textures, not to mention ideas, abilities, and abstract notions. He also created human beings with the built-in desire to emulate and enhance his natural design. In introducing our children to the astounding variety of sensual and intellectual experiences set in motion by our Creator God, we help them to comprehend the rich wonder of the mighty Lord's accomplishments.

When I think about my visual experience of God's greatness, many natural pictures come to mind—the white-flecked churning of stormy waves rushing to the shore and dashing against rocky cliffs; the familiar grandeur of my purple and red mountains blanketed with lush green evergreens or dotted with red, blue, white, yellow, and purple wildflowers; the colorful abundance of purple irises and yellow jonquils in the botanical gardens; the blinding brightness of mounds of sparkling white snow on the frigid mornings in January. These are all pictures of real places I have grown to love.

Other pictures are a precious tiny baby nursing and patting her mother's chest with a satisfied relaxation; the gentle affection of our golden retriever as she reaches for us with her paw; the shy red foxes with bushy, white-tipped tails that tiptoe across the forest floor and the deer and wild turkeys that scamper through our yard; autumn leaves bursting with color in late September; children sleeping in angelic form; a blazing bonfire; millions of stars sparkling in the midnight sky as we sleep on our deck.

The Lord has indeed given us an array of visual feasts to enjoy in his natural world. And he has also inspired the creative work of men and women through the ages who sought to respond to the beauty they saw around them with beauty of their own. Surely the spires of a Gothic cathedral are evidence of the Lord's amazing creativity working in the hearts and hands of visionary architects and skilled craftsmen! Surely a sculpture by Michelangelo or the graceful arch of a suspension bridge reflects this handiwork. Being able to enjoy these expressions of God-given creativity is also part of God's gift of visual enjoyment in the world.

Sounds are another reflection of God's creativity. The crash of the surf during high tide stirs in me a sense of wonder at his grandeur. Plaintive Celtic music touches me deep within. The breeze stirring the pine trees and jostling the wind chimes, the rowdy laughter of boys wrestling, my youngest daughter whispering, "I'll never move away from home, Mom. You are my best friend!"—all these sounds touch my heart.

Smell is another sense closely tied to emotion. For me, coffee brewing or bread baking in the morning is an enticing smell. The smell of barbecued brisket or brownies baking always reminds me of my mother. The aroma of wet autumn woods makes me think of walking to school on foggy and misty mornings during my early missionary life in Poland, and the smell of wood smoke brings delightful memories of picnics and weenie roasts.

And consider the abundance of flavors the Lord offers to enrich our lives. Our sense of taste is basic to the way we experience the world—that's why babies put everything in their mouth. Our sense of taste has such a direct path to our hearts and souls that it has come to stand for experience itself. "O taste and see," cries the psalmist, "that the Lord is good!"

The Lord has provided us with so many wonderful taste experiences. Remember the fun of touching a honeysuckle blossom to your tongue and tasting the nectar? There is also the built-in sweetness of crisp pears from Nana's orchard, the satisfying and refreshing zing of cherry tomatoes pulled off our own vines, the earthy and delicious taste of mushrooms from the forest floor. And then there are the arrays of delicious foods enhanced by gifted cooks employing their God-given creative powers: warm, sweet homemade cinnamon rolls; spicy, cheesy enchiladas; grilled salmon with dill; greasy, crisp, salty french fries; tangy apple cider; or creamy oatmeal heaped with brown sugar and walnuts.

Yet another way we can experience the wonder and variety of God's creation is through touch. When I think of the joys of touch, I think of Nathan's giving me a hand massage, the icy chill of an afternoon swim in a mountain lake, the furry head of a newborn nuzzling my neck, the cozy feel of flannel sheets on a winter's night, a hot bubble bath in which to soak, "tickling my soft back" (a phrase Sarah coined for our family) at night before going to sleep, or a gentle kiss that says, "You are special."

Not everything in God's creation seems immediately pleasing to our senses, of course. I personally find large spiders and insects scary, mosquitoes and chiggers annoying, and snakes creepy. The roar of an approaching tornado brings a sense of panic to my heart, and the sound of woodpeckers pounding on our house unnerves me. I dislike the smell of marigolds and wet dogs, can't handle the taste of raw fish, and avoid stroking porcupines or stinging nettles. Yet even these frightening or repellent experiences give testimony to God's magnificent inventiveness and power. Despite my personal feelings, in fact, I would hesitate to attach the label "ugly" to anything the Lord has made. In the words of Genesis, it is all "very good," and it all has the capacity to draw us and our children closer to him.

EXPERIENCING GOD'S CREATION THROUGH WORDS AND IDEAS

Because God created the world that we see, hear, taste, smell, and touch, we experience aspects of his wonder and majesty when we use our senses. But God's creation, like the Lord himself, transcends the limitation of sensate reality. His creation includes not only what we can perceive with our eyes and ears and nose and tongue and skin but also what we can think, imagine, and feel.

The ability to think and understand, for example, is part of God's creative wonder. So are mathematical principles and physics and chemistry and logic, the mysterious qualities of intuition, memory, and spiritual perception, the invaluable character traits of bravery, nobility, and integrity. And we, who are made in God's image, were meant to experience his power and beauty and creativity in all of these "invisible" realities as well.

One of the most effective ways to see these areas, with the eyes of our hearts, is through ideas expressed in words. John 1:1 attests to how integral words and language are to the Creator's presence: "In the beginning was the Word, and the Word was with God, and the Word was God." Jesus himself was the Word—a communication from heaven to earth. There is power in the written and spoken word that brings to mind the power of the Creator speaking a world into being: " 'Let there be light'; and there was light" (Genesis 1:3).

Scriptural examples of words that stir our hearts and define our ideas of God deepen our relationship with him. First Corinthians 13 helps us understand the meaning of unconditional love. The story of the good Samaritan in Luke 10 gives us word pictures from Jesus himself that portray realistic actions of God displayed in everyday circumstances. Psalm 23 shows us the comfort of God's love and guidance in our lives as we view him as a shepherd.

Similarly, literature, poetry, and great stories have, through the ages, demonstrated a capacity to stir our hearts and, at their best, to help us see God. A longing for purpose and meaning, which are abstract ideas, can be fulfilled with verbal ideas. Words also catalyze our lives into action and unite hearts and minds. In the written and spoken word (the result of creative effort by men and women made in God's image), we can encounter the reality of God's unseen creation.

ENCOUNTERING GOD THROUGH THE NATURAL WORLD

Helping my children to enjoy and appreciate God's handiwork in its many varieties requires a choice. It means I must take time to expose my children to the beauty and grandeur of nature, to stop to enjoy and admire it with them, and to choose to allow the intangible reality of God's design to fill our souls—time when the televisions and the computers are turned off, no phone calls are made, and activities are balanced so that quiet pondering and thoughtful enjoyment are a regular part of our days.

In our culture we have too often secluded ourselves and our children from the beauty and mysteries of God's natural creation. In the interest of convenience and progress, we have substituted man-made materials for the real thing. And while I believe that human creations can indeed be indirect expressions of God's creativity, I also believe that the farther we move from nature the more out of touch we can get with God's power and reality.

We may substitute silk flowers for fresh flowers cut from a garden or wildflowers plucked from a hillside. But while the silk flowers never wilt, they lack the incredible fragrance of roses or honeysuckle or lavender or the freshness of buttercups or Queen Anne's lace. And while the real flowers may wither, they also teach us lessons about the fragility and temporary state of this life that perfect artificial ones never could.

Even the food we eat tends to be prepackaged and institutional. The natural tastes of spices and herbs in homemade soups; the chewiness of whole-grain bread, pasta, or brownies with pecans; the natural sweetness of real fruit and the juicy crunch of fresh vegetables are replaced with vitamin tablets and commercial substitutes.

So many of us in our plastic, industrial world spend the bulk of our lives apart from any true natural beauty. We travel inside protected cars and feel the wind, rain, and snow on our faces only as we move from one enclosure to another. So many children in our industrial society grow up surrounded by glass and plastic, steel and asphalt. They spend most of their time with machines—televisions and stereos, game consoles and computers, and cars. They are rarely exposed to the natural elements that were meant to daily confront our soul with the greatness of God.

No wonder current generations seem to give in so easily to doubt and skepticism! They have had little opportunity to wonder at the greatness of God in the vast ocean or in the middle of a snowy blizzard or felt tiny when standing under the great canopy of stars.

There is something about the direct experience of God's natural world that tends to put our human doubts and questions into perspective. This is something Job learned near the end of his time of being tested by Satan. Job and his friends tried to figure out why God had allowed him to be tested in such a way. Our Holy God did not feel compelled to answer the questions Job and his friends asked. Instead, God's answer focused on the elements of creation that showed his greatness:

Who is this that darkens counsel
By words without knowledge?
Now gird up your loins like a man,
And I will ask you, and you instruct Me!
Where were you when I laid the foundation of the earth!
Tell Me, if you have understanding,
Who set its measurements, since you know?...
Or who enclosed the sea with doors,
When, bursting forth, it went out from the womb;
When I made a cloud its garment,
And thick darkness its swaddling band? (Job 38:2-5,8-9)

The Lord goes on and on in exclaiming the marvels of creation. His apologetic for the circumstances was simply the vastness of his creation. This passage clearly shows that God's perspective and wisdom and purposes are vastly different from our human, limited viewpoint.

We and our children also need Job's message. That's why one of the greatest gifts we can give our children is exposure to this magnificent Creator through the wonderful things he has made. Their appetites for life need to be built on those things that reflect the image of God through the work of his fingers. Practically speaking, that means that one of the most important things I can do as a mother is get my children—and me!—outdoors as much as possible.

Most children respond happily to spending time in nature, especially if the experience is cast as an exploration and they have companions on the adventure. Some love to hike and run and jump on the meadows and the rocks. Others are more thoughtful, prone to seeking out hidden treasures in the nooks and crannies of rocks and trees. But regardless of how they experience God's world, the spirits of all children seem to open up when allowed to interact with nature.

All of my children were vibrant and free when we climbed the rocky hills of Rockport, Massachusetts, and felt the spray of the cold ocean water on our faces.

Hiking nine miles into the woods, climbing over towering rocks in a flowing stream, and hearing the sound of hungry coyotes as we descended the last mountain before home is also a favorite memory—a story my boys have recounted again and again.

But even smaller, less time-consuming encounters with nature have proven beneficial to my children's souls. Driving out into the countryside, away from the city lights, to view the Milky Way or a comet has provided delight and awe. Even playing outside on a summer's evening, feeding birds in the backyard, collecting bugs and looking up their names, or taking a family walk around the neighborhood on a winter afternoon can be enough for a mini-adventure and an exposure to the beauties of God's world.

Any encounter with God's outdoors can make a difference. Over the long haul, the more time our children spend in natural settings, both wild and tame, the more deeply they will realize the magnificent message of Jeremiah 32:17: "Ah Lord GOD! Behold, Thou hast made the heavens and the earth by Thy great power and by Thine outstretched arm! Nothing is too difficult for Thee!"

FILLING OUR HOMES WITH BEAUTY
AND INSPIRATION

Proverbs 24:3-4 says,

> By wisdom a house is built,
> And by understanding it is established;
> And by knowledge the rooms are filled
> With all precious and pleasant riches.

Picturing my home as a sort of castle in which all the rooms are wisely adorned with "precious and pleasant riches," I have decorated and arranged my home environment in ways that help our children experience God's creation more richly. In particular, from the time they were very small, I have filled our home with items that appealed to their senses and fed their understanding of God's beauty and their appreciation of human creativity.

To delight my family's visual sense, for example, I have adorned our walls with pictures and art that support the highest goals for my children's minds.

Collecting gold-framed calligraphy scriptures from an artist was a practice we began one Christmas and have continued to do every year. In addition, snapshots of our family's antics and stages of life are framed and scattered throughout the house to serve as visual reminders of the importance of family. Colorfully framed prints of family, children, mountains, teapots, Viennese settings (where we lived), wolves and eagles for the boys, Victorian scenes for the girls, and collectible art prints from museums are strategically placed throughout the house. Large-format books featuring great art, historical battles, and photographs adorn coffee tables and hearths. We even keep baskets of favorite books and magazines in our bathrooms. I change these items around from time to time to give my children a variety of pictures to fill their minds as they rest around the home.

Rooms are painted with invigorating colors. Wildflowers, fresh garden flowers, or colorful leaves and pine cones bring the natural world into our indoor environment. I have planted hundreds of bulbs and flowers over the years to give us something fresh to put on our table from time to time. I do not have a green thumb, so I always pick hearty perennials that are indigenous to our area and require very little care.

The sounds of our home revolve mainly around music. We have some sort of music playing most of the day. (The house rule is that the music in our shared areas must be melodic and pleasing for everyone.) In addition to "canned" music, whenever possible we fill the house with our homemade music—piano, violin, guitar, and our enthusiastic voices.

Collecting books on tape and radio dramas has made our many and long car trips an auditory and verbal experience to remember with delight. Story tapes have entertained my children for at least a couple of hours when they were ill in bed. And the sound of "Mom's soothing voice" or Dad's deeply expressive one reading long, adventurous books out loud has always been a source of comfort for our brood.

Homey, familiar flavors also symbolize comfort for our family. We try to eat as healthfully and naturally as possible, with plenty of whole grains and fruits and vegetables. Mom's homemade chicken soup or cinnamon toast with tea or ginger ale with juice bring soothing comfort to anyone who is sick. (I have collected a few high-sided trays and small, flat baskets that sit easily on a bed and catch spills, and I keep a supply of pretty paper luncheon napkins to serve as a cloth in these "love baskets.") Whole-wheat cinnamon rolls are birthday breakfast fare, while homemade pizza with a specially adorned piece for each person is the standard for our family nights together. On nights when I'm out of steam, we enjoy snack meals—crackers or toast and cheese slices, bits of fruit, popcorn, and cold cuts, or cereal.

Smells are closely tied to tastes and foods. Half the joy of being home is following the enticing, familiar aromas of yeasty bread or simmering chili into the kitchen. Sunday afternoon teatimes with a special baked treat, fragrant candles, and steaming hot tea with milk and sugar shaped our children's palates from the time they were quite young.

Holidays reflect a different array of smells and tastes. Creamy potato soup and herb bread are traditional for Christmas Eve—a shepherd's feast to accompany our reading of the Christmas story. Brisket with twice-baked potatoes is a favorite company meal. Gooey donuts are a popular fare when other children spend the night. Most families are pretty good at sharing the tastes and flavors that make their family special.

Not all scents are food related, of course. The warm fragrance of a vanilla candle can drive away sickroom smells or help me relax after a busy day. The refreshing bouquet of rosemary in my cooking pot or almond hand lotion refreshes me. The woodsy smell of pine boughs on the mantel or the garden smell of flowers on the table brings the outdoors in, reminding us once more of the beauties of the natural world.

To appeal to our children's sense of touch, I fill our home with items that are soft, fluffy, and soothing to the skin. Loosely knitted baby blankets with silky edges are given to each child at birth and always placed within their little fingers when born. Each time I nurse or put my little ones to bed, I always cuddle them with the softness of these particular blankets so that they will have something familiar with which to comfort themselves when I am not there. And hand rubs, back scratches, and head rubs are a favorite "go to bed" ritual that has opened up many heart-to-heart conversations over the years.

ENCOURAGING A CREATIVE RESPONSE

Last week little Joy disappeared into the recesses of her room for about four hours. When I was finally invited in, she showed me an array of cards she had made for "everyone that I love." The joy on her face as she shared her masterpieces with me reminded me that encouraging my children's creativity is one of the most profound ways I can help them experience and understand the magnificence and creative power of God.

Creativity is such an integral part of the image of God within all of us. Creative expression isn't just limited to those who happen to be adept at arts and crafts or home decorating. Being creative in God's image encompasses a wide range of activities—from storytelling to house construction to cooking and crafts to music to basic problem solving. And being creative isn't limited to original ideas. Whenever we adapt an idea or try a different approach to an issue or give our personal spin to a particular endeavor, we are learning a little more about our God-given nature and the nature of our creative God.

A large part of fostering creativity in our own children is modeling it in our daily lives, allowing them to participate in our creative pursuits. And once again, these creative endeavors don't have to fall in stereotypical creative categories.

Gardening has been one of my favorite ways to enjoy God's creation, exercise my creative muscles, and involve my children at the same time. Although I am not a seasoned or an informed gardener, I love flowers and the process of growing them. When I visit greenhouses and smell the fresh soil and choose vibrant blossoms to plant at home, my spirit soars, and my children catch my enthusiasm. Whenever possible, I take them to the greenhouses with me. Each one gets five dollars for plants and a small section of our garden in which to create his or her personal place of beauty—a wonderful laboratory for observing the intersection of natural creation and human endeavor.

Another fun creative endeavor we have tried as a family is making applesauce. We go each fall to an orchard to pick apples. At home, each child has a part in peeling, coring, slicing, boiling, and mashing the apples into a chunky sauce with just the right touch of cinnamon and sugar. All of us rave about the wonderful fall treat because we all had a hand in making it!

Partly out of interest, partly out of necessity, I have become rather proficient at bread baking. I can whip up a six-loaf batch of dough in no time. Once it has risen, though, my children and I really enjoy unleashing our creativity. We turn that batch of dough into a variety of wonderful baked goods—cinnamon rolls, pizza dough, onion-herb bread, buns. Joy and I have even sculpted it into animal shapes.

Encouraging our children to express themselves with words and music has been an important way that Clay and I have encouraged creativity in our home. We have memorized favorite poems, scriptures, and sayings as a family. Computer-designed birthday cards with original poems or notes of appreciation and encouragement from each of our children are a standard for birthday breakfasts. We have invested precious funds in music lessons and instruments to help our children develop basic skills and a knowledge to creatively express their musical abilities. And from the time our children were very small, we have sung and played together, enjoying both the fellowship and the joy of creative expression.

An essential part of keeping the creative spark alive in our family is filling our house with tools and materials for creative endeavors. Boxes of stickers, paints, colored pencils, stencils, and bulk paper are always on hand for anyone who feels the need for artistic expression. Musical instruments are also at hand. Fabric and thread and old dress-up clothes from Goodwill (including army togs, helmets, swords, long dresses, hats, capes, shoes, scarves, and jewelry) become costumes for dress-up and impromptu theater. Seeds, trowels, garden tools, and small bedding plants encourage our children to try their hand at gardening. Left-over pieces of wood, nails, screws, and tape give my children things to build. Legos, blocks, trains, and dolls from my childhood encourage imaginative play.

Collecting how-to books on art, crafts, and hobbies became a habit when our children were quite small. One of our most dog-eared books describes how to make play-clay and salt dough and pictures various statues and figurines for children to copy. A book describing simple magic tricks engaged Nathan's interest in becoming an illusionist. This book planted seeds that grew into Nathan's performing as a magician for children's parties.

CREATIVE MOTHERING

I have often heard mothers say, "I'm not the creative type. I don't know how to bring such creative elements into my home. How do you think up all of those ideas? I'm not very artistic!"

I, too, have felt inhibited and insecure about my abilities in these areas, but I have learned to grow as I go along. It is possible that many of us have not practiced being creative or nurtured that capacity. Even more likely, I think we have limited the idea of creativity to arts and crafts.

We must remember that being made in God's image means we are like him—each of us. If he is creative, then we also have that potential—all of us. As mothers we have been privileged to be involved in one of God's most amazing acts of creation—bringing new life into the world. And we are involved in a task that requires us to improvise, try new things, and contribute to the development of a human soul. How can we say we're not creative?

God's creativity, like all aspects of his reality, is so much larger than what we usually imagine. If we have the Spirit of Christ in our lives, then he will inspire us with living ideas that cover the wide breadth of life's demands.

A wise and creative woman isn't necessarily that way all on her own. A wise woman has learned to imitate lots of other wise women; the creativity comes in adapting their ideas to her needs. I have gathered a wealth of ideas over the years by reading, watching people, copying the ideas of others, and scaling them to the needs and ages of my children, husband, and friends. I have also learned a lot by experimenting along with my children. We have learned together, with lots of failures and successes—and a whole lot of fun.

One of the most interesting things I have learned about exercising my creativity over the past eighteen years is that the comprehensive task of mothering is a creative endeavor in itself! A large part of the task of parenting is in learning how to be a creative problem solver in the face of thousands of challenging moments.

I often pray, "Lord, in the power of the Holy Spirit, help me to have your perspective on this moment (or about this child) as I face the issues of our day." This means I am seeking gentle and life-giving ways to steer my children on the path of life that will lead them to my dear Lord. Instead of relying on reflex reactions and "one size fits all" parenting techniques, I want to approach my responsibilities as imaginatively as possible.

For instance, I have learned that there are usually peaceful ways to motivate my children to do what I want them to do instead of always confronting them with harsh words and lectures. My children soften their hearts toward me much more quickly when given a cup of tea and a warm cookie accompanied with a beautiful note card or a back rub with soothing music or candlelight as a backdrop than when I give another lecture.

When I sense that the children are down or in a grumbling mood, I avoid further conflict by suggesting something that will soothe their frazzled nerves and calm their spirits. One of my children was feeling lonely and exhausted from schoolwork. Instead of a serious talk about the need to have a cheerful attitude (which I also do from time to time), I made him a special snack dinner, lit a candle in my room, and served him there before the others ate their dinner.

I often fail to serve my lectures in such an enticing way and instead am more of a nag. Yet I am learning to use my influence and minister to my children in gentle or inspiring biblical ways by exercising creativity in my own journey of motherhood.

From dealing with financial constraints, time limitations, illnesses, and hormonal teenage years, mothering requires all of us to exercise ingenuity and inspiration to live those years with grace while providing lots of food for thought and heart along the way. What a relief to realize that we are not alone in this. Remembering that all our creativity comes from the Master Designer himself can help us relax, do our best, and enjoy the ideas when they come.

KEEPING PERSPECTIVE

In order for our children to have the opportunity to develop fully, we as mothers must seek to provide them with a wide range of ways in which to experience God's many facets. When we care for their physical and emotional needs with grace and gentle care, they internalize an understanding of God's care. When we give them a righteous moral base by telling them what to do, modeling right behavior, and applying appropriate discipline, they come to know something of the Lord's righteousness and justice. When we teach them how to have healthy relationships by modeling unconditional love and encouragement and requiring them to serve others, they instinctively learn something about how God relates to humans and wants us to act.

Our mission as mothers is a comprehensive one. We are called to help our children develop appetites for beauty and excellence in the arts by exposing them to these things and to provide for their intellectual growth and education through stimulating discussions, carefully chosen movies, and worthwhile books. We train and instruct them in the knowledge of God and understanding of Scripture by sharing from the fullness of our hearts throughout the moments of our days. We build a sense of heritage, destiny, and mission for their future lives by establishing traditions in our homes, providing opportunities for them to work in the home, and showing them how to minister to the needs of others. And we do all this while attempting to keep our home in order and running somewhat smoothly!

The exciting part of our job is that there are limitless creative ways to give life and vibrancy to any of these tasks. But it's important to keep in mind that creativity in mothering is simply a means to an end, not our primary goal. In each area of training and life-giving provision for my children, my goal is to make the Lord real—his character, beauty, love, justice, truth, excellence, and purposes. My goal is to touch my children's hearts with the overwhelming wonder of his presence. As I seek to gently and lovingly expose my children to the natural greatness of God's being, my hope is that their own devotion will naturally arise out of the wellspring of their full hearts.

I need to keep in mind, however, that this will not happen overnight. Cultivating an appreciation of God's creation and the "in his image" creativity of our families is a lifelong habit. It takes years to develop and is built by the ways we choose to live each day.

A single visit to the ocean on one vacation will likely not be enough to produce a deep love and appreciation for God's creation. A single museum visit or concert will probably not instill a deep understanding of how God's creative image inspires people to create. But moment by moment, as we take time to reflect on creation, sketch a favorite mountain scene, write a poem of praise, or admire the new buds on a tree—and share all of these things with our children—we have the opportunity to cultivate an appreciation for God's creative greatness in their souls and invite a grateful, in-his-image creative response.

In the meantime, little children break the crayons, spill the paint, and fight over the brushes. Older children will squabble with one another or complain just when we'd like them to admire a sunset or the scenery. Yet a child's mind, desires, and understanding are still being shaped by a lifetime of being exposed to beauty and creativity—day in and day out.

As moms, we understand that childhood has many stages and that we cannot measure our success in these areas by focusing on one moment. Building an appreciative and creative spirit into our children requires our commitment to clean up many messes, to admire and encourage their creative efforts, and to give our children the freedom to explore and experiment, knowing that they will eventually mature into flourishing and creative adults.

TAKING JOY IN GOD'S CREATIVE GIFT

In the midst of all we're doing, however, we need our own frequent exposure to the wonder and beauty of God's creation to keep our souls nourished and our hearts renewed. There have been periods in my life when I could not think one creative thought. Sometimes just getting through the day, month, or year has been a challenge. Yet a part of the reason God has given us so much beauty and spectacular variety in creation is to encourage us with comfort, joy, and delight.

When we take time to enjoy what he has given us and to reflect on the wonder and beauty of his works, our souls will be fed with what we need to get through life. Beauty is not just something frivolous; it is essential to the foundation of our lives. Otherwise, why would God have taken so much time to create it as an essential part of his dominion?

One day not long ago I awoke in the early light of morning. I sat in a favorite chair that is positioned facing a mountain. A whirling snowstorm was blowing in clouds over the mountain, and the gentle snow drifting down onto the pine trees was a soothing balm to my then-frazzled soul. I put on some music, made a cup of tea, lit a candle, and allowed the moment to fill me with peace. It was in the beauty of this peaceful time that I spent my first few waking moments being reminded of the Lord's splendor and quietness.

This is the picture that I asked God to place in my mind all day as I progressed to the less peaceful moments, which involved cleaning the house, getting my children ready for the day, following them through their chores, disciplining attitudes, making meals, and completing phone calls. These few moments admiring God's creation stayed with me all day. But I had to take time to appreciate it and store it in my heart.

Our children will need hundreds of such pictures to store in their hearts in order to adequately face the battles in their lives. When we help to cultivate these pictures for ourselves and continually pass along a repertoire of natural beauty and the touch from God's hands, our children will indeed have reservoirs of soul food from which to feed for a lifetime.

FOR THOUGHT AND REFLECTION

Something to Think About...

"Mom, I feel like many of the Christians that we know are so boring and one-dimensional and tied to the rules they keep. I don't see or hear about anything real or exciting in their walk with God. I want a God who is as big as the dreams and passions of my heart. Do you think I'll ever find God to be like that? It certainly won't be by observing many of the Christians we know!"

The familiar dreams of my own teenage years echoed in the idealistic words of my teenager. All too often, it seems, Christianity is small-minded and limited to a few sets of dos and don'ts. Yet if Jesus set the stars in place and taught them how to sing and walked on water and raised the dead, then there is nothing small or limited about him. Until we teach the excellence and magnificence of our Creator God, our children will not be free to be passionate about him and his causes or fully creative in their response to him.

1. *Romans 1:18-20.* What has been a constant testimony of God's greatness throughout the ages? To what does the phrase, "His invisible attributes, His eternal power and divine nature, have been clearly seen, being understood through what has been made" refer? Why, then, is it important to expose our children to creation?

2. *Proverbs 24:3-4.* What does this verse say about a home? What does it mean to fill a house with "all precious and pleasant riches"? Does your home reflect this verse? What do you lack?

3. *Job 38:1-7* (actually, the passage extends from Job 38:1 to 40:2). What is God's answer to Job's friends, who lack understanding for Job's suffering? What is the point of this passage? What are some ways you can expose your children to the bigness and holiness of God?

4. *John 1:1-3.* Where was Jesus at the beginning of the world? What part did he play in creation? If we know him and have his life in us, how

should that reflect in the creative areas of our own life? How can you make creation and nature more a part of your life?

Something to Try...

Running through the waves at the seashore, climbing the mountains when the spring snows are melting, and splashing through an overflowing lake after a heavy rain have brought out pure joy and delight in my children. The reality of God is always more evident to me at these times when I am enjoying God's creation with my family. Being outdoors often seems to neutralize our children's attitude problems and bring peace to their souls.

- Plan a trip to the mountains, the desert, the sea, or the woods—whatever place of natural beauty is accessible to you—just to have an adventure with your children. If possible, this outing should include both active time (hiking or swimming), learning time (identifying plants or shells), and quiet, reflective time (a rest period under the trees or a campfire under the stars).

- Visit a bookstore or a library and bring home a book with pictures by a great painter or photographer whose work stirs awe in your hearts. Pour mugs of hot chocolate or cider and gather together on the couch to enjoy the book together.

- Buy each child a sweatshirt or T-shirt and puffy paints, and have a family craft time to design your family crest or coat of arms. Or write a story together, print it in a blank book, and let your children illustrate it.

- Plan an out-of-the-ordinary picnic and surprise your children with it. Pack your favorite foods in a basket and carry them to enjoy on top of a building, in the woods on a winter day, on the grounds of your local library, or even in your living room.

CHAPTER 11

The Ministering Mother

Bringing God's Purposes into Our Homes...and Beyond

The harvest is plentiful, but the workers are few.
Therefore beseech the Lord of the harvest
to send out workers into His harvest.

MATTHEW 9:37-38

D rive-home traffic had caught us as we made our way home from swimming lessons on a sweltering afternoon. As we exited the freeway close to our home, we found the cars were stacked up almost to the freeway. As we waited for our turn at the traffic light, Nathan observed, "Hey, Mom, there's a homeless man up ahead with a sign that says, 'Please help if you can.' Look how tan his face is! He looks like he's been out in the sun a long time!"

We had grown accustomed to the telltale signs of people who lived on the streets—tanned, weather-beaten skin was a giveaway.

"May I please give him a couple of dollars? He looks hungry!"

As we edged forward in the traffic jam, I gave Nathan my purse, and he found a couple of dollar bills. Finally we reached the man. Nathan handed out his meager offering with a smile. "God bless you!"

"Thanks a lot, son!" was the seemingly sincere reply.

As we drove over the exit ramp, the kids all agreed that the man looked forlorn and hungry. So we agreed to pull into a nearby fast-food restaurant and buy the man a meal. Should it be a chicken sandwich or a burger?

"Be sure to get him the value meal, so he can have a full stomach!"

We secured our aromatic meal, which tempted all of the kids to ask, "Please get us some fries too, Mom! They smell so good!"

When we returned to the exit ramp, our man was nowhere in sight. We drove around to look for him. Finally Nathan yelled out, "Look! He's almost across the highway on the other side!" We felt like treasure hunters with our booty in sight.

We navigated through the congestion and waved to the man to come to our side of the road, where Nathan presented him one food item at a time. "Here's a deluxe cheeseburger with the works. Here are some giant fries. Here's a large Coke. Hope you like it!"

The man's eyes widened as he said, "As soon as you gave me those two dollars, I thought I would see if I could get a burger for ninety-nine cents and still have money for a drink. That's where I was walking. But this is far more than I hoped for! This is a feast! Thanks sooooo much. You've made my day!"

We asked where he was headed. He replied, "When I get enough money, I'm headed home to Washington, and I can't wait!"

One of the kids said, "We'll pray for you. God bless you!"

To which he replied, "Will you pray for me now?"

At the end of our heartfelt prayers, we waved and told our anonymous friend good-bye. All the children were smiling as we finally arrived home, and I sensed once again that the Lord was stretching their little hearts with the memory of a man with a grateful smile.

The cost of our service to that man was almost nothing! It took very little money and hardly any time, yet the dividends in my children's lives will last for a lifetime. (I hoped we made a difference in his life as well.)

On another such occasion when we had shared some food with a homeless person, the man (who had only one leg and walked with crutches) grasped Nathan's hand and squeezed it, saying, "God bless you, Nathan! You are the only person who has stopped to help me all day long. I sure appreciate you!" This left such a lasting impression on Nathan that he prayed for the man each night for a month afterward!

Service to others in need is an essential part of training and instructing our children in order to cultivate in them a loving and obedient heart. Serving others is a way to live out what the Bible would have us believe in our hearts. It puts feet to the message of the gospel.

Clay and I have found, however, that service is best taught through a combination of modeling and instruction. It is by watching us give unselfishly of our money, home, time, and gifts that our children begin to think of themselves as stewards of all that they have. And it is in showing them what it's like to follow Christ by loving others that we live up to his calling in our own lives.

CALLED TO LOVE

One of the fundamental messages of the Bible is that all of us who belong to Christ are expected to extend his love to and to meet the needs of other believers and those in our community. We have a stewardship responsibility for which we will have to answer to God someday, giving account of the ways we have served him by reaching out in love to others.

In Matthew 25:31-46, Jesus spells out this responsibility clearly when he talks about the judgment of mankind at the end of time. In this familiar passage, Jesus tells us that certain people will be blessed because of the way they served others on earth:

> Then the King will say to those on His right, "Come, you who are blessed of My Father, inherit the kingdom prepared for you from the foundation of the world. For I was hungry, and you gave Me something to eat; I was thirsty, and you gave Me drink; I was a stranger, and you invited Me in; naked, and you clothed Me; I was sick, and you visited Me; I was in prison, and you came to Me.... Truly I say to you, to the extent that you did it to one of these brothers of Mine, even the least of them, you did it to me." (verses 34-36, 40)

Conversely, he says those who refuse to serve others in their lives will be rejected by God.

> Then He will answer them, saying, "Truly I say to you, to the extent that you did not do it to one of the least of these, you did not do it to Me." And these will go away into eternal punishment, but the righteous into eternal life. (verses 45-46)

Jesus clearly modeled the kind of life we are to lead as his disciples, and his ongoing teaching underlined our responsibilities. We are to minister to the poor, the sick, the needy, and the captives. We are to be careful lest our actions harm any weaker than we are. We are to love our enemies and forgive those who persecute us. And we are to take Christ's message of love and redemption to everyone—to the ends of the earth.

And yet we are not on our own as we try to follow Christ in serving others. God, in his wisdom, has equipped each of us to serve him. All of us who belong to Christ are given spiritual gifts from the Holy Spirit so that, in his power, we may serve others and meet their needs. Romans 12:6-8 as well as 1 Corinthians 12:4-30 give us a fuller picture of what these spiritual gifts encompass. First Corinthians 12:7, for example, reminds us that "to each one is given the manifestation of the Spirit for the common good." In other words, we are gifted by God so that we might serve and help others. We are to be God's mouth, hands, and feet as we minister to the needs of our fellow human beings.

Ephesians 2:10 even goes on to state that we and our children were made from the beginning to glorify God by doing his work: "We are His workmanship, created in Christ Jesus for good works, which God prepared beforehand, that we should walk in them." This takes us back once more to God's original design for blessing the world through families and casts a whole new light on what it means to subdue the earth and make it productive. From the very beginning, God's plan has been for all his people to find blessing, not only in their families, but in a godly heritage of doing good works.

DESIGNED TO SERVE

Helping our children understand that they were designed uniquely by God to serve the needs of others helps them to realize their position in God's kingdom. Each person will have an opportunity to live out a story of how God used them uniquely to bring his light into the world. The real foundations of a positive self-image are built upon the significance bestowed upon us by God in allowing us to be a part of the work of his kingdom. Whether that work involves leading someone to the Lord, feeding the poor, writing a note of encouragement to a depressed friend, visiting a lonely and unloved neighbor, it is all significant to the Lord.

There is a tendency to leave the work of serving others in the hands of the "professionals" or to those who have chosen as their life's work some sort of a ministerial vocation. Significantly, Jesus chose no professionals as his disciples. He chose common, ordinary men to do the work of God's kingdom. Spiritual qualifications in the mind of Christ are not determined by the degrees a person has earned at a university or a professional résumé but by the anointing of his Spirit and by a willingness to serve in obedience to God's commands. I believe that parents too often fail their children in this regard. They give a wrong impression about serving the Lord through the hypocrisy in their lives. We go to church as a family and listen to a sermon. On the way home from church we might comment to the kids, "That was a great sermon. There certainly are lots of needs in the world. God really has called us to share our faith."

Often the parent fails to take the initiative to share his faith or give to the poor or do whatever the pastor was recommending. The children then learn from their parents that it doesn't really matter if you obey God by actually doing good works. It only matters if you can articulate what you *should* do.

God will hold us all accountable for the wonderful opportunities we have to minister to others. The level of materialism in America, combined with the availability of Scripture and the freedom to invest our lives for him, provides us with a heavy weight of stewardship for our own spiritual heritage. He will also hold us accountable for not training our children or, worse, causing them to stumble spiritually (Matthew 18:6).

It doesn't have to be that way. The family as a whole can present a beautiful picture to others of the reality of the Lord expressed in a body of people. Jesus specifically gave those of us who know him the responsibility of reaching the world with his salvation and personally modeling his love to an often loveless world. As my children move beyond a simplistic understanding of their personal need for a Savior, our family then serves as the logical place where they can learn to value the lives of others by observing Clay and me as we serve others in real life.

The family can be such a wonderful picture of God's love expressed through the normal activities of daily life. I have been amazed at how often people have stopped to tell us how wonderful it is to see a family that is close or whose children are so polite. God's grace seems to cover us in the eyes of others as we seek to serve him together.

But how does a family specifically serve God and others? For us, the focal points for training our children and serving as a family have been hospitality, helping those in need, and evangelistic outreach. Through what we teach and model in these areas, we hope to pass along God's purposes to our children and to the families they will establish.

HOSPITALITY: SERVING THROUGH OUR HOME

Home is a natural place for children to learn the work of hospitality. Through the years, in the sixteen communities where we have lived, we have had many opportunities to model for our children the importance of opening our home as a place of ministry to others. Working together, we have prepared and served hundreds of meals to visitors. Hundreds of people have found a welcome and a bed in our home. And that doesn't include the children who hung out in our family room, the friends who dropped by for a chat or a Bible study, or the neighbors we've hosted for tea parties and open houses.

A couple of years ago in Colorado, we decided to hold a Christmas open house for our neighbors. This tradition had been passed down from my mother and father. Our children designed and printed the invitations. Then came the fun trek around the neighborhood to stuff the mailboxes with our cards, hoping for a positive response. Each child helped clean and decorate the rooms, make cookies and chili con queso (also traditional), heat the hot apple cider with cinnamon candies for flavor, light the candles throughout the house, and load the CD player with Christmas music.

Always before such get-togethers, we pray for those who will attend our party and review what behavior is expected from each child. When our children were young, we reminded them to greet our guests with friendliness and courtesy. "Serve the guests first, and be sure to direct all of the kids to a fun activity. Be sure no one is left out!"

On this particular occasion, fifty people showed up! Our children were amazed. They all giggled in the kitchen as neighbor after neighbor brought us more and more of the same poinsettias and cookies that were on special at the local grocery store. Many of the neighbors told us that they had lived in the area for fifteen years and had never met their other neighbors.

After our party, the children chattered excitedly about whom they had met. This began a campaign of praying for the families now that we had faces to go with their names. We have not always been fruitful in our attempts to reach out to our neighbors, but that night of hospitality opened doors for meeting needs and building friendships.

Opening our home to missionaries has given us another opportunity to teach hospitality as well as give our children a firsthand glimpse of ministries in other countries and the needs of people in another part of the world. Hosting international students studying at local universities has broadened our children's understanding of other cultures. Developing these relationships provides a perfect opportunity for our family to reach another person by sharing Christ with the students who will one day return to their countries. Hosting Christmas teas and mother-daughter teas and serving guests for our Mom's Night Out evenings has also given them practice in serving others.

As our children have learned to serve in our home, I have watched their confidence grow. They know what to do to make others feel loved and cared for, and they feel good about their ability to reach out in love. As a bonus, by serving others in our home, our children have learned to serve us. They have even surprised Clay and me from time to time by serving us a candlelight meal in our bedroom or bringing us breakfast in bed on Mother's Day and Father's Day!

Teaching our children to serve by extending hospitality to others has been a deeply satisfying experience for our entire family. At times, however, our home has been out of control because of too many people visiting, and I've been reminded of the need for wisdom and balance in this area. Because we have often lived in areas that attract tourists, our commitment to hospitality has occasionally taxed our children's patience. I have seen them weary of giving up their bedrooms, changing beds and washing sheets, helping cook for crowds, and baby-sitting young visitors. Two different summers we hosted more than sixty overnight guests in a three-month period.

I learned that when I allow serving others to destroy my family's routines, I can easily lose the point of training my children to love ministry. Staying exhausted for too long not only makes for a grumpy mother and grumpy children but also can sour the children on the idea of service. It is up to me as a mother to find a balance between reaching out to others and raising children who think of hospitality as a privilege.

SERVING THROUGH SEEING AND HELPING

Matthew 9:35-36 gives me a picture of Jesus' heart motivation for ministry that I hope to pass on to my children::

Jesus was going about all the cities and the villages, teaching in their syna-
gogues, and proclaiming the gospel of the kingdom, and healing every
kind of disease and every kind of sickness. And seeing the multitudes, He
felt compassion for them, because they were distressed and downcast like
sheep without a shepherd.

This passage tells me that children must learn to see people as Jesus did and
feel as he felt. Instead of seeing the multitude and seeing them with disdain and
scorn—or as an overwhelming drain on his time—Jesus felt compassion for
them.

Selfishness and self-absorption seem to be the most natural expression of sin
in our family. We can be pretty harsh in judging other people's immoral behavior and lifestyles. We also tend to want the best for our family and let others fend
for themselves.

Yet Jesus saw the crowds as they really were. He saw their need for leadership, protection, healing, and nurture, and he responded by reaching out to
them in love and by doing what he could. This is the way we need to teach our
children to serve. They need to see as Jesus saw and then reach out to others in
compassion, as he did.

The home is a natural place to teach such habits of seeing and serving.
Encouraging a small child to take a cold drink to Dad when he is mowing the
lawn on a hot day is helping to establish a pattern of thinking about the needs of
others and responding. Writing encouraging cards or notes for a child who is sick
models the kind of thoughtfulness and caring that can open hearts to Christ.

To make this a lifetime habit, I have encouraged my children to reach out
to each other since they were quite young. Older children are asked to read to
younger children or play a game with them from time to time. Helping a sibling do his chores or fix his bike or button his coat is a small way to practice for
helping those in need—or being a good parent someday.

In addition to helping each other, though, children need to be taught that
reaching out to others beyond the family is important too. Noticing the needs
of others and serving them is not natural to sinful people. It is a habit that comes
with training and modeling. At the same time, I've learned a lot from my children's generosity of heart and eagerness to help others. Yes, they can be incredi-
bly self-centered, but their eyes and hearts can also be more open than mine, and

they tend to be less hampered by the kinds of questions that plague adults, such as who deserves help, what kind of help is appropriate, or how motives might be construed. Even as I teach them, I find that they help me to grow and stretch toward being the kind of compassionate server I want to be.

Life presents all of us with daily opportunities to reach out to others, and the more we respond to these opportunities, the more we all learn about serving others. Our children need to see us reaching out in love, and they need to be included in our acts of service. Taking meals to families when someone is sick or in the hospital is a constant need for those in our church. Making plates of cookies with notes of encouragement or appreciation is a favorite tradition of our family. Helping another family pack for moving or cleaning someone's home gives my children a look at the real-life needs of others.

Giving money and possessions is another habit that is developed through teaching and modeling. When Sarah was very small, Clay and I were asked to teach and sing in a homeless shelter. We took our two little ones with us to share a meal with the precious residents of the shelter. Sarah looked wide-eyed at the many weary adults we met. She asked, "Why do all of these people have to live in big rooms together? I would think that they would rather be home in their own beds!" When we explained that none of these people had enough money to have their own home, she got big tears in her eyes and said, "Then I think we should help them buy their own homes!" When we returned home, she emptied her piggy bank (eighty-seven cents) and asked me to send it to the director of the shelter. I sent her investment along with a letter to the man in charge. A week later Sarah received a personal note from the director as well as a receipt for her donation. He thoughtfully expressed that because of generous people like herself, many people were able to have "full tummies" and could go to bed in a comfortable, safe place without worry.

This experience made a lasting impression on Sarah and was the beginning of her understanding that she had the ability to use her life and resources to help others. Her offerings have seemed like a small thing to many people, but I believe it was the important first step that started Sarah on the road to becoming a generous, unselfish person.

Allowing children to have their own money to give and to have a say in how the family money is spent gives them a vital sense of their own ability to help. At times, when we have extra money because of a speaking engagement or new book contract, we have a family meeting and allow our children to help us decide where to give a tithe of the money. Donating to an orphanage in Romania was a choice that seemed important to one of our children. Supporting a Christian relief organization in Afghanistan seemed a timely contribution to another child. Giving to a beloved missionary was a third choice. Teaching our children to see themselves as people who have a contribution to make to the world comes in the small ways we serve repeatedly in life's dailiness.

SERVICE THROUGH EVANGELISM

Meeting the physical and felt needs of others is a steppingstone to their deepest need, which is to come to a living and abiding relationship with God. The battle of this life from beginning to end is about knowing him and giving him our allegiance. God has designed us to know him intimately and to experience his love, grace, and forgiveness. Through a long history of human sin, God persisted in trying to bring his rebellious people back into communion with him, even to the point of sending his own Son to die, rise from the dead, and redeem us.

Sharing this reality with others is the most important act of stewardship to which we are called. Yet for many of us, modeling this type of service for our children seems to be the most difficult task of all.

When we approach the task of sharing our faith, we often picture a huge task of reaching the whole world for Christ, and this seems too formidable. In reality, though, sharing our faith is often as simple as loving others and gently showing them the source of our love, the Lord Jesus.

About a year ago the board members of our ministry offered to pay for one year of housecleaning help so I would have more time to write. Overjoyed at this wonderful gift, I began trying to find someone who could help me regularly. A team of precious women, sisters-in-law, came my way, and over time we developed a friendship. They got to know my children and saw how we operated in our home. This led to questions about our work and my writing and finally opened the door for heartfelt questions about their relationships with God.

Several weeks ago we had the opportunity to sit down for a cup of tea together, and I explained from the Bible how we can know and experience God's love personally. What a sweet time of fellowship we had as we talked and prayed together.

Later that night Joy, who had listened as we talked, said, "Mommy, I liked it when we got to talk to our friends about Jesus. That was nice. Maybe I'll get to do that someday."

This experience came to me in the normal routine of my home life. Such opportunities to witness do not happen often, but when the Lord presents an opportunity, I try to be ready. The chance to get to know these women and to share my heart happened over a long period of time as we developed a relationship.

Outreach in our home has also been expressed in a variety of other ways. We have hosted Bible studies—church-based groups as well as gatherings for moms, mothers and daughters, fathers and sons, neighborhood groups, and groups for kids. Some years we have a variety of groups meeting in our family room; other years we have had no groups at all. Yet whenever we have opened our home, our children have seen us share with others, be involved with their lives, and pray for them.

We have exposed our children to larger outreaches as well. Clay became a believer through the ministry of Andre Cole, a Christian illusionist, and has recounted the story of his conversion many times. Consequently, Nathan has gotten quite interested in "Gospel Magic." He began with a few small illusions and then proceeded to sharing his skills at birthday parties, our moms' conferences, and churches.

In the midst of praying for God to open up opportunities for Nathan's life, Clay found out that Andre Cole was coming to our city for an evangelistic outreach. Clay immediately called to offer his help and our boys' help with this effort. Before long they were praying for those who would attend the meetings, taking tickets, and ushering at the event.

Our children were involved in the whole outreach from beginning to end—and what a wonderful learning experience that was for them. It was one thing to tell them that God wants us to reach the world with his message. It is so much more effective to give them an opportunity to contribute their time and energy alongside us in real-life ministry. Such experiences have helped put the spark in their lives that has motivated them to view themselves as part of a team who will tell others all over the world about Christ.

Serving Wisely

Anyone who has seriously undertaken a life of service to others quickly learns that though giving can be deeply fulfilling, it can also be frustrating. The people we give to are not always grateful or even friendly. Sometimes they may take advantage of us. Reaching out to others can bring us ridicule or rejection, and trying to meet too many needs on our own power can cause us to feel overwhelmed—as our family came to feel during the summer of too much hospitality.

Even as we involve our children in love and service, we need to prepare them for times when service brings painful consequences. We need to teach them how to love wisely and count the cost. Most important, we need to help them understand *why* we are reaching out in the first place—and the vital importance of an active dependence on God in all we try to do.

Simply put, if we serve others because we expect to be rewarded with warm feelings or the praise of others, we will eventually be disappointed and perhaps turn bitter and cynical. If we try to serve on our own power, we will inevitably run out of steam or let our sinful motives sully our efforts. If we focus on following Jesus, however, in loving people as he loved and loving others *because he loved us,* we will find a buffer for our disappointment. And if we give out of obedience to him and in dependence on the Holy Spirit, we will be both empowered and sustained.

We give to others because that's the kind of people we want to be—obedient, loving people. We give because God first reached out to us with his love, and it is our privilege to give to others from that love. It helps to point out that we can't really know the ultimate outcome of our efforts; we have to trust God for that. We may think we have failed to help someone, when we've actually planted a seed that God will bring to fruition later.

It is always a good idea, of course, to help our children exercise good judgment as to *how* we serve. If we choose as a family to give money to a charity, it makes sense to research it to be sure the money we give will actually reach the needy. If I am alone in a car with my children and spot a homeless person on the roadside, it might be wiser to bring him food or give him money instead of giving him a ride. Perhaps we might offer food or clothing or even furniture instead of money to someone in need if we suspect that person might have trouble handling the cash.

Ultimately, though, I believe we will be judged more by our compassion and our willingness to give than by our caution and circumspection. Sometimes we have to risk being exploited or having our service misused as we obey Christ in reaching out and trust him for the outcome. This is something we have tried to teach our children and to model for them. I would rather my children see me err in giving too much than to let caution be an excuse for callousness. But I also want them to know *why* I make the choices I do. Most important, I want them to be intimately acquainted with the person who motivates all my attempts at service and outreach.

OUR GREATEST CHALLENGE

As his disciples were congregated on a mountain in Galilee after his resurrection, Jesus gave them the instruction that has historically been called the Great Commission. He instructed them in this way:

> All authority has been given to Me in heaven and on earth. Go therefore
> and make disciples of all the nations, baptizing them in the name of the
> Father and the Son and the Holy Spirit, teaching them to observe all that
> I commanded you; and lo, I am with you always, even to the end of the
> age. (Matthew 28:18-20)

That should be so easy to do! Those of us who have had the great privilege of knowing the Lord Jesus personally, of experiencing his generous love and acceptance in our own lives, and of knowing his forgiveness for all our short-comings and deeds of unrighteousness know what it is like to have true peace and a sense of centeredness. How natural it should be for us to want to share this wonderful God with others!

Though it should be something that we do naturally and enthusiastically, the sin nature in our lives causes us often to shy away from doing so.

In Matthew 9:37 we read, "The harvest is plentiful, but the workers are few." I have often wondered why this is so. Why, if someone really knows the Creator of the universe as his personal Father, would he not willingly and thankfully let as many as possible know of him? As I have pondered this question, I have come up with a few answers (as well as more questions).

What if God intended his love and purposes to be passed down from one generation to another through the intimacy of a mother to a son or daughter or a father to his little boy or girl? Such a transmission of truth would be natural in the context of a comfortable relationship. As a parent walked hand in hand on a mountain trail and observed the patterns on a moth or the multicolored stripes of a rock formation, it would be natural to talk about the wonders of God.

As a little one rests in bed and tearfully expresses guilt and sorrow about a lie that was told, the cost of the payment for our sin and the beauty of redemption and forgiveness would be easily discussed with a heart that is open. In this context, sharing our faith seems something that each of us would do. Making disciples of my children is certainly part of my view of the mission of motherhood.

I also want to pass on a legacy of outreach to my children. I was convicted by the Lord when I was a young believer that, to follow Christ and to be close to him, I needed to adopt his heart for redeeming the world. As a young woman, I was fortunate enough to become involved in the ministry of Campus Crusade for Christ. Through that staff, I received excellent training in how to give a personal testimony and share my faith.

When the Lord brings people across our path who show a spiritual hunger or have deep personal needs, Clay and I share Christ with them—and to make sure our children know what we are doing and why. One afternoon, when Sarah was eight years old, she rushed into the house and said, "Mom, you need to help me quickly! I've been playing with the little girl across the street, and we started talking about Jesus. I told her all about how she could know him, and I want to read through one of those little books with her to explain it all!"

Sarah had seen us use some Four Spiritual Laws booklets as we shared Christ with others, but we didn't know she was paying attention. She took one of the booklets across the street to her friend's house and read through it with her. And the little girl told Sarah she wanted to believe in Jesus and know him personally! The two prayed together that afternoon. We were amazed that the Lord used our little one to lead someone to himself when we had never formally taught her how to do it.

As our children matured, we realized that as we sent them into life from our home, we wanted them to sense that God had a purpose for their lives. We used to say to them, "I wonder what your major in college should be? I wonder how you will make money to support your family?" In the past few years, however, we have begun to speak to them in different terms. We have told them that someday they will have to give an account for the privilege of knowing Christ and understanding about his kingdom. These days we say to our children, "I wonder in what way God would have you invest your life for his glory? How can you use your gifts and strengths to bring others to him or to further his kingdom's influence on this earth?" Then we discuss these issues.

This does not mean we think all our children should go into full-time Christian work. We simply believe that *all* believers—our children included—should use their lives, homes, families, and professions as platforms for sharing Christ with others and living out his purposes. A child may go into politics and become a moral and godly leader or become a nurse or doctor to help those who are ill or suffering. But whatever our children choose to do with their lives, we want them to understand that they were "bought with a price," that God has prepared "works" for them to do, and that they, like the disciples, can be a part of the amazing things that God is doing in the world.

I know that God will hold me accountable for the treasure of life that I hold in my hands—the hearts and souls of my children. It is immensely important, then, that I pass on this legacy to my children of seeking to follow this Great Commission. Jesus intended that one of the greatest gifts we could give our children was the baton of eternal life, to be passed on from one generation to the next. Surely, then, helping our children develop a heart for God and his kingdom work must be my fundamental priority as a mother. The specific ways in which we train our children to reach out to others—whether we teach them to give a "cup of cold water" to the homeless or urge them to become missionaries to a foreign country—make little difference. It is in discovering what it means to be part of God's redeeming work in the world that will excite our children's heart to meet the needs of others. By giving them tracks upon which to run as they learn to reach out to others, we are also helping them to build bridges of love back to their own hearts. We help them receive love by learning to give it to others. The gift of service to others is a gift of training we give our children that will serve them endlessly the rest of their lives as they are caught up in bringing God's redemptive love to the world.

For Thought and Reflection

Something to Think About...

As a young single missionary in Vienna, I felt inadequate to reach out to people. I couldn't speak German except to ask, "Do you speak English?" and a few other survival phrases. At Christmas, when one of my friends said that she would be hosting a Christmas tea and planned to share Christ in story form at the end of the tea, I thought of a young girl who was a nanny for some friends of mine. She spoke a little more English than I spoke German, but our communication was limited.

Still, I took her as my guest to the tea, where my friend shared her story. As soon as our party was over, my young guest hurried out the door saying that she was late for an appointment. I assumed she was not interested in our message and didn't give it much thought.

About six weeks later, however, she called and asked if we could get together. We met for coffee. "What I heard at your party," she told me in her halting English, "was what I was longing to know all of my life. I went home and started to read the Bible. Is that a good thing to do? Can you tell me more?"

I was surprised that it had taken so little to lead her to the Lord. But I learned once more that it is not our effort or expertise that the Lord needs for us to minister to people—or to teach our children to love and serve others. All he needs from us is a faithful and willing heart. He'll do the rest.

1. *Matthew 28:18-20.* What does it mean to make disciples of Christ? What is the difference between just leading people to Christ and making them disciples? How do we apply this to raising children?

2. *Matthew 9:36-38.* When Jesus saw the multitudes, what did he feel for them? What needs did he see? How does this passage apply to people today? Why is the harvest of people plentiful and the workers few? What are some specific ways you can help cultivate a heart of compassion in your children?

3. *Matthew 25:34-46.* What is the essence of this passage? How does our service to others reveal our understanding of what it means to follow Christ? How do we pass this aspect of service on to our children? Are there people in your life right now who need the love and service your family has to give? Perhaps a friend of your children is in need of your compassion.

4. *Romans 12:9-21.* These verses give a basic overview of how Christians are to treat others. What are some specific tasks that we are called to accomplish? What specific challenges could you give to your children to give them practice in these areas.

Something to Try...

"Mommy, you would be so proud of me! I just helped Nathan and Joel clean up the den, and I didn't even get mad when they told me what to do!"

"What do you mean, Joy?"

"Well, you know we have that tape where Steve Green says to do everything without complaining? For some reason that came to my mind when I was with the boys, so I decided not to complain!"

I have been amazed over the years at how Scripture memory exercises (such as the Steve Green Bible tape) have helped my children apply biblical concepts. When we help our children learn Scripture, we are opening up channels for the Holy Spirit to speak directly to their hearts and to teach them the ways of the Lord.

- Memorize Romans 12:9-18 with your children.
- Help your children bake cookies (or homemade bread or another treat) and deliver them with "I appreciate you!" notes to five people whom the Lord brings to your mind.
- Host a neighborhood picnic in the summer or a holiday open house at Christmas. Prepare your children to see this as an opportunity to reach out to neighbors in order to minister to them. Begin praying for the families who respond. Seek opportunities to reach out to them as a family, and look for opportunities to share Christ with them.

❧ Adopt a foreign exchange student through International Students, Inc., or find out if the college in your town provides such a program. Seek first to help and befriend this student, and watch for opportunities to share Christ with him or her as well.

❧ Try this! We used to eat oatmeal one evening each week to symbolize to our children the poverty level of many children in the world. We would put the money we saved from not having a big meal (five dollars) into a money jar. We would also throw our extra change into it. When it reached fifty dollars, we would decide as a family where to send the donation—usually to a missionary or nonprofit group who served in underprivileged nations.

PART FIVE

A MOTHER'S HEART *for* ETERNITY

CHAPTER 12

The Faithful Mother

Finishing the Journey with Endurance and Grace

Therefore, do not throw away your
confidence, which has a great reward.
For you have need of endurance,
so that when you have done the will of God,
you may receive what was promised.

HEBREWS 10:35-36

As I rested on the warm brown sand, my back against the small hill, I had a perfect view of all that was dear to me. It was a golden moment that I knew would quickly pass and might never come again, so I painted a picture of it in my mind to store away for future times when I would need it to comfort me.

Sarah was running gently toward the almost-bashful incoming tide, her long, light brown hair shining in the sun. She was splashing as she went like a child in full delight, so happy to be in the actual place of her storybooks. Joel and Nathan laughed and shouted at each other as they waded in ankle-deep, crystal-clear, blue gray water, searching for flat, rounded stones to skip over the water. Little Joy diligently carved in the wet sand with her large white shell to see what impressions she could leave that would outlive the wash of the tide. Clay walked gingerly along the shore, collecting polished stones. When we got home, we'd put the stones in a glass bowl as a memento of this cherished time in a place we'd long dreamed of visiting.

For many years our family loved the *Anne of Green Gables* movie series, based on Lucy Maud Montgomery's books. We made an event of watching these films each autumn as the leaves began to turn color and drift to the ground. Snacks in hand, drinks poured, we'd watch with rapt attention as the story of red-haired

Anne and her adopted family unfolded on the screen once more. Following on the heels of Anne's story was the *Road to Avonlea* series, with a lovely home setting, laughing children, involved adults, and sweet stories that all turned out well in the end.

"Maybe someday we can visit Prince Edward Island to see the Anne of Green Gables house and visit the real homesites of Lucy Maud Montgomery," Sarah had said hopefully one day. "I wish I could see the Lake of Shining Waters," Joel chimed in. "I want to see the woods where all of the children walked and played," added Nathan.

As soon as we checked into airline prices, however, we realized that such a trip was far out of our reach. So the children continued to hope and pray for the fulfillment of their desires. For years they prayed sincere, innocent prayers with faith-filled expectation: "Dear Lord, if it is your will, please let us someday go to Prince Edward Island. Help Mom and Dad to get to speak up there so we can afford to go. Thank you, Lord. Amen."

"Just keep praying!" was my constant reply when they asked me about it. And finally it happened. Clay and I were asked to speak at a regional conference for parents in Saint John, New Brunswick. Even though our schedules were booked, I asked Clay, "How can we refuse a conference that the children have been praying about for so long?"

The rest, as they say, was history. Now we were actually playing on the shores where Lucy Maud Montgomery had lived and grown up, storing up the heart memories that would play a part in her enduring stories. And as I sat there enjoying the scene, I found myself pondering questions I had often asked before: What has drawn us so strongly to these books and to these shows? Why have these themes sustained our interest for so long?

I believe it is the clear picture they present of a redemptive family where love and forgiveness are given in the midst of petty failures and frequent mistakes, where home is a secure haven in which to be comforted, encouraged, inspired, and trained. Montgomery's beloved stories depict qualities of family love and community life that we all long for—a longing placed by God in the depths of our heart—but so seldom seen today. They reflect tender relationships between ordinary adults and children, relationships in which both adults and children are honored, and respect is the backbone that holds them together. And they reflect for us a hope of what we might become as a family.

In a way these stories reflect my vision for what I was attempting to build in my family—a family that is close and loyal, loving and living together while building a godly heritage that would be strong for generations. Though the Montgomery books are not explicitly biblical, the close family life they depict was exactly what Clay and I wanted in our home. We added biblical training and a Christian world-view to the mix and sought to create an old-fashioned family life and love.

As I pondered these thoughts, I was drawn back to the picture before me. How blessed I was to see that the kind of family I had dreamed of was indeed, by God's grace, standing before me. Yet it had been years in the making, and the process had been fraught with challenges every step of the way. Like my children who faithfully prayed and waited for their dream trip, I had spent years praying and faithfully working to live out the dream that was in my heart. Like them, too, I had wondered if my dream would ever come to reality. But now I could see that, like our Prince Edward Island vacation, it, too, was really happening.

For one thing, I could see that we were a close family who mutually shared values, a love of the Lord, a close and loving relationship, and a desire to spend our lives together, serving the Lord and building his kingdom on earth through the stewardship of our lives. The dream Clay and I had of a shared family life had been communicated to our children over and over in the course of our daily lives. Now we were seeing the fruit of this training in our family loyalty and a real sense of who we are as "the Clarksons." My children were delighted to have their mom and dad playing with them on the shore. They viewed us as partners and sustainers of their own lives, and this gave me a sense of great joy.

I could see, too, how our marriage had weathered many storms as we had held on (sometimes with white knuckles!) to standards of unconditional love and commitment, grace and forgiveness through the difficult times. Through the stresses of our sixteen moves (six international ones), periodic financial difficulties, frequent job changes, the inevitable pressures of ministry, and long hours of work, we kept building our relationship. The personality differences and preferences that hammered at our emotional core had taken their toll, but time and commitment had molded us into more mature, patient marriage partners. Even during those years when I was at home alone with small, sick babies and Clay had to work far too many hours, we somehow held on. We had made a "forever" commitment at the altar—"for better or for worse." This promise before God had kept us going in our dark times and rewarded us when we tasted the fruit that unconditional love and patience can build. We were determined to build together a godly heritage that would pass on righteousness to the next generation.

Now, much older and more experienced, I'd found it a deeply fulfilling blessing to learn to partner with my sweet husband and to realize we had indeed built what we always hoped to build. There is an inherent reward in perseverance—the knowledge that when we were tempted to quit, we still chose the path of obedience. This knowledge brought me peace.

I reflected on the sweet and enthusiastic relationships my children shared. Sarah, who was beginning to fly with her own wings, was still committed to nurturing and encouraging her brothers into young manhood—this in spite of the years of putting up with their rude and loud boy noises and comments. She had learned to laugh at their humor (at least most of the time). She had made it through the extremes of hormones, the dark loneliness of many years without a close friend, the pressures and responsibilities that are inherent in being a first child in a large family. Though graduated from high school and in the process of seeing her first book published, here she was, playing in the ocean as innocently as a child and enjoying it to the depths of her soul.

Joel and Nathan, though extreme opposites, were learning to share life-giving comments with each other instead of constantly quibbling. Loyalty and graciousness were taking root bit by bit in their lives as they pushed through each challenging day toward maturity. Diligent work habits were slowly replacing laziness, and their hearts for God and his Word were beginning to bloom.

Seeing my young men beginning to develop their own skills and personalities was a special pleasure. My gentle Joel had become a talented and skillful acoustic guitarist with a wonderful dry wit. He was the one we called on to fix the computer or order an airline ticket. Nathan, our extroverted comedian, had become a practiced Christian illusionist and dreamed of performing before thousands. And he, who is generous with his affection, would occasionally bring me and his sisters a card with a long-stemmed rose. (So they were paying attention to me after all!)

Joy just continued to be like her name—a source of constant joy. She was learning to read and ride a bike and was delighted at the many worlds that were opening up to an enthusiastic six-year-old. She was thrilled to be splashing in the freezing water without fear.

I reflected on my years of performing the endless mundane tasks of motherhood—picking up mountains of socks, supervising numberless naps, and cooking thousands of meals of which only a portion were appreciated. I had wondered if my children would ever eat vegetables and actually like the whole-grain breads that Clay and I preferred. Now there was a sense of "Mom, you are such a good cook! I love our pizzas and homemade bread and soups! (But please don't serve spinach or okra too often.)"

There had been hours of constantly settling fusses over petty issues, continually straightening our home, only to have it messy within a short time. There had been myriad books read, lessons supervised—and still feeling inadequate to do it all. Inadequacy, in fact, had been my familiar and constant companion, overcome only by "His strength is perfected in my weakness" choices of faith. I had had so many moments when I doubted that anything was being built into the hearts of my children, when my belief that all of this mattered for eternity was all that kept me going, one step at a time. Now I was seeing that every ordinary act of faithfulness really had mattered greatly and had shaped our children into wholesome, interesting, thinking people.

Now I can see clearly just how worthwhile the journey has been. The reward of a shared sense of humor and the pure enjoyment and love of being together shows me how glad I am that I held tight to my vision. These children, now towering over me in their grown-up bodies, are just the kind of people I want for friends. Indeed, I consider my family to be my very best friends. How thankful I am that God, his Word, and his Spirit kept me pressing faithfully onward. God, my precious Father, has himself been my guide and friend as I struggled forward. I have sensed his patience as I have needed to grow, his love and grace when I have failed, his instruction when I needed to learn how to build in reality what he has placed in my heart to do. Simple passages from his Word have given me pathways upon which to walk forward in my journey toward biblical motherhood.

As I look around me, though, I see so many other precious moms floundering and tempted to give up. I see moms who struggle, as I struggled, with a sense of inadequacy and failure. Many are lonely, feeling unsupported by their families and their communities as they work to give their children what they need. Many are confused, questioning the choices they have made and worrying about the factors in their life they can't control. And many are simply tired, running low on the energy they need to be the mothers they truly want to be.

For all these mothers and for those who have yet to encounter moments of discouragement, I want to share a little of what—besides the grace of God—has helped me to continue on this worthwhile journey.

AN INSPIRING VISION

The truth is, parenting can be hard. We parents are to be shepherds watching over our children's lives—guiding, protecting, and determining what is best for them. And sometimes it seems that wolves are waiting at each turn in the path to woo our children into their clutches. Diligent parents must confront these wolves again and again, and sometimes we must do battle for our children's souls. Establishing a godly heritage will come at a great cost.

Those who are able to maintain this vigil and avoid the strong clutches of ungodliness are those who have a clear vision—a well-defined picture of what God has designed the family to be. The mission of motherhood becomes clearer through each battle won as we walk with our Lord. Our vision gives us the ideal we pursue. It defines the decisions we make, the priorities we keep.

When I was a young single missionary living in Austria, one of my favorite retreats was a village in the lake district in the Austrian Alps. Hallstatt is a thousand-year-old town tucked between a towering mountainside and a deep lake. To get there, I had to take a train from Vienna. I would step off the train onto a small platform standing all by itself on the *other* side of the lake, then walk a few steps to a dock where a boat would take me the rest of the way to Hall-statt. As I stood at the back of the tiny boat, with the soft spray of the lake blowing in my face, I always noticed the remains of a small rock castle built on the side of the mountain.

One weekend I had taken my mother and a friend to visit this favorite retreat. We dined on a lovely deck outside our quaint hotel, which fronted the water, then retired to our rooms. Within an hour, however, a ferocious storm engulfed the whole area. The electricity in the town suddenly went off. We looked out our third-story windows and saw, in the darkness, that the deck where we had recently eaten was now flooded with violent, tossing waves.

As we peered fearfully across the lake, everything seemed to be moving side-ways and up and down. The high winds were blowing the torrents of rain side-ways, the trees were bent over, and everything seemed to be caught up in the violence of the storm. An enormous flash of lightning illuminated the black sky. And suddenly I saw the outline of the stone castle, standing constant amid a storm that was shaking everything else to its core.

I have never forgotten the sense of strength and solidity I felt, gazing at that old structure that had not been daunted by centuries of such storms. It has become to me a picture of what God has created a home to be.

Though cultural storms attack violently each day, a solid Christian home can be a protective fortress, a haven of peace for all who live there. Those inside its walls are protected, nurtured, and nourished in body, heart, mind, and soul. Such homes need a director, guardian, and caretaker, which is what God had in mind when he designed the role of mother. Homes that are being established and protected by the mothers who have a clear vision of their God-designed role can bring refuge and life and hope to a generation of children who need to grow strong in order to be able to battle the storms they will one day face.

In my own life, I know that what kept me going through thick and thin (besides God's grace) was this clear picture in my heart of what I wanted to attain. I nurtured this vision in my heart. I read books that undergirded it. I prayed through Scripture that encouraged me in my conviction. Whenever possible, I shared it with others, and I found that the act of passing along my vision helped solidify it in my heart. Most important, I constantly visited my vision for motherhood in times of discouragement and doubt. I prayed that the Lord would keep it fresh in my heart, and he honored that prayer. On so many occasions, it was what carried me through.

A PERSEVERING FAITH

And yet I have learned that a vision in itself is not enough to keep me going through the hard times. What I've also needed is good, old-fashioned perseverance—a deep, unwavering commitment to stay the course and not give up.

A few months ago, shortly before giving my final message at a Whole-Hearted Mother conference, I was walking down a hotel hallway toward my room. A woman with red, swollen, tear-filled eyes grabbed my arm and begged me to spend just a couple of minutes with her.

She said, "You know, when I started out this race of motherhood, I was committed to the ideals that you were talking about. But over the years I became worn down by the responsibility of my children and all the pressures that seemed to call them away from me. I began to make one little compromise after another. I let my children do some things that were against my desires. I allowed them to become too attached to the values of their peers. I didn't take the personal time that they needed from me to talk and to pray, didn't make the necessary effort to discipline them and to play with them. Now my oldest daughter has run away from home. I have lost her. Please tell others my story so that they will not make the same mistakes I did. I hope it is not too late to redeem my relationship with my other children, who are still at home."

The woman put her finger on this character quality we mothers need so desperately—this quality of persevering in faith.

I have observed that many women start off well, with strong convictions and high dreams and ideals, but when they get into the trenches, they give up. Perhaps when each of us sees our inadequacies, we are tempted to give up and doubt our abilities to withstand the strong cultural forces and still exert influence over our children as mothers. Many moms eventually relinquish the authority that God designed them to have and the responsibility of raising their children to others—the teachers at school, the church youth group and its leaders, or even the children's peers.

But while people can certainly be a blessing to our children, enriching their lives, God has given the stewardship of children's lives to parents, not to institutions or even the church. Our relationship with our children is the one he desires to use to help train them for their life's work. Deep inside, children know that. God has preordained that they want the love and approval of their own parents most of all.

But this task of stewarding children's lives is not a short-term process. There is no quick list of rules that can be followed in one short year that will ensure success. The mission of motherhood requires grit. It requires perseverance. And that often means years of repetitive and mundane tasks, years of repeating yourself, years of wondering whether anything you do or say makes a difference. "Clean up your room!" "Please talk to your sister kindly!" "No, I'm sorry. Just because everyone else is doing it—that doesn't mean we can do it!"

Hebrews 10:35-39 is a passage that has been an anchor to my soul as I faced this need to stay the course in my journey of motherhood.

Therefore, do not throw away your confidence, which has a great reward. For you have need of endurance, so that when you have done the will of God, you may receive what was promised. For yet in a very little while, He who is coming will come, and will not delay. But My righteous one shall live by faith; and if he shrinks back, My soul has no pleasure in him. But we are not of those who shrink back to destruction, but of those who have faith to the preserving of the soul.

Where do we get this kind of endurance? To me, just understanding that it's part of the job of motherhood has helped. Plain old stubbornness has probably helped as well. I don't like to fail, so I keep on trying. In the long run, though, I think the only thing that will give us sufficient strength to persevere is an enduring faith.

We must choose to believe that God himself will eventually reward our choices and efforts to raise a godly heritage for his glory. It is for him and his purposes that we must endure, trusting that he who promised is faithful. Being godly parents is no guarantee that our children will choose to respond to all that we have taught them. Yet trusting God's timing, submitting to his design, and obeying his Word are always the right biblical choices for us to make.

Hebrews 11:1 reminds us that "faith is the assurance of things hoped for, the conviction of things not seen." I have to trust that though I am constantly confronted by my children's immaturity or lack of responsibility or foolishness (or hampered by my own shortcomings), the seeds of my training and my years of watering with love, faith, and prayers will indeed someday mature the fruit of a godly character. I must choose to believe that it matters that I am choosing to be with my children and slowly build their character instead of pursuing a full-time career where the results of my labor may be more immediately tangible.

Hebrews 11:6 goes on to say that "without faith it is impossible to please [God], for he who comes to God must believe that He is, and that He is a rewarder of those who seek Him." My hope is in the unchanging character of God—that indeed he will reward my faith efforts to obey him, trusting that his way is indeed the best way. His Spirit will accomplish what concerns me and my children. He himself will build both them and me into all we need to know and be.

A Tenacious Trust—and a Willingness to Fight!

There have been times in my life as a mother when I didn't feel like I could bear one more day of messes, fusses, and all the needs that threatened to engulf me. There would be times when I was dealing with a habit or a sin or an attitude of one of my children, and I would feel like a total failure. I'd think, *I'm making a wreck of this child. I'm failing as a parent. What if this child rejects the Lord? Grows up to be a failure? Stays as selfish as this? What if I am misleading all of these moms in encouraging them to sacrifice many of their own goals for the sake of mothering? Who am I to tell them all these things?* I would be overcome by my feelings of inadequacy, failure, fear of the future and what it holds for my children.

My only choice in these times when I reached the bottom of my heart was to do again what I had practiced so many times—to keep trusting the Master and Lord of my life. And as I poured out my heart—my fears, my inadequacies, my weariness, my concerns about my children, and my own lack of love for some of my own family members—I found solace for my soul and strength for my heart. The Lord would encourage me to trust him, to wait on him and give him time to work, to hold on to his promises, to not compromise my convictions, and most important, to persist in my love and my prayers for the little ones he entrusted to my care.

Before Jesus was crucified, he told Simon Peter that he (Peter) would turn his back on him: "Simon, Simon, behold, Satan has demanded permission to sift you like wheat; but I have prayed for you, that your faith may not fail; and you, when once you have turned again, strengthen your brothers" (Luke 22:31-32).

Throughout Scripture we see that Satan continually seeks to destroy that which is precious to God. He came to Eve in the garden. He tried to destroy the faith of Job. He even tempted Jesus. Now, at the end of Jesus' life on earth, Satan was seeking to subvert the man Jesus had chosen to be the leader of the disciples. Yet Jesus' response was that he had prayed for Peter and that after Peter had failed and repented, he would once again turn back to Christ and strengthen the other disciples!

Jesus also prayed specifically for all of his disciples the night before he died: "I do not ask Thee to take them out of the world, but to keep them from the evil one" (John 17:15).

We need to recognize that Satan seeks to destroy our children's desire to walk with God. Peter himself, after having experienced years of spiritual battle, described Satan as a ravenous wild beast: "Your adversary, the devil, prowls about like a roaring lion, seeking someone to devour. But resist him, firm in your faith, knowing that the same experiences of suffering are being accomplished by your brethren who are in the world" (1 Peter 5:8-9).

When we understand Satan's plan to steal what belongs to God, we can recognize that one of our greatest tasks in regard to our children is to be a spiritual warrior for their souls. Soldiers must be aware of the battle and prepared to fight with adequate weapons in order to win. We are equipped with God's Word ("the sword of the Spirit," Ephesians 6:17) and are admonished to pray the same way Jesus prayed for Peter.

Our children will be tempted to stumble. They will be prey to Satan's attacks and his efforts to draw them away from God. No matter how diligent our training, how inviting our home, how deep our wisdom, our children will be tempted and must learn to develop their own faith. Yet, as mothers, with God's strength and companionship, we can be champions for their souls and walk with them through their times of temptation and struggle. We can support them in prayer, encourage them through the Word, and love them as Christ loved Peter and the other disciples.

I am so glad that, by God's grace, I didn't give up when times were difficult and I was tempted to look for other solutions besides the Lord. As we were walking together one day, Sarah said, "Mom, something has just clicked in my heart! I feel that I've been given so much and have been so blessed in my family. I have this burning desire to help other young women find their way. You won't believe this, Mom, but I'm thankful that you would never let me off the hook and always helped me to see my sin and to bear with me long enough to change my ways. Thanks, Mom! I love you a lot!"

How surprised I was by what she said, and yet how glad I was that somehow God had kept me going through all those difficult years. The fruit of a mature child tasted sweet to my heart and soul.

A LITTLE PERSPECTIVE

In recent years I have learned firsthand that the need for wise mothering doesn't lessen as children grow older. Indeed, having three teenagers in the house has really stretched my mothering muscles. My oldest three are good, fun kids, but they are subject to the same hormonal shifts and growing pains as other kids their age. I never know when one of mine might erupt over a seemingly minor issue. A simple request like "Could you please empty the dishwasher?"—something we have all done thousands of times over the years—might get a dramatic response like, "Everyone in this house eats too much and uses far too many dishes! All we ever do is empty the dishwasher. We should all try fasting for a week!"

My teens also have an opinion about everything and are usually sure that their perspective is right. Each child who has learned to drive, for instance, is sure that he or she knows how to do it better than most of the other people on the road. Their bantering and bickering often rubs against my midlife need for quiet and calm.

What's a mother to do? I am trying to remember that much of the behavior I find so unsettling is simply normal for kids who are growing and changing way too fast to handle everything with grace.

One evening I sighed loudly and slouched onto the couch, hoping someone would notice what a martyr I had been just to get through that stressful day. My six-foot-two older son sat down beside me, draped his long arm around my shoulders, and said, "Lighten up, Mom. We are all okay, and we'll make it just fine. Being loud and aggressive and bantering with you and Dad over any and everything—that's just a guy thing. We just love to joust verbally to show our manly side. We just want you to notice how competent we have become! But underneath, we are still your devoted boys!"

After thinking about his insightful comment, I have relaxed a little and tried to learn to live through yet another growing stage of life. Joel was telling me that I needed to get a little perspective—to step back from the daily grind a little and take a bigger view of what was happening. This, too, is a great help in keeping me going through the years of difficulty and moments of just plain tedium.

Keeping a sense of humor at the forefront has been a must. The more I can laugh at my difficulties, the less power they will have over me. I really think that God made children funny as a gift to help parents survive. There have been so many times when a silly or strangely perceptive comment has been enough to diffuse a tense situation and change my mood from gloomy to encouraged. And learning to laugh at myself—my organizational shortcomings, my midlife mood swings, my little personal quirks—has truly been a godsend, a reminder that, as serious as life and motherhood are, most of my daily ups and downs are not *that* serious. (After all, God is still in charge!)

Enlisting allies in my mission of motherhood has been another way that I have found not only perspective but desperately needed encouragement and support. For many years, wherever I have moved, I have sought to invite other mothers into my home for a Mom's Night Out. These are times we always eat something delectable, relax together, and share our hearts. We might spend a little time in the Word and close in prayer.

Often I would start out one of these evenings being extremely frustrated with my children or housework. Others would share their frustrations too. Even if no one provided solutions to the problems, just sharing what we were experiencing and feeling made us feel better. The companionship of others helped me realize I wasn't the only one facing the challenges of overwhelming housework or stubborn children.

Another very helpful source of perspective and encouragement for me has been the company and advice of a couple of older women. Meeting with them and probing their minds for wisdom and experience helped to give me perspective on my life. I chose women whose lives I respected. Taking the initiative to seek out these women, ask for their help, and meet with them opened the doors for several strong and supportive friendships—and a lot clearer view of how I was doing as a mother.

A final, important source of perspective and encouragement for me over the years has been taking the time to see that my own basic needs are met. I really do want to be a servant to my family. But I've found that a mother whose emotional well is dry cannot continue indefinitely to give to others without cratering. And I've come to believe a mom who takes the time to enjoy life and fill her own heart with the pleasure and joys that God intended us to experience will offer her children hope for their dreams and joy along the way.

Seeking to get enough rest after exhausting periods, talking with friends to commiserate, having a quiet time to myself each day, getting away from all of my responsibilities on a short trip, and reading good books have been my ways of refilling my well and finding refreshment and perspective. I have really made an effort to add fun back into my life along with my many duties. Shopping in antique malls for old treasures, visiting new tearooms, going for long walks daily, or taking French cooking lessons are just a few of the ways I have had my own adventures. As a bonus, I have found that this practice of taking time for personal refreshment has given my children a model for ways that they, too, can find refreshment for their souls.

A SACRED TRUST

It is not perfection that God expects from mothers. There is no perfect personality that does the job best. It is not our background or training or the way we keep house that qualifies us to be godly mothers.

God designed mothers to partner with him in his eternal work, and he has promised to reward our faith and our faithfulness. The precious children he has placed in our hands are hoping that we will be faithful and endure so that they will have a reason to hope and an example to follow in their own lives.

It is for the children's sake that we give our lives. We are protecting future generations that they might be strong for the battle of life. We are the real, in-the-flesh, tangible picture of God's loving hands, strong arms of protection, and encouraging words of hope to our children.

Nathan is my son "in whom there is no guile." He always keeps me on my toes and clearly states what is going on in our family and in my relationship with him. In his honesty, he has always pointed the way for me as a mom. When Nathan was eleven, we were reading a historical book together. As we closed on an exciting chapter about a battle in the Revolutionary War, he looked over at me and said, "You know, Mom, I hope I can be a hero like the one in our story someday. And I think every kid kind of hopes their mom and dad will be heroes for them and will spend time with them so they can have a heritage to be proud of. When I know you believe in me and when you spend time with me, I feel like I might do something great with my life and be a hero too!"

Nathan articulated a desire that I believe is in each child's heart—that their mom and dad will invest the time it takes to be a living hero for them. Each child longs for a heritage in which he can have pride; a home where he can see the faithfulness of God lived out every day; a family in which love is constant, forgiveness and grace hold everyone together, and faith and endurance conquer all obstacles. This is the kind of foundation upon which a child can begin to build the fortress for his own life.

Each of us, as mothers, must continually endeavor to make the right choices so that our children receive such a foundation. Nathan hopes for this, as do Sarah, Joel, Joy, and each of the children whom God has entrusted into your hands. May God's grace sustain us all in this great calling, and may we see eternity changed because of the commitments of our hearts lived out for his glory. May God's strength sustain you as you embrace the heroic mission of motherhood in the days and years ahead.

꧁꧂

FOR THOUGHT AND REFLECTION

Something to Think About...

"I don't understand you!" said one mom as she left the room in which I was speaking. "It sounds like all you ever do in your family is sit around being spiritual and talking about spiritual things! That doesn't sound like much fun for my children!"

Since I try to dress up and appear professional when I speak, people sometimes get the wrong impression about our family. We are all extremely human and display flaws that accompany our humanity. The personalities of my children tend to be extreme—some too loud and crude, some too quiet and timid. We certainly experience the typical ups and downs of normal kids and parents. And we *do* have a lot of fun. And yet I consider all of this sometimes hectic life as intensely spiritual—not because we are particularly holy, but because we are redeemed and live in the joy and grace of God.

In fact, it is because of God's greatness and beauty and design that our family has had so much fun. The memorable times of camping under the stars (though we froze and got wet from an early morning rain), boating on the ocean (two children became seasick and taught us patience), enjoying a wonderful play, watching favorite movies huddled together on our king-sized bed (while fighting over who has the most pillows), and dancing in our living room to a rousing Scottish jig all helped us to celebrate the joys that God has placed in our lives.

It is not only the knowledge of holiness that we must pass on to our children. It is a personal relationship with a God who is far greater, bigger, more adventurous, stronger, and better than anyone I will ever know. He is the source of joy that gives me the strength to keep going during the hard times, the mundane times, the intense times, and the fun times as well.

1. *Hebrews 11:6.* What does this verse say pleases God? What kind of faith does God require in order for us to make it resiliently through motherhood? For what do we have to believe God, and for what reward are we waiting?
2. *1 Peter 5:8-9.* What kind of battle are you up against in seeking to build a godly heritage? Who would love to discourage you in your commitment to biblical motherhood? Who was the first woman he tempted? What were the consequences?
3. *Ephesians 6:10-18.* Whose strength must we use to fight our battles? What specifically does Paul tell us to do to fight the battle well? Look at verse 17. If we have God's Word in our minds, how will we use it to put away all thoughts of inadequacy or guilt?
4. *Hebrews 10:35-39.* According to this passage, what do we need to finish this task well? What does endurance mean? What are the issues of endurance in your own life? Give them to God in prayer and leave these issues in his hands and trust his timing.

Something to Try...

I have a little corner in my room that gives me great pleasure. A small recliner nestles next to the fireplace and a window with a mountain view. A small CD player sits beside me on the floor with a box of my favorite music. An old tea table with a vanilla candle, a coaster for my teacup, and a stack of my favorite books wait for me each afternoon. I almost always take fifteen to thirty minutes out of each day just to be alone and relax with my favorite things—and recharge my spiritual and emotional batteries so I can persevere with the important mission of being a mother. Other favorite refreshers include early morning walks in the mountains, week-long adventure trips to new areas with the kids (no cooking, no cleaning up messes, no phones or e-mails!), lunch or breakfast dates with a friend who loves me, dinners or dates with Clay (no kids allowed on these!), and special days when Clay takes the kids out for the day and leaves me to do whatever I want—eat, sleep, watch a movie—in my own home!

❧ Have a quiet time of reflection and make a plan for refreshing yourself in the next six months. On a sheet of paper, make a list of ten different things you could do in a fifteen-minute period to refresh your spirit (do stretching exercises, enjoy a cup of coffee, weed a section of your garden). On additional sheets, list ten different refreshing activities that require an hour or more (a movie matinee, a long hike, a browsing session in an antique store) and ten possible refreshing activities that take a whole weekend (a car trip to a nearby city, a religious retreat, a getaway with a group of old girlfriends). Use these lists as a resource to schedule your "sanity time"—at least fifteen minutes daily, an hour or two weekly, and a weekend refreshment at least once every six months.

❧ Spend time talking to God and give over all the worries and stresses that you have tried to bear alone. Thank him that "He who began a good work in [your children] will perfect it until the day of Christ Jesus" (Philippians 1:6)!

Resources for Mission-Minded Moms

Many of the following books may be found through our Whole Heart Catalog (available online at www.wholeheart.org or by calling 800-311-2146).

Barnes, Bob. *A Little Book of Manners for Boys.* Eugene, Oreg.: Harvest House, 2000. This book covers the same ground as *A Little Book of Manners* by Emilie Barnes but is specifically targeted to the different needs and tastes of boys. There's nothing "mushy" about this book.

Barnes, Emilie. *A Little Book of Manners: Etiquette for Young Ladies.* Eugene, Oreg.: Harvest House, 1998. Written for girls aged six to ten, told in simple story form, and delightfully illustrated, this book introduces basic good manners, explaining the whys as well as the hows and stressing a loving attitude over simply following rules. (Also look for Emilie Barnes's other delightful Emilie Marie books for girls: *Let's Have a Tea Party, The Very Best Christmas Ever, My Best Friends and Me, Making My Room Special,* and *Cooking Up Fun in the Kitchen.*)

Clarkson, Clay. *Heartfelt Discipline.* Colorado Springs: WaterBrook, 2003. This is not just one more formula for how to discipline your young children but rather a fresh biblical reexamination of what the Bible says about childhood and discipline. *Heartfelt Discipline* presents a faith-based approach to teaching and training your child that is relational rather than confrontational, focusing on your role as a godly guide who directs, corrects, and protects your child as you walk together along the path of life. This book reflects much of the philosophy that Clay and I developed over the years in our own home. Of course, he is one of my favorite authors. I love the way he thinks and expresses life-giving ideas!

————. *The Twenty-Four Family Ways.* Monument, Colo.: WholeHeart Press, 1999. A great devotional tool for teaching children the Bible, instilling biblical values and Christian character, and strengthening their relationship with the Lord. In addition to explaining twenty-four family values, or "ways," it is also filled with carefully selected scriptures, character-quality definitions, and 120 family devotional outlines. Comes in flip-book format and includes a color poster.

Clarkson, Sally. *Seasons of a Mother's Heart.* Fort Worth, Tex.: WholeHeart Press, 1997. Although I wrote it specifically for homeschooling moms, I hope this deeply personal book will also lift the heart of any mother who is trying to live closer to God's design for motherhood. Each brief chapter contains a short Bible study, engaging small-group discussion questions, practical ideas for living the Word, a thought-provoking quote, and a meditation drawn from my experience as a mother.

Clarkson, Sarah. *Journeys of Faithfulness.* Monument, Colo.: WholeHeart Press, 2002. This is our Sarah's first book! It grew out of her desire to encourage serious young women like herself to be faithful to God wherever they are in life's journey. Sarah uses fiction to retell the stories of four young women in Scripture—Mary of Bethany, Esther, Mary the mother of Jesus, and Ruth—then follows with her own reflections on faithfulness, four Bible passages with questions for discussion or personal reflection, and three "Journey Journal" pages for readers to record their own thoughts. Perfect for young women in their 'tweens and teens.

Demoss, Nancy Leigh. *Lies Women Believe.* Chicago: Moody, 2002. This wonderful book exposes forty of the deceiver's lies to women today about God, themselves, sin, priorities, marriage, children, emotions, and circumstances. Nancy Demoss offers godly, biblical counsel on how to counter those lies with God's truth and how to find freedom to live in the grace and forgiveness of God.

Green, Steve. *Hide 'Em in Your Heart Bible Memory Melodies.* 2 volumes. Nashville: Chordant/Sparrow, 1991. It's amazing how many scriptures our children have remembered from the songs on these CDs (we started using them when they were available as audiotapes). Frank Hernandez wrote the catchy, child-friendly, Scripture-only songs. Steve Green makes them come alive for kids with his remarkable voice.

Murray, Andrew. *Raising Your Child to Love God.* Minneapolis: Bethany, 2001. Andrew Murray—nineteenth-century pastor, missionary, author of more than 240 books, and father of eight—left us a thoroughly biblical and practical journey through what it takes to raise a child to love and serve God. The fifty-two short chapters of this book overflow with godly, timeless wisdom and principles.

Richards, Lawrence. *It Couldn't Just Happen.* Nashville: Word, 1994. Larry Richards provides satisfying answers to your child's challenging questions about the authority of the Bible, the nature of man, the origin of the world, and much more. It is filled with lively and informative text that does not talk down to young readers, as well as helpful drawings and photos. Good for casual or serious reading for preteens and up.

Schaeffer, Edith. *What Is a Family?* Grand Rapids: Baker, 1993. Edith Schaeffer, wife of the late theologian Francis Schaeffer, lays out a mother's-eye view for the Christian family in her classic 1976 book. Her words inspired me as I began my journey to motherhood and are still fresh to me today.

Schoolland. Marian M. *Leading Little Ones to God.* Grand Rapids: Eerdmans, 1995. In this time-tested and proven gem from 1963, you and your little ones will learn together about God, Jesus, the Holy Spirit, salvation, and other basic Bible truths of the Christian life. Each of the eighty-six brief devotions includes a text about a specific Christian doctrine, a suggested Bible reading, discussion questions, a memory verse, and a suggested hymn to sing. It's written for younger children, but the Scripture references can be turned into an outline for a study of basic Bible doctrines for your older children.

St. John, Patricia. *Stories That Jesus Told.* Harrisburg, Pa.: Morehouse, 1995. Skilled storyteller Patricia St. John retells thirty of her favorite parables of Jesus. Her delightful writing, combined with realistic illustrations, is a delight for any lover of stories—and a wonderful way to recreate for little ones the fresh excitement of listening to our Lord's storytelling.

Trumbull, Henry Clay. *Hints on Child Training.* 1891; reprint, Eugene, Oreg.: Great Expectations, 1993. No matter how many new parenting books we see, this is still our favorite. Trumbull's 1891 classic rings with clarity and wisdom, going straight to the heart of thirty timeless issues of child training. This book by Elizabeth Elliot's great-grandfather contains the godly, practical wisdom of an experienced and dedicated Christian father of eight. I highly recommend this book for all Christian parents but especially for those with young children.

Vos, Catherine F. *The Child's Story Bible*. Grand Rapids, Mich.: Eerdmans, 1989. This classic story Bible, written in 1935, reads like literature. Unlike too many of today's Bible story books that are either simplified to death or crassly trivialized by commercial tie-ins, *The Child's Story Bible* is clean, clear, and precise. Vos stays true to the biblical text, adding illuminating insights and perspectives that bring each Bible story to life. Thirty-nine classic, full-page, color illustrations elegantly supplement her dignified text. Ideal for reading aloud.

Our Twenty-Four Family Ways

Concerning AUTHORITIES *in our family…*

1. We love and obey our Lord, Jesus Christ, with wholehearted devotion.

2. We read the Bible and pray to God every day with an open heart.

3. We honor and obey our parents in the Lord with a respectful attitude.

4. We listen to correction and accept discipline with a submissive spirit.

Concerning RELATIONSHIPS *in our family…*

5. We love one another, treating others with kindness, gentleness, and respect.

6. We serve one another, humbly thinking of the needs of others first.

7. We encourage one another, using only words that build up and bless others.

8. We forgive one another, covering an offense with love when wronged or hurt.

Concerning POSSESSIONS *in our family…*

9. We are thankful to God for what we have, whether it is a little or a lot.

10. We are content with what we have, not coveting what others have.

11. We are generous with what we have, sharing freely with others.

12. We take care of what we have, using it wisely and responsibly.

Concerning WORK *in our family...*

13. We are diligent to complete a task promptly and thoroughly when asked.

14. We take initiative to do all of our own work without needing to be told.

15. We work with a cooperative spirit, freely giving and receiving help.

16. We take personal responsibility to keep our home neat and clean at all times.

Concerning ATTITUDES *in our family...*

17. We choose to be joyful, even when we feel like complaining.

18. We choose to be peacemakers, even when we feel like arguing.

19. We choose to be patient, even when we feel like getting our own way.

20. We choose to be gracious, even when we don't feel like it.

Concerning CHOICES *in our family...*

21. We do what we know is right, regardless of what others do or say.

22. We ask before we act when we do not know what is right to do.

23. We exercise self-control at all times and in every kind of situation.

24. We always tell the truth and do not practice deceitfulness of any kind.

By Clay Clarkson (copyright 1997 Whole Heart Ministries). A devotional guide for parents using these "ways" may be ordered through www.wholeheart.org.

ABOUT WHOLE HEART MINISTRIES

Whole Heart Ministries is a nonprofit Christian home and parenting ministry founded by Clay and Sally Clarkson in 1994. WHM is dedicated to encouraging and equipping Christian parents to build a biblical home and a godly heritage by nurturing, discipling, and educating their children at home. Sally is the author of *Seasons of a Mother's Heart* and coauthor of *Educating the Whole-Hearted Child*, both published by WHM. She has also encouraged thousands of mothers through her WholeHearted Mother Conferences and audiotapes since 1998. WHM also publishes Bible study and devotional materials to help parents raise wholehearted Christian children, as well as reprints of inspiring books from the Victorian era. The Whole Heart Catalog, published annually, offers hundreds of heart-building, faith-strengthening, "best in their class" books and resources for Christian parenting. The Whole Heart Online Web site is an always-growing, dynamic resource filled with helpful content and our WHOnline Bookstore. To learn more about Whole Heart Ministries or to join our mailing list, please visit our Web site or contact us by mail.

www.wholeheart.org
e-mail: mail@wholeheart.org

Whole Heart Ministries
3761 Highway 109N, Unit A
Lebanon, TN 37087

Sally Clarkson is available for speaking engagements on a limited basis, since she is still focusing her energies on her children who are still at home. For information about her availability, please contact Whole Heart Ministries.